15.69

BROTHERS

By Peter Goldman and Tony Fuller
(with Vern E. Smith and others)
Charlie Company: What Vietnam Did to Us
The Quest for the Presidency 1984

By Peter Goldman (with others)
The End of the World That Was

By Peter Goldman
Civil Rights: The Challenge of the Fourteenth Amendment
Report from Black America
The Death and Life of Malcolm X

By Vern E. Smith
The Jones Men

Standing, from left to right: Vern E. Smith, Terry E. Johnson, Peter Goldman, Monroe Anderson. Seated, left to right: Jacques Chenet, who took the photographs in the book, and Sylvester Monroe.

BROTHERS

BLACK AND POOR—
A TRUE STORY OF
COURAGE AND SURVIVAL

SYLVESTER MONROE AND PETER GOLDMAN

with Vern E. Smith, Terry E. Johnson

Monroe Anderson, Jacques Chenet

A NEWSWEEK BOOK
WILLIAM MORROW AND COMPANY, INC.
NEW YORK

Contemporary photographs by Jacques Chenet.

Library of Congress Cataloging-in-Publication Data

Monroe, Sylvester.
  Brothers : black and poor—a true story of courage and survival
    1. Afro-Americans—Illinois—Chicago—Biography.
I. Goldman, Peter Louis, 1933–   . II. Smith, Vern E.
III. Title.
F548.9.N4M66   1988   977.3'1100496073   [B]   87-35028
ISBN 0-688-07622-X

Printed in the United States of America

First Edition

1 2 3 4 5 6 7 8 9 10

BOOK DESIGN BY BARBARA MARKS

TO

ALL

THE

CHILDREN

IN

ALL

THE

PROJECTS:

KEEP

ON

KEEPING

ON

CONTENTS

CONTENTS

FOREWORD

I am an invisible man. No, I am not a spook like those who haunted Edgar Allan Poe; nor am I one of your Hollywood-movie ectoplasms. I am a man of substance, of flesh and bone, fiber and liquids—and I might even be said to possess a mind. I am invisible, understand, simply because people refuse to see me . . . When they approach me they see only my surroundings, themselves, or figments of their imagination—indeed, everything and anything except me.

Ralph Ellison, Invisible Man

Thirty-five years after the publication of Ellison's great American novel, the blacks who come to manhood in our inner cities are still, for the most part, invisible. We have met a few of them, eloquently revealed, in memoirs—James Baldwin's, Claude Brown's, and Malcolm X's leap vividly to mind—and a few more, brilliantly drawn, in the fiction of Ellison, say, or Richard Wright, or John Edgar Wideman. But those are the works of extraordinary people; it is the ordinary men, the brothers on the block, who elude our gaze and our understanding. There are reams of newsprint about their poverty and their delinquencies; there are libraries of sociology about the circumstances of their lives. They are the cast of the urban middle-class nightmare, the objects of widespread prejudice and fear. And yet they have a way of disappearing into the cityscape of our minds. We see them mostly from a safe distance, if at all; we rarely hear them speak for themselves about themselves about their lives, their victories, their defeats, and their dreams.

This book is a group portrait of twelve such men, a story of lives formed in the want and violence of the housing projects on the black South Side of Chicago. Most were in their middle thirties when we encountered them. They had come of age in the 1960's—a time, we thought, of widening opportunity for the black poor. But the great public events of the day—the struggle against segregation in the South and the war on poverty in the North—played out at a vast distance from their lives. A few were touched by the vogue for affirmative action and two were delivered by it. Most were not. They grew up in the isolation of the ghetto; they lived, often, in fatherless households; they drifted through school, rarely finishing; they got involved in petty crime and warring gangs; they came of age too young, men-children taking jobs, getting married, and fathering babies before they were out of their teens. They dreamed the American Dream, but as they approached middle age, their hopes had mostly been checkmated by circumstance. The wonder was not that so few succeeded but that so many survived.

They opened their lives in the spring and summer of 1986 to a team of four correspondents and a photographer from *Newsweek*. The sons of the ghetto are not normally welcoming to strangers, and the fact that the reporters and the cameraman were black was not itself enough to gain them entrée; to let down one's guard can be a dangerous and even a fatal mistake. But one of the visitors was one of their own, Sylvester Monroe, Vest to the brothers he grew up with in the projects and the gangs. Monroe introduced his new colleagues to his old homeboys over dinner at a South Side restaurant called Army & Lou's one evening in the spring. His word was character reference enough; over the months that followed, interviews took on some of the intimacy of friendship, and the correspondents became part of the furniture of the lives they observed.

For all of them, the assignment was a voyage of discovery, an exploration of the world behind the all too familiar statistics of material need and social disorganization. For Monroe, it was a trip through a time warp into his own past. He had gone away to school early in his teens and was making a successful career at *Newsweek,* most recently as a Washington correspondent specializing in politics and minority affairs. But he had married a girl from the projects and had never lost touch with his roots. He was part of two worlds, and there were days working on the story when he felt as if he had never left home.

The resulting report was a collaborative effort, like most works of newsmagazine journalism, but it was in large measure the story of Vest's world. He contributed a memoir of his own coming of age and interviews with several of his friends. Others of the dozen lives were reported by Vern E. Smith, chief of the magazine's Atlanta bureau and a co-author of two past *Newsweek* books; Terry E. Johnson, a national affairs writer based in New York, and Monroe Anderson, a correspondent in Chicago. The basic reporting spanned four months, with numerous follow-up visits and calls; it occasionally led the reporters into delicate and even dangerous situations, moments at which their safe-conduct was the bond of trust developed over time between them and their sources. The accompanying portfolio of pictures is the work of Jacques Chenet and is itself the product of patient photojournalism; Chenet typically spent a day or so just getting acquainted with his subjects before shooting the first of hundreds of frames. The collective effort had an intensity of the sort the magazine might bring to covering a presidential campaign or a war. Our subjects responded by trusting us, literally, with their lives.

We have tried to honor that trust, to present the brothers as they see themselves and would have the world see them. The form of the book is ours; the content, and the language, are theirs. Few have led wholly blameless lives; some have strayed into crime and drugs; one has been an outlaw since his teens and is now paying the price, in prison. They have been as candid about their vices as about their virtues; they allowed us, that is, to see them whole, as men, not statistics, with all the strengths, weaknesses, hopes, and vanities that are part of the human condition. It is important to note that they are not a scientific sample of all black men in America, or even of black men raised in the Chicago projects. It is fair, on the other hand, to say that they represent an accurate slice of life as fashioned in our urban ghettos and that their stories come to a not untypical range of happy and unhappy endings.

We published those stories first, in much shorter form, in the March 23, 1987 issue of *Newsweek;* this version is three to four times as long, and we hope it has gained accordingly in texture and depth of field. We are indebted to many friends and colleagues for helping us make both versions happen. Our editor-in-chief, Richard M. Smith, made an extraordinarily bold commitment of manpower in the field and space in the magazine to a subject that had elsewhere fallen from journalistic fashion; in this, he honored a *Newsweek* tradition at least a quarter century old. Maynard Parker, the magazine's editor, oversaw the project with intelligence and energy; he was ably assisted in the closing stages by Peter McGrath, a senior editor whose normal watch is foreign news. Tony Fuller, our national affairs editor, inspired the story in conversations with Monroe, and senior editor Lynn Povich was a source of counsel and help. Our picture editor, Karen Mullarkey, and our art director, Patricia Bradbury, brought their skilled eyes and caring minds to the magazine version of the story. Melanie Cooper, the senior researcher on many past *Newsweek* special projects and books, was a major contributor to this work—the guardian not just of its factual accuracy but of its fidelity to the lives and the trust of its subjects.

We are grateful as well to our old friend and editor at William Morrow, Bruce Lee, for his faith in this story; and to Rollene Saal for reuniting us with the house that published an earlier *Newsweek* book, *Charlie Company: What Vietnam Did to Us,* with happy results. Helen Dudar, the writer and critic, was as always the first reader, and the wisest. We are collectively grateful to the women in all our lives—to Helen, to Hattie Kelley, to Marie Smith, to Janet M. King-Johnson, to Joyce Anderson, and to Cheryl T. Chenet.

Most of all, we owe our thanks to the people who walk these pages. to Gregory Bronson, to Edward (Half Man) Carter, to Everette (Pee Wee) Fisher, to Edward Hamilton, to Herman (Moose) Harper, to Billy Harris, to Roy (Honk) Johnson, Jr., to Ulysses (Sonny) Spruiell, to Steven Steward, to Charles Ray Stingley, to the late James

Bonner, and to their parents, wives, lovers, and friends. We hope that their stories will be one small step toward acquainting America at last with its invisible men.

A personal postscript: My teammates on this project and I have frequently been asked why a white editor was chosen as the principal writer of what is otherwise so wholly a work of black journalism. The suggestion is that it must have been *because* I am white. The real answer is that I am a writer; newsmagazines have traditionally considered writing and reporting to be separate specialties, and I happened to be the resident subspecialist in long-form narrative journalism.

Still, the division of labor has always seemed odd to outsiders, and the response is therefore not always satisfying to people who raise the question of my race. Of them, I ask only what Dr. Martin Luther King Jr. once prayed for his children: that I be judged not by the color of my skin but by the content of my character, or in this case by the work I have produced in partnership with my colleagues and friends.

—PETER GOLDMAN

New York City
January 1988

PART I

VEST:

AN

INTRODUCTION

BY

SYLVESTER

MONROE

They say you can't go home again. So when I returned to the Robert Taylor Homes and Prairie Courts, I was filled with deeply mixed emotions about being back in the South Side Chicago housing projects where I grew up. I was journeying back to my past, and I didn't know what I would find.

It wasn't that I was afraid. I'd been back many times in the twenty years since I left, in 1966. But this time I was returning as a reporter, retracing my life and those of my friends. What had happened to us, to Half Man and Honk, Pee Wee and Billy, and what did it say about growing up black in America? Perhaps, I concluded, by exploring our lives, we might find answers to why it is that black men seem destined to become an endangered species. Why it is that they—we—finish last in practically every socioeconomic measure from infant mortality to employment to life expectancy. Through portraits of our lives together and apart, I thought, we might find some answers.

What concerned me was how my old friends would react when I asked them to be the subjects of a *Newsweek* special report on black men. Some of the brothers were a bit skeptical and even suspicious at first.

"Vest, are you the Man?" Sonny Spruiell asked when I initially explained the project to him. He meant was I with the police. When I assured him I was not, he still had reservations. "I don't have to talk to any white people, do I?" he asked me.

Another, Greg Bronson, also agreed to participate, but with reservations of his own. He was an angry guy, a nationalist, and he told me up front that he was not at all convinced that the story would ever be published. "Those white people you work for are never going to do a positive story about black men," he insisted.

So I was more than a little surprised when all the guys I approached agreed to be interviewed. I was even more surprised by their incredible openness and candor. Why would they want to bare their lives on the pages of a national newsmagazine? Part of it was personal, a favor to an old homie from the projects. But more importantly, they did it because we asked. That's a rare opportunity for young black men, to speak to the readers of a national magazine and now a book about how they see themselves and the world in which they live. "Nobody ever asked me what I thought about *anything*," my old buddy, Edward (Half Man) Carter, told me.

So it was that on a crisp, clear morning in the fall of 1986, ten of my oldest friends gathered on the rooftop of one of the sixteen-story buildings that make up the Taylor Homes to be photographed for the cover of *Newsweek*. We were eleven middle-aged men, reunited by a magazine story, but bound together long before that, I thought, by a common ghetto background, a quarter century of friendship, and the inescapable fact of our blackness.

My own journey back to that rooftop began years ago, when I was a young boy listening to my Mississippi-born grandfather and uncles talking about the discouraging limits placed upon black ambition, black dreams, black hope. "A black man can't do this or that," they'd say. "They ain't never gonna let a black man be this or that. And if he gets too big, they'll kill him."

I grew up hearing the men's anger raging in the recesses of my mind. But another, more hopeful voice resonated there as well. That voice was my mother's. I remember her telling me over and over again that I could be whatever I wanted to be, if I just worked hard enough. "For a black man to get ahead in this world, he's got to work twice as hard and be twice as good as everybody else," she'd say. What mattered was that he *could* get ahead. I doubt that she really believed a poor black kid from the projects could be anything he wanted to be. But I think she knew, intuitively, that if I and my brother and sisters were to have any chance at all, we had to have something to reach for, something to hope for. As a young, single mother of seven, she never had much more than that to give us. But if she'd given me nothing else, I would always be grateful for that, perhaps her most important gift of all—the capacity to dream.

Generally speaking, poor people in projects like the Robert Taylor Homes don't place much stock in dreams. They see little point in it. And back then, even I knew that harboring such an outrageous ambition as wanting to be president of the United States was tantamount to tilting at windmills. I might as well have wanted to be the Incredible Hulk. Though my mother was fiercely ambitious for us, she never pushed us toward any particular vocation. She just wanted us to want to be *something*. I couldn't really understand it then, but what she was saying was that being poor was hard; being poor without hope is deadly.

When I left Chicago for St. George's School in the summer of 1966, via a special outreach program called A Better Chance (ABC), all eleven of us were still in school. And at the wide-eyed age of fourteen or fifteen, we still had dreams. Some of those dreams were larger than others, but for the most part we still believed that with hard work, determination, and a little bit of luck, a black man could make it in America. After all, it was the sixties, and things were changing.

What I wanted to be, from the time I was fourteen years old, was a writer. I never imagined that I could or would become a correspondent for a national magazine. I just knew that I wanted to make a living someday putting words on paper. I read F. Scott Fitzgerald and dreamed of writing a novel of my own. I even started signing my name S. Vest Monroe, feeling a bit miffed that my mother had not given me a middle name. The dream gave me hope. And my mother's constant pushing convinced me that education was the best fuel to fire the dream.

"Education," she would say, "is the last best hope for the black man."

Having to leave the safety and familiarity of home to get it was as difficult a decision as any I've ever made. In fact, if it had been entirely up to me, I might never have gone to St. George's at all. I was quite happy at Wendell Phillips High back home, making straight A's, running on the track team, and discovering the wonders of women. Besides, I'd already worked up my own scenario for success: I'd graduate from Phillips, go to the University of Illinois-Chicago Circle Campus, and take my best shot from there.

Now I was being told that I could do better, but it meant my leaving home to attend an all-boys boarding school in Newport, Rhode

Island. It might as well have been the other side of the universe. Not only would I be away from my family and friends, there wouldn't be any girls and barely any other blacks at all. In fact, when I arrived at the front steps of St. George's on a damp, dark September night in 1966, I was one of only five blacks enrolled in a student body of slightly more than 200. It was culture shock on a jarring scale.

The first person I met was Gil Burnett, who taught biology and was my faculty adviser. He looked like William Colby, the former director of the Central Intelligence Agency, and the rumor among students was that he had once been a top-secret CIA operative himself. He seemed nice enough to me, extending a warm welcome to the Hilltop, as St. George's is called, and helping me get squared away. But something seemed to bother him as he stood there sizing me up for the first time. I had dressed in my best outfit—a wide-brimmed Dunlop hat, dark glasses, Italian knit shirt, reversible pleated baggie pants, and brown-and-white Stacy-Adams wing-tip shoes.

"Do you have other clothes?" he asked finally.

"Yeah," I said. "Just like this."

The next day he took me in his Land Rover to the Anderson-Little knitting mills in Fall River, Massachusetts, and bought me a blue blazer, two pairs of gray flannel slacks, and a plain pair of black tie shoes. My Stacy-Adamses would not do for Sunday chapel, he said.

I was thankful for the new duds. They gave me the look of a New England preppie. But I still felt like a fish out of water. More than a few times, I wondered why I had ever agreed to leave Thirty-ninth Street in the first place. Never had I felt more alone—or afraid. My one consoling thought was that it wouldn't be for long.

The main reason I was there, I reminded myself, was to please my mother and Mr. Lovelace, the Chicago public school teacher largely responsible for getting me my scholarship to St. George's. My mother had given me an out, or so I thought. Sensing that I wasn't sure about the whole idea, she had said to me at the outset that she thought it was a wonderful opportunity and that I would never forgive myself if I didn't at least go and see what it was like. If I didn't like it, I could always come home, she said. Though I myself knew, in some vague sense, that going to St. George's would alter the course of my life, it didn't make it any easier to accept what I had to give up in order to take advantage of it. Secretly, I resolved to stay at the school for exactly two weeks, long enough to make a good show of it, and then head for home.

After roughly two weeks, I had what I thought was the greatest stroke of luck: I got sick, so sick in fact that I was admitted to the school infirmary. It was perfect. I'd call my mother, tell her what a god-awful place boarding school was, and catch the first thing smokin' for Chi-town. To make my pitch even stronger, I decided to ask the infirmary nurse exactly what was wrong with me.

"Hey, Doc, what've I got, anyway?" I asked when the nurse brought around the nightly milkshake, which I suspected was laced with castor oil or something worse.

"Oh, I think you're suffering from a really bad case of nostalgia," she said.

I hadn't the foggiest notion what *nostalgia* meant, but it sounded pretty serious to me. Wonderful, I thought. There's no way Mom won't let me come home now.

I went to the phone, already planning my return to Robert Taylor.

"Hey, Ma," I began.

"Hey, how you doin'?" she answered.

"Not so good. I'm sick as a dog, Ma. This place is always cold, the sheets are damp, the food is terrible, and now I'm in the infirmary."

"What's the matter with you?" she asked.

"I can't keep anything down," I said. "The doctor says I've got a really bad case of nostalgia."

"What else did he say?" she asked.

"Nothing really, but I think I ought to come home, OK?"

"Sure, you can come home, but under one condition," she said without any change in her voice.

"What's that?" I asked.

"The only way you're coming home before you're supposed to is in a box," she said.

It was one of the hardest things she'd ever had to do, she confided years later. But she also knew it would have been a terrible mistake to do otherwise. It was three months before I got home again, for

Christmas vacation, and somehow I managed to survive. I even found myself actually beginning to like the place, and its teachers who tempered their no-nonsense classes with a touch of compassion. Geoff Spranger, my English teacher, challenged my intellect with the great works of literature, increasing my love of language. Chaplain Hays Rockwell's philosophy classes fired my imagination. I discovered that my capacity for learning hadn't been stunted by life in the Taylor Homes.

Looking back on it, I was pleased that in a way I was showing what black boys were capable of. Yet there was a faint disquiet. What bothered me was that some people found it easier to pretend I was something else.

"We're color-blind here," a well-meaning faculty member once told me. "We don't see *black* students or *white* students, we just see students."

The problem was that I wasn't sure he really saw *me* at all. This was a time when enlightened white liberals still espoused the theory of America as a giant melting pot into which we poured an odd assortment of ethnic and cultural backgrounds and mixed them into a red, white, and blue goulash with a star-spangled base. If an Irish brogue or Australian twang remained, it was generally considered a charming remnant of a proud heritage. But somehow black skin never quite fit the recipe. Too much melanin always seemed to spoil the stew.

Another teacher was surprised at my reaction when he implied that I should be grateful for the opportunity to attend St. George's, far away from such a dreadful place as the Robert Taylors.

How could I be, I snapped back, when my friends, my family, everyone that I cared most about, were still there? But you're different, he continued. That's why you got out.

I'm not different, I insisted. I'm just lucky enough to have been in the right place at the right time.

I was lucky in other ways, too. Growing up in the Taylor Homes didn't afford me the advantages of many of my wealthier classmates. But in other ways I was on equal footing. Love and support and a sense of self-worth could only come from within the family structure. And as my mother and others proved, it could happen whether there was one parent or two, a few kids or a houseful.

What that teacher failed to understand was that my background was not something to be ashamed of. Instead, like the old James Brown song of the sixties, I wanted to "say it loud: I'm black and I'm proud!" One of the greatest frustrations of my three years at St. George's was that people were always trying to separate me from other black people in a manner strangely reminiscent of a time when slave owners divided blacks into "good Negroes" and "bad Negroes." Somehow, it seemed, attending St. George's made me a good Negro in their eyes, while those left in Robert Taylor were bad Negroes or, at the very least, inferior Negroes.

It is perhaps one of the great ironies of my life that so much of it has been spent trying on the one hand to get people to see me as a black man, and on the other not to write me off or apply some damnable double standard when they do. That was the purpose of the all-black, eight-member Afro-American Association that I helped found in the middle of my second year at St. George's.

By late 1968, in my senior year there, it was becoming "fashionable" to have black students on a white campus. And that's when I started considering colleges.

"I'm thinking about Stanford," I told college adviser Bill Schenck.

"You're going to Harvard," he said. Top St. George's graduates traditionally went there.

And so, in the fall of 1969, I entered the ivied halls of Harvard full of expectation. Academically, it was all I had hoped for, a stimulating intellectual community of some of the best and brightest minds, black or white, in the country. But the disquiet grew louder. Even though there were, relatively speaking, a lot more blacks at Harvard than at St. George's, the sense of being a fish out of water persisted.

By the time I was a sophomore, I was leading a nearly all-black existence, rooming, eating, and socializing exclusively with blacks at a school considerably less than 10 percent black. My only real association with whites was in class. It was not an antiwhite statement, though many interpreted it that way. For us it was simply a matter of survival, a circling of the wagons in what felt like hostile territory. Feeling isolated and misunderstood, we turned inward.

Even at Harvard, it seemed, people were still trying to whitewash our blackness away. Why couldn't we just be what we were? It was beginning to dawn on me that even with a prep school background and Harvard, the pathway to my dream might still be a rocky one. Occasionally, memories of the dashed hopes of my uncles would pop into my head. But I'd quickly dismiss them by telling myself that it was different now.

Despite the growing unease, my ambition to become a writer still burned bright. A summer as a copy boy at the *Chicago Defender* had whetted my appetite for journalism. The next summer I was hired by *Newsweek* as a messenger and copy boy at the 1968 Democratic National Convention. Watching the magazine's reporters at the convention cinched it—I wanted to be a *Newsweek* correspondent. Three years later I got my first of two reporting internships in the magazine's Chicago bureau. Then, three weeks after I graduated from Harvard, I became a full-time correspondent in the Boston bureau. I was twenty-one. The dream had come true.

My mother had been right. I'd worked hard, caught the break I needed to get out of the ghetto, conquered my fear of St. George's, and mastered the curriculum at Harvard from the classics to calculus.

Looking back, as I walked into my office on the first day, I felt a little like the celluloid underdog Rocky Balboa on the museum steps in Philadelphia. We made it, Ma, I thought quietly to myself.

Still, for a long time, a part of me never really believed it. I kept hearing my grandfather's and uncles' voices saying, "Black men can't be *Newsweek* correspondents." I have worked for the magazine nearly fourteen years as I write this, but like many so-called successful blacks, I still find myself occasionally looking over my shoulder. For my grandfather and my uncles were right, too: Race is an inescapable burden for every black man.

To help me bear that burden, I married my childhood sweetheart two days before the start of my senior year at Harvard in September 1972. For me, the marriage was more than the affirmation of our love. I took great comfort in the fact that Regina was from the same Taylor Homes building that I had grown up in. No matter where I went or what I did in the white world, I could always come home to the warmth and understanding of a black woman who was from the same place I was from.

BROTHERS

Though economic class is rapidly dividing America into a nation of haves and have-nots, race remains an overpowering fact of life for blacks that still tends to overshadow everything else. What the men in my family were saying is that it doesn't matter whether you are rich man, poor man, beggar, or thief—if you are black, there's an artificial ceiling on your ambition. Even today the sight of a young black man evokes an image of someone dangerous, destructive, or deviant. Many people still perceive blacks, especially black men, as less intelligent, less productive, and generally more violent than the rest of society.

I didn't have to go back to the Robert Taylor Homes to understand that. I see it almost constantly wherever I go. Recently, I waited forty-five minutes one evening on Sixth Avenue in midtown Manhattan before a cab finally stopped for me. As more than a dozen of his fellow cabbies had taken one look and passed me for a "safer" white fare, I stood there wanting to scream out in anger and frustration: "Hey, I'm one of the good guys, I work for *Newsweek*, I went to college; I'm not going to rip you off!" It's the same in other cities, and it's not just cabdrivers. More than a few times, I've stepped onto an elevator and noticed a woman clutching her purse a little tighter under her arm, or I've been walking on a deserted sidewalk with a black male companion, when a white couple spots us and suddenly decides to cross the street.

To be sized up, categorized, and dismissed all within the space of a nervous glance solely on the basis of race is more than annoying; it's demeaning and damaging to the individual and collective psyche of an entire people. It's like being handicapped by a severe birth defect. My own psyche has not gone unscathed.

There's a recurring, Kafkaesque dream I have in which I'm shaken out of a sound sleep by a large, laughing white man standing over me and saying in a deep southern drawl: "Okay boooy, wake up! The party's over. You know you ain't no real *Newsweek* correspondent, and that degree you got from Harvard ain't worth the paper it's written on. You still just a nigger!"

He's the villain of my dreams, but sad to say, he exists in real life, too. I encountered one on the telephone when I was a reporter in Chicago. We were discussing affirmative action.

"I'm not givin' up one iota of anythin' for a black man to get ahead," the angry caller shouted. "If blacks didn't make it in the sixties, it was because they didn't want to. Blacks have had their time. That's why some of us have formed a group called SPONGE."

"What's that?" I asked.

"The Society for the Prevention of Negroes Getting Everything," he answered. Our conversation ended shortly after that.

Even among people of goodwill, I find that the mere mention of race often prompts a fit of hand-wringing and heavy sighing as if to say, oh no, not *that* again. Indeed, race relations is old news, it seems, unless somebody gets killed. Sometimes I get the feeling people are thinking, "Why are there still Negroes?"

The fact of the matter is that there are. And we aren't going anywhere. Nor should we. What strikes me most about retracing the lives of my homeboys from Thirty-ninth Street is how easily our lives could be interchanged. Some of my friends like Roy (Honk) Johnson, now serving eight years for armed robbery, turned their back on a system they figured offered none of us much hope.

What Honk didn't say, but what is clear to me now, is that where opportunity revealed itself, a chance for success followed. Where it did not, the predictable occurred. I wondered what Honk's life might have been had it not been circumscribed by race; if he had gotten the same opportunity to succeed or fail as every other American.

Because he didn't, many of his nightmares are real. For me, it's meant waking up in a cold sweat or weathering a few uneasy moments now and again. I had one of those moments a few months ago while I was back in Chicago reporting this story. I was standing in front of the Taylor Homes building where I grew up, rapping and jiving with some of the old crowd like we used to as teenagers. Suddenly I had the strangest feeling. It felt so familiar, so natural to be standing on the corner of Thirty-ninth and Dearborn. I imagined that when we were done, all I had to do was walk to the elevator, ride up to the twelfth floor, and go home to apartment 1201.

"Wait a minute!" I said, shaking myself. "This is crazy. I'm not one of the boys on the block anymore. I'm a journalist, and I live in Washington, D.C."

I left Chicago the next day, moved partly by the urge to reassure myself that the feelings I had on Thirty-ninth Street really didn't matter. Ironically, where I went was to St. George's. I'd graduated from there eighteen years ago, and now I was back to participate in graduation day exercises as a member of the board of trustees.

As I sat in the opulent chapel, draped in cap and gown for the school's traditional Prize Day service, a world away from Robert Taylor, that, too, seemed surprisingly comfortable and natural. It struck me that I am as at ease on the "hilltop" as I am on the "low end" on Thirty-ninth Street. I was at home in either, though I am neither a true preppie nor a real ghetto gang-banger; I am rather the peculiar product of an even more peculiar hybrid American experience.

I thought about all those years I'd spent at St. George's, Harvard, and *Newsweek,* trying to find my way back home. Why had it taken so long to realize that if you are born black in the U.S.A., it doesn't matter much where you go in this country or what you become; you can never really get away from home. Like it or not, there is at least a kernel of truth in that old, and otherwise distasteful, adage, "You can take the Negro out of the ghetto, but you can't take the ghetto out of the Negro."

By the time I went back home for the *Newsweek* piece, I knew that I had never left.

PART II

COMING

OF

AGE

IN

THE

GHETTO

TREY-NINE

My mother comes from the Mississippi Delta, Vest said, *and she'd come up from shanties down there to one kind of tenement after another in Chicago. She was ecstatic when we moved into the Robert Taylor Homes—this would be January of '64. I think she thought, I've got my children in a place where they'll be warm in the winter and they won't have to worry about being bitten by rats. And it* was *nice. It was without a doubt the best place that we had ever lived. It looked neat. Everything worked. My brother and I had our own room. But I went back while I was working on this story, and I was talking with Honk Johnson about what the place is like.*

And he said, "Could you live down here?"

And I said, "Yeah, if I had to." I said, "I've been here before."

And he said, "No, that's not what I mean." He said, "You'd go to jail *if you had to. But would you live down here?"*

And I thought about it, and I said no. If I had a choice,

there's no way I'd live on Thirty-ninth Street again. Honk
does business there, but he wouldn't live there either. Nobody
would live there if they had a choice.

Honk Johnson, entrepreneur, stood leaning against a parked car
out back of the building they call Trey-nine one Saturday in the summer of 1986, basking in the bright morning sunshine and in his own
midnight reputation as the baddest dude on Thirty-ninth Street. "Roy
Johnson Jr., a.k.a. Big Honk," he mused aloud, imagining what his
police file said about him."Known dealer, known killer, chief of this,
chief of that. Don't F with him." The image, once a source of pride,
had lost some of its old power to please him. His belly was churning
threateningly after a night's drinking at Cigar's Lounge and a noseful
of bad heroin, and ahead of him, if he didn't get lucky, lay a stretch
of hard time for armed robbery; *all* time is hard time when you're
pushing thirty-five. Honk had been feeling his mileage lately and was
thinking about retiring from The Life after twenty years as—his own
phrase—a hell of a nigger.

But the sun was warm, the barbecue was popping on an open
grill, and Honk was enveloped in the fine sixties sound of Martha
and the Vandellas floating up from the car radio: "Come and get
these memories, come and get 'em . . ." The project was a house
of memories for Honk; the song itself was one of them, and as he
hummed along with it, his mood mellowed. He still looked sharp in
his sporty yellow sweater and his Louis John shades, with a floppy
Borsalino riding low over his marcelled hair. Hats like that had been
a signature of his from boyhood on, broken down mean the way
Capone used to do; it was Honk's homage to Chicago tradition. "I
wear big hats, shoot big guns," he liked to say with just the right
edge of menace, only today he didn't need that edge; today no one
was calling old Honk's hand. At Thirty-ninth and Federal, he was
royalty, a visiting feudal prince come down from the suburbs to the
projects to mingle with the people.

"Wha's happenin', Honk?" a teenage boy said, edging gingerly
into the prince's orbit. The kid was wearing a leather jacket, and his
hair was a Jerri-curled pile of glossy black ringlets.

"Hey, man, what's up?" Honk answered languidly. If he remembered the kid's name, he didn't trouble himself calling it.

A girl followed, pretty and pouty in a black and white pantsuit. "Hey, Honk, what happened to you last night?"

"Got tied up," he said. "I *told* you, I'm gonna come down there and knock on your door."

She leaned close, hands on hips, trying to see through his sunglasses into his graveyard eyes.

"Well, Honk," she demanded, "*when* you comin' by?"

The shades were like curtains over his intentions, and Honk hid behind them, sputtering something and dancing out of reach. He was a married man now, an outlaw emeritus, looking for something more than quick hits; still, it was nice being wanted. In the view from downtown, Honk was a statistic, one more bit of evidence confirming what social science calls the pathology of the ghetto. At Trey-nine, among his rappies, he was somebody. At Trey-nine, Honk was home.

Trey-nine was shorthand for 3919 South Federal Street, the northernmost in a two-mile Stonehenge of red-and-cream brick high rises called the Robert Taylor Homes in memory of the first black director of the Chicago Housing Authority. Mayor Richard Daley had cut the ribbon in 1962, with a homily on the great liberal dream of public housing; it was still thought, in that innocent time, that you could deliver the poor from their desperation by heaping up great piles of bricks and mortar around them. Honk was one in a group of schoolboys who settled into the project soon thereafter, manchildren of ten or eleven, their lives bound together by their age, their address, and the common condition of growing up in the want and isolation of the ghetto. They had been born to what was becoming a threatened species in our culture and our postindustrial economy: black men struggling for life and livelihood in the rotting inner cities of America.

They were Vest Monroe's crowd, and they were much like the friends he had left behind at another, older project, Prairie Courts, not far to the north and east; they were in fact a fair slice of preadolescent life in ghettos across the urban North. They were mostly the children of refugees from the poverty and racism of the backwater South. Only a minority had fathers at home. None had money, except what they could scrabble up themselves in minimum-wage jobs or on the street. They gave one another nicknames, Honk and Half Man and Pee Wee and Moose and Brainiac, and they passed through the rites of boyhood together; they learned to read, write, do sums, play ball, drink wine, sing doo-wop, jive with girls and—a necessity in the ghetto—fight with fists, sticks, stones, knives, and, ultimately, guns.

All had dreams—variants, usually, on the American Dream of home, family, and material well-being. Some, like Vest, tried to make their way in the mainstream. Some, like Honk, became outlaws. Some zigzagged between the poor outer margins of the economy and the street. A few among them succeeded, against all odds. The majority would not—not, at least, by the conventional measures of success in middle-class America. They were still trying, still getting by, but the closed-in world they were born to, like the projects they grew up in, was heavy with the expectation of their defeat, and most would, in some measure, succumb.

So much more had seemed possible when their generation first moved in. Trey-nine was new then, and like them it had a look of unspoiled innocence and hope. There were no rats or roaches there. The gangs hadn't arrived—not yet. Neither had the pestilence of drugs. The paint was fresh. The lawns were green and flowered. The elevators worked. The stoves and refrigerators were new. There was heat and hot water and breathing space, at prices poor people could afford; in those days a three- or four-bedroom flat rented for an average of $60 a month. Billy Harris's mother, broke and alone with six children, felt as if she were moving into a palace. Ed Hamilton saw it as a place where life began—a *good* life no matter what the rest of the world thought of people who live in the projects.

But for too many of the newcomers, it turned out to be a place where hope died. Projects like the Taylors, in Chicago and elsewhere, were built by design in those parts of town where black people already lived and were intended to keep them there. Rather than break up the ghetto, the planners rebuilt it, straight up, with all its poverty and all its debilities piled sixteen stories high in crowded vertical neighborhoods. Other projects rose to the north and south of the Taylors, and an expressway was routed past them, effectively cutting them off from the surviving white neighborhoods nearby. The twenty-eight buildings that made up the Taylor Homes became a city within a city, poor, black, insular, dependent, and dangerous. The official population by 1986 was 19,000, the great majority of them mothers and children. Perhaps 5,000 men were *around* at any given moment, living off the books, but two-parent families had always been a minority and were becoming a rarity. The most forceful lesson of fathers to sons at the Taylor Homes lay in their absence; to be a boy there was, and is, to apprentice at being an invisible man.

Honk Johnson's own father had floated in and out of Honk's boyhood; the family's move from the tenements to the projects was not so much an escape from the problems of ghetto life as a change of venue. Roy Johnson, Sr. was a hard-working man, a tailor and presser by trade. He always kept a job, but he was a drinker and a lady's man as well, and after siring his fourth child, he began running the streets. By the time the Johnsons moved into Trey-nine, he had moved out of their lives; to stay home would have been to live surrounded by the evidence of how little material support he had to give his growing brood. All he did was got 'em and named 'em, his wife, Ernestine, thought—that and whup them when they disturbed his peace.

Their rearing otherwise fell mostly to her. She was a good woman, a resolute Christian raised in the church in Alabama and brought north by her own daddy, a steelworker, in quest of a better life. She was thirteen then and pretty as a model, but when her path crossed Roy Johnson's at a social club called the Black Spider on Thirty-ninth Street a few years later, she was lost. She married too young, at seventeen, and had too many children, a baby a year, until there were eleven and she was overwhelmed by their sheer number.

She did what she could, seeing to it that they went to church and stayed off the streets, but she felt powerless to affect which ones would turn out good and which, like Honk, would not. She did not buy Honk's own theory, which was that the deprivations of his childhood had made him what he was. A lot of kids have a hard time, she thought; *she* had had a hard time, long passages of poverty when her daddy would be laid off and her mama had to bring home the leavings from the white folks' kitchen for their dinner, and she had come through all right. No, something else was making a couple of her sons come up wild, and it did not seem to help when she let Roy senior back in the house to be father to them. He seemed not to want them around; it was as if it got on his nerves just *seeing* so many children and so many needs beyond his power to satisfy.

Mrs. Johnson accordingly began to question whether she had been right to take him back. The undependability of men as husbands was a fact of life in her world, a part of the way things were. It's a *lot* of women don't have their husband, she thought in her stoical way, and they got by; so could she. She sometimes imagined that the way things turned out was somehow her fault. Sometimes she thought that if she had been bad, her boys would have come out better. Sometimes, in her despair, it seemed to her that the worst people had the best children.

Her second son, Roy junior, mystified her most of all; it was as if Trey-nine had taken him away from her and sent him back a stranger called Big Honk. He was an undersized child through his teens, a runty boy with innocent eyes, but he had taken a wrong turn early in his life—had got obsessed with having to be poor and wanting to be rich. Mrs. Johnson tried in later years to figure out precisely when and why he had gone bad, as if she were a doctor chasing a particularly elusive virus. The first offense she could remember was the day when, still a small boy, he stole $10 from her dresser drawer and pretended he had found it. His daddy whupped him, but his sins were growing in number and order of magnitude before the family ever moved to the projects, and the flat of his father's hand was not enough to stop him—not for more than a few weeks at a time.

Neither was Roy senior's example, which, when he was home, consisted mostly of hard work and inexpensive pleasures. Little Roy's role models instead were two older boys who ran with the Egyptian Cobras, one of the fighting gangs that were sprouting up on the West Side. He was only seven when their paths crossed; they were thirteen and fourteen. They had been in and out of jail two or three times, which did not disturb Roy, and they always had money, guns, and style, which fired his schoolboy imagination—turned him *out* just watching them walk that walk and talk that talk. They looked to his wide eyes like someone you could *be,* and he tried.

His primary education in The Life was thus already well advanced when, at ten, he found himself in the Robert Taylor Homes. His mother, like most in the project, imagined that raising children would go better there, that it would get them away from the worst influences of the ghetto on their young lives. Things worked out that way with some of her children, but not with little Roy. Trey-nine became his finishing school instead, a seminar in the economics of crime.

As a grade-schooler, he developed his skills filching franks at the ballpark, a game that interested him more than the one on the field. "They hit a home run!" one of his homies would yell, and Honk would be thinking, F the home run—gettin' me some more of these good hot dogs. His folks had taught him better, but the argument that it was wrong to steal had no force whatever for Honk as against the countervailing facts that he and his friends were broke and hungry and that stealing was fun. White folks be eating hot dogs while Honk and his homies *starving*. It was as simple and inequitable as that, and once he had righted the scales of justice to his satisfaction, he would go home too full for dinner.

He hungered for cash as well, and he was precociously good at hustling it. Not out to do no crazy, he thought, just tryin' to have money. At age twelve, he first tasted codeine cough syrup; *every* MF drank syrup, he guessed, in those days before the children of Trey-nine had discovered harder drugs. At thirteen, he was trafficking in it, scoring it by the gallon from a West Side connection and pocketing $200 or $300 a day in profits. By the time he turned fifteen, he was an accomplished B&E man, he and his band of rappies plundering the shopping center across the street for carts of food and racks of clothing and reselling it at Trey-nine at bargain prices.

He dressed their piracies up in Robin Hood costume—stealing from white people for *our* people, he liked to say. The mothers in the building got the first chance at the loot, and at the lowest prices. But to Honk's great regret, his own mama wouldn't buy any of it, not the merchandise and not the liberation-front line; everybody's mother except her got some of the spoils. Honk couldn't even flaunt his success at home. He had to act like a broke MF around his parents; his mother, being a Christian, would have disapproved of his bankroll, and his daddy, being a presser, would have been hip to the designer labels in his clothes. But his poor-boy game did not fool Mrs. Johnson. Her second son was growing up as hard and glittery as a dime-store pinkie ring, and by the time his new friends renamed him Honkie, for his light skin color, she barely knew him anymore.

His American dream was wealth and, as he came to understand later, glory—an assertion of size in a world that discouraged it in male blacks. When he turned seventeen, he declared his independence of adults, at home and in school; their time for telling him stuff was over. Nigger has to make a mark for himself, he thought. The boys of Trey-nine were getting to be men, and the question was what kind of men they were going to be.

He knew *he* wasn't going to be like his daddy, slaving at some tailor's shop for chump change, and he wasn't going to bump along from one minimum-wage job to another like some of his Trey-nine homeboys were doing, Half Man and Hamilton and them. Some people, that was the way they really wanted to go: find that little job and starve while you work your way up. But Honk was born to hustle. He figured he could stand out on the corner looking sharp in his Stacy-Adams wingtips and hundred-dollar hat and *think* up more money in an hour than a dude like Half Man made in a whole sweaty day.

He sometimes thought in later years that he might have done better after all taking a job and working his way *toward* something besides easy money. But he wasn't gaited for the workplace, and after a couple of short-lived tries in his teens, little old part-time gigs, he walked away from it for good. He had trouble taking orders from anyone, and besides, he thought, he couldn't *buy* no hundred-dollar hat with no job he could have got.

He had been a bright boy in school, when he applied himself. But no teacher had ever reached him, and the talent went undeveloped. The only heroes he ever had were the studs out in the street holding that paper, the green kind with pictures of dead presidents on it. The fact that they kept disappearing to the joint or the graveyard didn't deter him; Honk wanted what they had, that quick bankroll overnight. He wanted it all, and if you couldn't dunk a basketball like Billy Harris, or bring home straight-A report cards like Vest Monroe, it was hard to imagine how to get it legally. In the projects, a boy coming up didn't even know what to dream *about*.

So Honk dropped out of high school and the work force and became what the brothers on the block call a player: a trafficker in anything the law disallows. In the years thereafter he would scheme, rob, deal, pimp, kill, and make money, a lot of it, more than most of his homies had to show for a lifetime of straight-up. He didn't know nothing about no working, he liked to say, because there wasn't no money in it. The dudes would come home from their twelve-hour slaves with their $15 and Honk would be out on the corner, sharp as a MF, styling, profiling, and waiting for the party. He'd hear some stud complaining about how he couldn't get no job, and Honk would answer impatiently, "Nigger, you don't *need* no job." He himself had never had a real one, unless you counted the army, and he only joined that because he had to; he had caught a grand larceny case at seventeen and was given his choice, the army or the joint. He had never even learned to fill out an application form. But he had never wanted for anything, not money *or* glory. All Honk had ever thirsted for was more.

"One year as a millionaire," his homeboy Little Jimmy was saying the day of the barbecue at Trey-nine. "That's all I want. Let me have that, where I can do whatever I want."

Honk shook his head no. He was feeling better, having first thrown up and then anesthetized his stomach with a plastic cup of wine. But the notion that enough was enough was heresy to him.

"You wanna stay rich from now on, hunh?" Little Jimmy said. "You wanna be a ol' Howard Hughes. Shoot, if you had a million bucks right now, you still wouldn't be satisfied. If he had ten million," Jimmy went on, turning to a visitor, "he *still* wouldn't be happy."

Honk grinned. "What I wanna get enough of it for?"

"If he got ten million," Little Jimmy said, "he want twenty."

"Wanna try to live forever," Honk said, leaning, rail-thin, into the wind. "See how *that* sounds."

"Immortality?" Little Jimmy said. "You can forget it."

Honk sipped his wine, his smile now masking his feelings; mortality and its analog, prison, were in fact very much on his mind. He *had* achieved a kind of royalty on Thirty-ninth Street, but it had turned out to be a very small principality, a corner left behind by the white man, and most of the dudes he had met and passed on his way to eminence there were either dead or in jail. He glanced up at Trey-nine, eyes slitted against the sun. He was still a regular commuter, taking care of business *and* pleasure, and his mama still lived in the Taylors with his younger brothers and sisters. But the project no longer had the freshness he remembered from his boyhood, or the promise. It was an OK place to visit. He just didn't want to live there anymore.

From the upper stories, you could still see the spires of downtown Chicago, but they remained as distant from Trey-nine, and as unreal, as the Emerald City of Oz. The project had become a city of lost hope—of dudes younger than Honk with no money, no home, and no prospects hustling the few dollars left on the street; of barely adolescent girls with babies, living starved lives on welfare and the impermanent affections of their men; of little kids growing up vicious, wilder even and more conscienceless than Honk himself had ever been. The old lawns at Trey-nine had gone bald, the brick was graffitied and scarred, and the open-air galleries running the length of each floor had long ago been screened in with steel-mesh fencing. Its purpose was to stop people from falling over the five-foot railings. Its effect was to make it look as if they had been sealed in—as if, Honk thought, they weren't *supposed* to escape. If you came from Trey-nine, he thought, scanning its chipped brick face, prison was just a change of address. If you came up in Trey-nine, like he had, prison was where you were *from*.

FATHERS AND SONS

I *remember once after my stepfather left, he was going to take me to a Harlem Globetrotters game,* Vest said, *and he told me he'd be by and pick me up at six o'clock or something—the game was at seven-thirty. I must have been, oh, ten or eleven years old. And I remember waiting and waiting, and I kept watching out the window for his car. He had a little Pontiac, a '56 or something. It got to be eight, nine, ten, and he didn't show up, and finally my mother said, "He's not coming." And I said, "Yes, he is. He* said *he was coming." Knowing that the game was over.*

And then he came in the next day, and he said, as he usually did, that something had come up. He asked me if I still loved him. And of course I said I did, and all was forgiven. But inside, to deal with the pain, I told myself that I would never depend on anybody or wait for anybody for anything like that. So those things made me self-sufficient, in a way.

What else it does is you grow really close to your mother, and you get what you need from your mother. But the dark side was not having a role model at home. At eighteen, I found *myself a father. I finished school, but when I was twenty-one we started living together as a family, and all of a sudden I looked at this little girl and said, "I'm her father— what am I supposed to* do?*" That's what you don't learn. You see* Father Knows Best *on television, and you say, "Is that the way it's supposed to be? But it can't be like that, given the circumstances that I'm in." I knew the father was supposed to bring home the bacon and pay the rent and provide food, but what did it really mean to be a father? I didn't know. I never had one around to see.*

One day in the middle 1980's, Billy Harris bumped into his father on the street near Trey-nine. They had been nearly strangers since the day in Billy's boyhood when his parents broke up, leaving his mother alone with six children, a moldering tenement apartment, and a future on welfare or short wages. Hey, the old man must not care about us, Billy had told himself, and the feeling, in his wounded nine-year-old heart, was mutual. He had to grow up before he could meet his father on common ground and see him as he was coming to see himself: one more black man crossed out of the picture by the unseen hand of the system.

That system, in Billy's eyes, was a game rigged against black men, and his father, having figured the odds, had thrown in his hand; the pleasures and dangers of the street were preferable to living at home with his defeat. The day the old man split, the Harrises became another bar-graph ghetto family—poor, fatherless, and imprisoned in the underclass—and their move to the Taylor Homes in 1963 only reaffirmed the sentence. Men were a ghostly presence there, as transient and trackless as bedouins in the desert. Boys like Billy had to find their way to manhood on their own, making it up as they went along.

Their mothers tried. They were still a powerful force at Trey-nine in the early days—you didn't want *any* of them to catch you being bad—and Amanda Harris was one of the strongest. She had journeyed her own long, hard road from her beginnings as the daughter of poor Mississippi sharecroppers, the first of their seventeen children. She was twenty-eight when she made her way north, one in a sixty-year exodus of blacks from the cotton belt to what the sociologist E. Franklin Frazier once called the city of destruction. She was an innocent there, and she soon fell under the spell of a factory worker named Willie Edwards, fifteen years her senior. His sweet-talking Chicago ways ran cross-grain to her plain country piety, but she married him and bore him five sons and a daughter.

They were Edwards's only legacy to her, and she raised them according to her own scriptural ways. She was an uncomplaining woman; she would not speak ill of her husband after they broke up and would not consider remarrying. Instead, she accepted the burden of rearing their children as hers alone. She believed in education, though she had only got as far as the eighth grade herself; all *her* children could say their ABC's and write their names before they ever saw the inside of a schoolroom, and all of them eventually made it to college. She insisted on their moral education as well, drawing her rules from the Bible and enforcing them with a frown. Billy would be tempted to do wrong, and there she would be in his mind's eye, his old girl, watching and willing him to do right.

She ruled from apartment 305 by a stern code. The building lights at Trey-nine lit up at eight at night, and that meant curfew time for her boys—a signal, as if by her own hand, that they were to drop whatever they were doing and come on home.

"Mama, it's so *embarrassing*," Billy finally protested. He was twelve by then, and his big brother Willie was fourteen; some of their buddies were already fooling around with girls and guns, and they had to march upstairs like *children* when those lights came on.

"OK, then," Mrs. Harris said, "I'll come down."

"No!" Billy squawked. "That's even worse!"

She relented, but only barely; if they saw her on the gallery with a white towel over her shoulder, she told them, that meant get on upstairs or else. "If you come up," she said, "I won't come down. But if you embarrass me, then I'm going to embarrass you."

They came up.

What Mrs. Harris could not provide her boys was a male role model in the straight-up life, a man in the house bringing in a regular pay envelope and presiding over the family. Such men were scarce in the Taylors and getting scarcer—nine families in ten living there today are headed by women—and Billy, in any case, had grander ambitions. He wasn't made to be a preacher, which was what his mama wanted, and he didn't want to grow up part of what he saw as the garbage all around him, the crossed-out brothers floating through the projects like driftwood on the tide. He wanted to be different, to stand out, to be *respected*, and he wanted it in a hurry.

The hard way there was too slow for Billy, and too chancy. He was good at school, even exceptional when he tried, but he didn't like going; you got beat up by gang-bangers on the way there and back, and even when you were safely inside, the other dudes played the dozens on you—machine-gunned you with insults about your mama or your threadbare clothes to see if they could make you fight or cry. Billy was a dreamer, and ghetto schools were not about dreaming; they seemed to him designed instead to *discourage* hope and freeze the black poor where they were, living in public housing and subsisting on welfare. Boys particularly felt pressured to drop out early, on the grounds, frequently expressed to them, that no one from the projects was likely to come to anything good. Billy, being dark-skinned, believed that those pressures intensified in direct relation to how black you happened to be. The front-office jobs and the fun pupil assignments, like messenger or monitor, seemed always to go to people of lighter complexion—lighter, anyway, than his.

Billy stayed in part to please his mother, though he did not have much faith in success through study. You had to believe in the system to go for that, he thought, and Billy was a precocious unbeliever. He saw cats he knew going crazy because some honky gave them a B instead of an A, when A's never got them anywhere anyway; they don't put articles in the paper about your last test score, he thought, and they don't reward you in the end for cloistering yourself and being the class egghead that nobody likes no F'ing way.

You could see brothers like that years later down on Thirty-ninth Street, the walking wounded, stoned on wine, dope, and disappointment. They had been hellacious students once, guys who really thought they could be doctors or lawyers if they worked hard enough; then they got scratched from the game, and it destroyed them. They couldn't even get themselves a *hustle,* 'cause they were too full of book learning to know the barest essentials—trivial S like what reefer costs out on the corner. Billy wanted success, too, but he wasn't going to go after it the way they had. He didn't want to wait in line for a Good Housekeeping Seal of Approval from some damn white man to tell him who he was or what he could be.

He had discovered that for himself at age eleven, when he first picked up a basketball and saw with the force of revelation that God had made him to play the game. Basketball is both pastime and narcotic in the ghetto, the cheapest high on the street. The hoops were already there, courtesy of the Chicago Housing Authority; your mama could get you a ball with a couple of books of S&H Green Stamps, and you wore sneakers anyway—everybody did, all the time, because they were both stylish and cheap. It cost practically nothing for black boys to buy into the dream, and the rewards were visible daily in the papers and on TV, the million-dollar payouts to dudes who looked and talked just like them. Not many brain surgeons or bank presidents came from the projects, but ballplayers did, dudes you *knew* from the schoolyards. In Billy's young eyes, it was one of the few accessible ways to stand out and *be* something, and not just blend into the ruined human landscape around you; a way, that is, of differentiating oneself from one's father. The parks and playgrounds swarm day and night with thousands of youngsters auditioning, in their fantasies, for fewer than 300 openings in the big-time professional league, and Billy became one of them, another black kid with a basketball jones.

He knew the odds—knew that, living where he did, it was statistically more likely that he would get blown away by some dude with a piece and a problem than that he would make it to the pros. He felt with equal certainty that he would do it. He said so in the school newspaper at Crispus Attucks—the other eighth-graders snickered behind their hands—and he repeated it at home. "Mama," he said, "I'm gonna be a professional basketball player, and I'm gonna get you a house and everything you want." *He* would be the provider, the man of the family. His mother tried not to smile.

His game was not in doubt. He didn't even have to *learn* it; it was his as if by birthright. His older brother Willie had been the reigning playground superhero at Trey-nine, and Billy had to fight clear of his shadow first. But as he grew to young manhood, a spidery six-foot-three-inch skywalker with unsmiling eyes, sure hands, and a certain arrogant disregard for the law of gravity, Willie Harris's baby brother became the main man. His only peer then was Honk Johnson's brother Reg—*Mister* Reg on the courts, out of respect for his game and his devastating right hand in a fight. He and Billy tested one another like gunslingers in a game of H-O-R-S-E one day, an epic shootout that ended in stalemate only when the light was gone and their aching young bodies sued for peace. After that, they teamed up, Butch and Sundance, and were next to unbeatable; they would spot the other side twenty-two points in a twenty-four-point game and still win most of the time.

Billy began with all the requisite motor skills, that mysterious interplay of mind, eye, muscle, bone, and ganglia that allows one man to play better than anyone else. He was blessed with an exceptional shot, inside or outside, he said one day, cataloguing his gifts as if he were a shopkeeper taking inventory; he had exceptional jumping ability; he could handle that rock above average; he knew how to pass. But Billy had more. Billy had *flair,* a sense of the possibilities and the theater of the game.

He called it imagination, and it was what separated him from the run-of-the-court players, all those dudes who couldn't even picture themselves doing certain things with a basketball. Billy couldn't imagine not being able to do them; he simply did, again and again, until they had become part of his game. The great ones had that genius, guys like Dr. J then and Michael Jordan now, the showtime superstars who gave it that little extra shake-and-bake something— that poetry of motion that people paid to see. Billy, having no false modesty, placed himself in their league. The main difference between them and him, he believed, was that they got a chance to show their artistry, where all he got was crossed out of the game.

His career had in fact almost ended before it began. He transferred out of his district to a mostly white school, Lindblom High, and was told, when he went out for the freshman team, that they were out of uniforms. All the white players seemed to have them; it was the blacks who had trouble suiting up. Billy didn't need to be told what the score was. He simply assumed he wasn't wanted and went home, to the ghetto and Dunbar High.

The cost, as he understood later, was in the quality of his education; he didn't have to work as hard at his academics as he might have at Lindblom, because no one at Dunbar demanded it of him. The profit was instant stardom. He was lighting it up, twenty-five and thirty points every game, fifty-seven one magical night in his senior year. College recruiters began appearing at Amanda Harris's door, courting her as if she were a debutante, and her mailbox at Trey-nine was stuffed with recruiting letters from coaches around the country.

Billy was on his way to glory, or, anyway, a taste of it. It didn't last long, and it was all a faded memory by the day, years later, when he encountered his father in the street; he had become, by his own description, a celebrity without cash, another tapped-out ghetto brother with a reputation and not much more. He had six children of his own with three women, and they were all growing up fatherless in the projects, just as he had. He *thought* about them, and when he had money he gave them some, but he had never learned to be a parent. He had become his father's son, and for all their estrangement, Billy felt a sense of connection when they met that he hadn't known for years.

He found himself, after a while, at his father's place. Billy's brothers and his sister had visited him as kids, and the old man had given them money. Billy, encased in scar tissue, had never been there; the distance between him and his father had been too great, like an unhealed wound. But chance had brought them together, man to man, and as they talked, Billy began to understand his father's past and his own.

His parents might have held their marriage together in spite of their differences, he thought, but the economics of the ghetto had been stacked against them, and so had the rules of play. Those rules made it easier for a poor woman to qualify for public assistance if she were single than if she were married; if you had some dude somewhere, you couldn't even get what you needed to feed your kids. So Willie Edwards had made the last gesture within his power as Amanda Harris's husband. He gave her back her maiden name and left.

For the first time, Billy saw his father as victim rather than villain, a casualty of the way things were. Hey, he thought, women were raising families then, and a lot of these dudes, hey—there was nothing else they could do *except* disappear. It was the system that had driven his parents apart, a system built, Billy thought, to keep poor blacks locked into that little class the Man had reserved for them. The evidence was all around him; most of the kids at Trey-nine were growing up in fatherless homes. But just being gone didn't mean that Billy's father had forgotten his family. At a point in their conversation, Edwards got down his scrapbooks. Billy leafed through them. The old man had clipped and saved every newspaper story that ever mentioned Billy's name. Every single one, Billy thought, turning the pages. He hadn't stopped caring after all.

SATAN'S SAINTS

Before I moved to the Robert Taylor Homes, Vest said, *the most experience I had with gangs was these guys who stopped you at lunchtime and hit you up for a nickel or a dime. They were basically shakedown artists, and if you didn't come up with it, they'd sort of rough you up a little. I never got roughed up—I gave away a lot of nickels and dimes. Or I did until this one day Gregory Bronson and I decided we're not going to give up a dime. This guy, his name was Bruce, asked us for a dime, and we said no. "What you mean, you're not going to give up a dime?" And Gregory had a pop bottle in his hand, and he broke it. I don't even think he intended to break it, but he did, and he said, "This is what you're going to get—you're not going to get a dime." And much to our amazement, Bruce backed off. Said, "I didn't mean it, I was just kidding." And from that day on, he never tried to shake us down again.*

But when I got to the Taylor Homes, the gangs were growing, and we decided to start one for protection. We got tired of these guys coming around. I wasn't in the politics of it; one day I was there, and the next day I was a Satan's Saint, or whatever they said I was going to be. But I was in it. It was safer to be in than out. The one thing you did not want to do was stand out from the crowd. And gangs were different then. Now, gangs are about making money, and we never made any money in the gangs. It was sort of you go out and you fight some guys—fistfights, or sticks and stones, or somebody might even get shot—but it was just sort of for the hell of it. We'd just go out and jump on somebody, and we never really went after anybody except in retaliation for something they'd done to us. It wasn't money—it was about turf and honor and all that.

Sonny Spruiell was lounging with some of the brothers on the benches outside Trey-nine one day in the mid-1960's, checking out the happenings, when an apparition came floating up Dearborn Street in their direction: a lone young dude wrapped in a flowing black cape with a blood-red lining. Some of the older tenants, with a practiced sixth sense for trouble, began easing off the set into the building. The boys did not. Teenagers coming up in the projects had to be both tough and wary of strangers, and they sat tight until the dude was almost in their face.

"My name is Jesus," he said, pronouncing it *Hey-soos* in the Spanish way, "and these are my Disciples."

He flung the cape wide. It flared crimson and black, like a battle flag, and the project came magically alive with armed invaders, members of a gang called the Devil's Disciples from down on Fifty-third Street. No one had even seen them coming; they just appeared, swarming over the grounds with pistols and shotguns like a posse chasing rustlers in the Westerns, and it wasn't much comfort that they were only passing through on their way to battle at Stateway Gardens, the next project to the north. Sonny thought of himself as a hard guy, a hope-to-die nigger, but there he was with his partners, trembling like frightened children at the *crack-crack* of gunfire in the air. He glanced at the grown-ups cowering on the second- and third-floor galleries. They ain't gonna look out for us, he was thinking. We're gonna have to look out for ourselves.

Till then, they had not done very well at it. Gangs were pandemic on the South Side, warring tribes who called themselves Disciples or Del Vikings or I, Supreme Cobras or, rising to primacy among all of them, the Blackstone Rangers. Visiting sociologists kept finding things to romanticize about them: the sense of identity, family, and pride they brought to young lives in the anarchy of the ghetto. But the people who actually lived there were frightened by the gang-bang-ing—the term meant gang war, not gang rape, in Chicago—and their fear rose as the arms race in the street escalated from rocks, chains, and Louisville Sluggers to real guns and live ammunition.

Trey-nine was in a particularly vulnerable position, standing alone on a block. It was the only building so exposed in the whole long row of projects stretching end to end like penitentiary towers down the South Side. Its solitude made it easy prey to gang-bangers from Stateway to the north or from the other Taylor high rises, clustered three per block, to the south. Just leaving the grounds meant tres-passing on some enemy's turf, a crime punishable by a beating or worse. You could not, for example, walk farther north than Thirty-seventh Street without some Del Viking trying you, with fists if you were lucky, with bullets if you were not. It got so bad that Half Man Carter started carrying a .22 pistol to school and kept packing it until the day he decided it was no longer worth his life to get there.

It had taken time for the contagion to spread inside Trey-nine. Applicants for the projects were screened in those days, with family stability as one of the criteria, and the mamas' Mafia still enforced some semblance of discipline; it was said that if one of them caught you doing wrong, she'd whup you first, then send you home for a second hiding at your own mother's hand. There were rules then, and parents who cared enough to enforce them. We wasn't orientated to no gang-banging, Honk Johnson mused long afterward. We all had *curfews,* so what the F we look like trying to be a *gang?*

But gangs, and gang fever, were everywhere around them. The boys of Trey-nine were surrounded by predators, and the Disciple raid brought home how vulnerable they were, even on their own home territory. They were too open a target, Sonny argued. Any dude look-ing to make a reputation could just walk on in and kick ass.

They had called a council of war the day after the invasion, gathering by habit on the twelfth-floor gallery outside Vest's apartment, 1201. His place was their informal clubhouse; his mama preferred that he and his buddies hang out there, on the theory that if she could not be sure precisely what he was into, she would at least know where he was. Sonny was there, along with Pee Wee, and Honk, and Half Man, and Moose, and Vest, and Nate the Albino, and a stud called Crazy Horse who lived across Fortieth Street but hung out with the Trey-nine brothers and knew about guns.

Sonny was a casebook underachiever, a bright and athletic boy who sometimes flunked tests on purpose so as not to look too serious about school or anything else. His preferred image was cool, the brother off the block, and he took charge of the meeting.

"I'm tired of running," he began. "I'm tired of seeing everybody that's supposed to be protecting our building run. We got to do something."

What they did was add yet another to the patchwork of private armies on the South Side, each claiming proprietary rights to its bit of real estate and its women; for people who owned nothing, those were the only possessions worth fighting about. Trey-nine's new entry into the field was called Satan's Saints, a name connoting that they were good guys who could turn evil when crossed. They didn't really think of themselves as a gang, not at first; they were the same boys who played ball and sang R&B together, only this time their objective was business, not pleasure, and the business at hand was mutual security. They were like wildebeests, Ed Hamilton would reminisce years later. They were herding together for their own protection, and once they got their thing tight, couldn't *no* strange MF walk in the building without first saying what he was doing there and who he was going to see.

Their warring was all cowboys-and-Indians then, a game, Moose Harper thought, until people started getting killed. They began as children playing grown-up, and their role models were gunfighters and gangsters in the movies, not the bruised and footloose men who had brought them into the world. When they wore the colors of the Saints, they took on both an aura of danger and the possibility of respect—a respect their fathers had too often been denied.

Even their early adventures in banditry had a kind of boyishness about them. Once, they gang-mugged a stray white hitchhiker, roughing him up a little until they discovered that he had no money; then, feeling sorry for him, they gave him some of their own. The principal weapon in their street wars in those days was a line of tough talk called woofing or, actually, *wolf*ing—playing wolf, like a dog does, to scare enemies away. Moose himself was a master at it, a boy in Bogart clothing. There was in fact a gentleness about him, the soft core of a child whose secret and seemingly unattainable wish was that his own father love him. But he carried a loud voice in a large body, and his fearsome nickname preceded him into battle—*Here come Big Moose*. Not even the Trey-nine boys knew where the name really came from: a puppet named Herman the German Moose on a kiddie TV show popular in his early childhood, before he moved into the project. They thought *Moose* described his size and strength. It didn't, though the effect was just the same; his name and his murderous mouth bought him a lot of prestige without his having to fight for it.

The formula didn't always work. Once, some Del Vikings raided a ballgame at Trey-nine and took all the bats, so Pee Wee Fisher said the magic word—"Moose"—and Moose faced off against the invaders. "Where you going with these bats!" he demanded loudly; it was a threat, not a question, and after some further bogarting by Moose, the Dels backed off. But they came back twice that day and again the next, bringing reinforcements—*big* reinforcements. The first time, Moose ran, escaping through the heavy midday traffic on Thirty-ninth Street. The second time, he bombed a Del raiding party with bottles from the gallery outside his thirteenth-floor apartment, adding a remark or two on the chastity of their mamas. The third time, the Dels arrived in force, demanding a chance to settle accounts with Moose in single combat.

"OK," Moose answered. Then he checked out the combatant they had in mind. The dude was huge. Goliath time, Moose was thinking, and he didn't feel as lucky as David. He lost interest.

"I think me and the guy who took the bats, me and him should go head-up," he said.

"No, I'm not gonna go head-up with you," the guy said, ducking behind Goliath. "Here's my brother."

"Wait a minute," Moose said, half pleading, "my thing's not with him—it's with *you*."

"*I'll* fight the big dope," a voice said at his elbow.

Moose stared. It was little Ed Carter, the kid they called Half Man because he looked, acted, and fought like a man tenanted in a boy's small body. He was five feet four in sneakers, but he had stone hands and cobra eyes, and if he was scared in battle, he never let anyone see it. He sized up the Dels' champion with his half-hooded gaze, looking unimpressed.

"Ed, you gonna get killed," Moose said.

"He don't intimidate nobody," Half Man said, and then, to the dude: "C'mon."

The two started rumbling at Thirty-ninth Street, wailing like World War III; they fought up to Thirty-seventh, then back down to Thirty-eighth, and when they quit, Half Man was the one left standing. The Del Viking was in ruins, and so was Moose's Bogart reputation. The biggest Satan's Saint had let the smallest do his fighting for him, and it was weeks before he could hold his head high again.

Fists by then were obsolescent weapons in the territorial wars in the ghetto; guns began appearing in the projects and on the street, and some of the Saints had the feeling they were getting in over their heads. Zip guns came first, a treacherous one-shot contrivance home-made with some wood for a butt, some inner tubing and a nail for a firing mechanism, and a length of car antenna for a barrel. They were usually fired wildly from a great distance and were at least as much danger to the shooter as to his target. You always turned your head away for safety's sake when you got off a shot; Sonny, for one, had no idea if he hit anybody or not, and neither did anyone else. But other gangs were laying up real guns, raising the stakes, and one day Crazy Horse led some of the Saints to his mother's place across Fortieth Street. They followed him into his bedroom. He turned back the mattress. Nestled on the springs was a sawed-off shotgun. The Saints, having been shot at, had the means to shoot back. Like it or not, they were armed for war.

Not all of them liked it. Crazy Horse was hard-core, and so were Sonny and Ed Hamilton and some of the others. But Moose hated gang-banging once it turned deadly—we wasn't *really* no hard guys, he recalled years later—and even Pee Wee, one of the Saints' main men, was losing his heart for it. He had been watching guys get *doggish,* moving up that escalator from clubbing to stabbing and then shooting each other; they were boys with guns, caught in their grown-up games, and Pee Wee's enthusiasm was fading as the slugs hit closer to home. One day, one of his Trey-nine partners almost caught it in a fight with the Four Corners Rangers. The dude took a bullet through the little bitty space between his skull and his brain, and Pee Wee was thinking, man, this S is *real.* Naw. Unh-unh. No mo' for me.

He saw how real things were the day they put on their black Saints' jackets, fueled up on sweet wine, and went hunting for a Del Viking who had pulled a gun on one of the Trey-nine brothers. The dude had challenged their prestige, and they knew they were going to shoot him; being children at warfare, they just didn't know how it would feel. They found him in an alley under the el tracks between State and Wabash, leaning against a car. He had a .38 stuck in his waistband, out where they could see it. He looked like he had been drinking.

"Mighty Satan's Saints!" Crazy Horse yelled. The code required that you "represent" what gang you were from.

"Mighty Dels!" the dude yelled back. He upped the .38 and started shooting, but one of the Saints beat him with a single shotgun blast from six feet. It hit the dude in the shoulder. His body fell forward. His shoulder was still stuck to the car.

The Saints ran back to Trey-nine. They were suddenly boys again, and they were scared, even Crazy Horse, the baddest brother in the gang; when the police came for him, he was shaking like everybody else.

"Pee Wee, you think he killed him?" Sonny whispered.

"I don't know, man, I don't know," Pee Wee answered.

The answer drifted back later: Yeah, the ol' boy died. There had been nothing personal in the shooting, and there was no dancing on his grave afterward; they even felt a distant fraternity with him. The dude had represented wrong, and hey—it was automatic then that they were going to butt heads. When you were a gang-banger, things happened.

And got worse. The strength-in-numbers impulse that had moved them to organize in the first place got them entangled in mergers with larger, deadlier gangs. They hooked up first with the I, (for Imperial) Supreme Cobras, headquartered across the street at Stateway Gardens, and while they were still getting used to being Cobras, a guy named Cody came around from the Blackstone Rangers to court them. The Rangers were the biggest and most notorious youth gang of them all, a Balkan empire spreading by force of numbers and arms across the South Side, but Cody came in peace that first time. He talked all about what an honor and privilege it would be to affiliate with the Rangers. The crowd from Stateway agreed, and the Cobras became the I, Supreme Rangers. Some of the Trey-nine brothers were unhappy about it, but the leadership of the gang had passed from their hands, and they had no choice but to follow along.

A few weeks later, Cody came back and found them idling on the benches outside Trey-nine. Some of the dissidents were calling themselves Satan's Saints again, and Cody's displeasure was clear.

"I want everybody to go to the meeting tonight," he said.

"What meeting?" someone asked.

"Stones' meeting," Cody said.

"We ain't no Stones," someone else answered.

Cody hit him.

So they went to the meeting, at a South Side church; the white clergy there had become persuaded that the Stones were a potential force for good in the community, Junior Achievers with guns, and allowed them to use the place for their weekly gatherings. The Trey-nine brothers took seats in the back and looked around, hearts pounding. Jeff Fort, the reigning Black Prince of the Stones, was in the pulpit, and some of his men were policing the aisles with rifles and clubs. It was "truth night" in the realm, a show-and-tell demonstration of the virtues of honesty, and if someone dozed off in the pews, one of Fort's enforcers would go upside his head with a pool cue to command his full attention.

In the pews, someone was introducing a new recruit, a little dude with a large reputation in his own neighborhood branch of the Stones. "And you know what, Jeff?" the guy presenting him said suddenly.

"He say he F'd you up. He told us that when he was in jail with us."

"*What?*" Fort exclaimed. "Send him up onstage."

The dude slunk up, looking scared.

"I hear you say you whipped my ass," Fort said. "Is that true?"

The dude was in no position to deny it. At a signal from Fort, two huge bodyguards materialized, one on either side.

"Get him!" Fort commanded.

The two of them took turns hitting the dude in the ribs, the punches landing so hard they lifted him off his feet. He was a tough little MF, and he took their best, shot for shot, till their hands were sore from hitting him. Someone produced a belt or maybe a bullwhip—memories differed—and they laid on ten lashes. Slavery days, Sonny Spruiell was thinking in the back benches, only the dude still wouldn't break.

Someone finally brought out a .38 revolver. He dropped in a single round, spun the cylinder, and put the muzzle to the dude's head. The choice is yours, the Stones' management told him. At the moment they pulled the trigger, he could sit still and take his chances like a Stone-to-the-bone Ranger, or he could knock the gun away from his temple.

Everybody in the house figured the dude would go for option B, in which case the slug, if it went off, would be coming straight at them. At truth time, guys were diving for cover under the benches.

They heard a *click* down front.

Heads poked up over the pews. The dude had sat still, accepting the one-in-six possibility that his brains would wind up splattered over the altar. He had passed the test. He had heart. Fort awarded him an on-the-spot commission as warlord of his home gang.

But in the back of the church, the newly made Imperial Supreme Rangers of Trey-nine sat shaken by the show. Their young lives were surrounded by violence, and some of them were already feeling hardened to it; still, there was something raw, something cold, about justice Ranger-style, emanating as it did from the barrel of a gun at point-blank range. Vest Monroe was scared and didn't mind saying so. Ed Hamilton was hoping no one could see how hard his heart was thumping. Moose Harper broke out in hives and wound up in the hospital; he had shot at guys, and been shot at, but he knew he could never do it that way—not that close. None of them was feeling particularly imperial *or* supreme, and most of them didn't much care about being Blackstone Rangers anymore.

JAMES BONNER

James Bonner was the one who always told us that we had to stand up for ourselves, Vest said, *and we couldn't let people walk over us. "You have to be a man—don't be a sissy." In fact, James Bonner would* make *us fight. There was a guy we called Mike Feet, because he wore like size fourteen or fifteen shoes. He was about six three or six four, but he didn't like to fight and he didn't fight. So James Bonner gave him this piece of advice: "If you don't like to fight,* start *the fight. Then there won't* be *no fight. While the other guy still talking, hit him. Knock him out." And he taught Mike Feet to do that. Mike would hit you one time and you'd be down with your eyes rolling back in your head before you'd said what you wanted to say. That was James Bonner's way. He didn't wait for trouble. He said, "If you get beat, you get beat, but fight," and if it didn't work out, if you got beat up, James Bonner would clean up for you.*

The real security force at Trey-nine, the cavalry you sent for when the enemy was at your borders, was the one-man gang they called James Bonner. They *always* called him James Bonner, as if it were one word run together, never just James or just Bonner; it was like a magic incantation you said to ward off danger. There were figures like him in urban black folklore, renegade heroes with fast guns and tombstone minds, only James Bonner wasn't no fictional bad-ass like Stackolee or Sudden Death. James Bonner was the real thing.

James Bonner was built inside and out like a barrel of blasting powder, 260 pounds of muscle, nerve, and violence on a five-foot-eight-inch chassis, and nobody *ever* knew how many MF's he and his sawed-off shotgun, Betsy, had taken out of the game. It was enough to understand that, as his brother Moe liked to say, James Bonner didn't brook no BS, especially not when the interests of Trey-nine were involved. He was the guardian of its gates, the enforcer of its codes, the man of the house to its fatherless boys; he was, dependably, *family* in a community where impermanence was otherwise the norm. It was James Bonner, six or seven years their elder, who looked after the Trey-nine brothers and, in his raw way, taught them right from wrong. Never mind what *I* do, he would say of his own outlaw life; *you* don't do that. He cared enough about them to tell them not to be like him.

His lessons in manhood and morals were reinforced by periodic pops upside the head and by the certain knowledge that in a jam James Bonner would do their violence for them. Once, for example, he brought home some food from the chicken shack where he worked and was frying up dinner for a bunch of the brothers when he heard a commotion outside his sixth-floor apartment. He came churning out of the kitchen to the screen door. It was so thickly clotted with soot and lint that he could see out without anyone seeing in. He scanned the scene. On the gallery, a couple of Del Vikings with .22's had got the drop on the Trey-nine boys—*his* boys—and were lining them up against the wall for a pistol whipping or maybe worse.

The deal was just going down when the screen door flew open. Heads turned. James Bonner stood filling the doorway, his shotgun leveled at the invaders.

They froze.

''Drop 'em, MF's, or I'll kill you,'' James Bonner growled.

His eyes were like open coffins. The Dels gave up their guns and ran.

Sometimes, he didn't even have to appear; sometimes, the mention of his name was enough. A girl named Carolyn gave a party one night, and some of the brothers were there, Vest and Moose and Sonny and Ed and Half Man, along with their ladies. The light was red and low. A Temptations record turned on Vest's portable phonograph, gaited slow for dancing. Carolyn's mother had stepped out to go marketing. The mood was getting mellow when a sharp rap sounded at the door.

Carolyn opened it a crack.

A dude named Kilgore, a gang leader from Stateway Gardens, poked his foot inside. A platoon of his partners crowded up behind him.

"Y'all havin' a party?" he asked. "Can we come in?"

"No," Carolyn told him.

"Aw, baby, why not? We just wanna come in and party a little bit."

"I said no!" Carolyn answered. She slammed the door on Kilgore's foot. He yanked it out, swearing loudly. She bolted the door, but as she turned back to the party, the window on the gallery exploded inward, showering glass into the living room. She opened the door again, and the gang-bangers poured in past her, howling for blood.

"Get out, get out!" Carolyn screamed. "The party's over!"

"Naw, it ain't," Kilgore said. "It's just beginning."

Vest was trying to rescue his record player when Kilgore slugged him in the eye. The phonograph went out the window. Vest fell to the floor, curling up under a rain of fists and feet. He could hear people screaming and furniture breaking and someone saying, "Naw, Baylord, don't hit him with the couch!"

Vest looked up.

Kilgore's enforcer, a gap-toothed 200-pounder named Baylord, had tipped a massive sofa on end and was about to send it crashing down on Vest's head. Vest was lying there, counting down to darkness, when a voice said, "Here come the Bonners with the heat!"

The alarm had reached the Bonners' apartment, 609, and James and his brother David had come charging up four floors to the rescue. But there was no longer a rescue to be made; by the time they appeared in the door, pistols in hand, the Stateway raiders had disappeared like a mirage in the desert.

Sometimes, more forceful demonstrations were necessary. Once, Sonny was playing his own South Side remake of *West Side Story,* warring with a dude from an enemy gang, the Russian Rangers, over a Trey-nine girl named Jean. The Rangers stole onto the grounds one night to settle matters and found Sonny's partner, Honk, hanging out in front of the building. One of them put a gun in Honk's face, marched him upstairs to Jean's apartment, 502, and ordered him to call Sonny out.

"Sonny, come outside," Honk said.

"In a minute," Sonny answered.

"Man, come out *now!*" Honk yelled.

Sonny peeped out. He could see Honk but not the gun in his back.

"Man, come on," Honk said, begging now. "*Please* come outside."

Sonny stepped out. The Rangers closed around him, and their leader, Bubbles, commanded: "Go get Jean."

Someone fetched her.

"Jean," Bubbles told her, "you been messing around with *this* guy." He gestured toward Sonny's competition, a dude called BB. "And you go with *this* one," Bubbles said, indicating Sonny. "Choose who you want."

Sonny and BB stood side by side, watching Jean deliberate. It was as if they were two pieces of merchandise and she couldn't make up her mind between them. The longer she took, the hotter Sonny got.

"Whoever you want," Bubbles prompted her, "choose him, and then that's gonna be the end of it."

"Well," Jean said finally, "I want Sonny."

Bubbles sent her home and declared the war over. "BB, this the end of it, don't mess with her no more," he said, and then, to Sonny: "OK, that's the end of it. We gonna let it go."

He and his party of raiders started downstairs, Bubbles and BB and Moses and Muscle and Skill. But the war had only begun for Sonny. Still boiling, he ran upstairs to 609 and banged on the door.

James Bonner appeared.

"James, they in the building!" Sonny sputtered, breathless. "They just pulled a gun on me!"

James Bonner disappeared inside, going, Sonny guessed, for Betsy. Sonny went off in search of more men and more guns, then caught up as the Rangers were walking out of the building.

James Bonner put his shotgun up their nose. "OK, you dirty MF's," he said, "which one of y'all got the gun?"

The Rangers surrendered it.

"Shoot 'em, shoot 'em!" Sonny screamed. He was jumping up and down.

"No, Sonny," James Bonner said.

"Give *me* the gun," Sonny begged. "Let *me* shoot 'em."

"No," James Bonner said, louder this time.

"Then let me shoot this MF right here." He pointed to BB, his competitor for Jean. "I'll blow his ass away."

"Sonny, *no*," James Bonner said. "They ain't coming around here no more."

They did come back, as it turned out, cruising past Trey-nine one night soon thereafter in a broken-down ruin of a jalopy. Some of the Trey-nine brothers were lolling around James Bonner's car, sipping beer and Orange Rock. The jalopy slowed. A couple of Russian Rangers leaned out, talking trash.

"F it!" James Bonner said; they were calling his hand, so he popped the trunk of his car, got out his shotgun—it was never far away—and took aim at the intruders. The driver floored the accelerator, pedal to the metal. The hulk didn't respond. It was laboring along at twenty miles an hour when James Bonner pumped the gun once and fired. He hit the rear window. It disintegrated. The Russian Rangers never came back.

James Bonner by then had become a folk hero around Trey-nine. In the sight of the law, he was another ghetto hard case, a trafficker in stolen goods and spilled blood. To the boys under his protection, he was a strong, brave, and even moral figure in his fashion; he did way more good than bad, Mr. Reg used to say, and the bad, he *had* to do. Like the time in later years when one dude from the building, a treacherous dude called Piggy, shot another to death at the shopping center and afterward put out word that he was going to take care of James Bonner, too. James Bonner never waited for trouble to come to him. When he heard about the threat, he got his shotgun, walked into Piggy's apartment, caught him with his old lady, and blew his head off.

James Bonner did a year and four months in prison for the killing. But no one at Trey-nine blamed him, not even Ed Hamilton, who was tight with Piggy and would have got blown away, too, if he had been there. James Bonner was everybody's big brother, Ed said, and if he killed Piggy, it was—it must have been—in the best interest of the building.

A BETTER CHANCE

I *didn't want to go to away to school in the first place,* Vest said. *I had never stayed away from home for more than a weekend, let alone lived in what was really a white community. I was very insecure about a lot of things, even knowing how to set a table. I didn't know which side the fork went on; at home, we'd just come in and get something to eat. So there was that—are these people going to think I'm stupid? And there was the work. I remember my aunt telling me, "You're going out there and those guys are going to be really smart.*

64

Doctors' sons, lawyers' sons, and Hattie's son.'' My mother's
name is Hattie. And I was really afraid I couldn't do the
work. In fact, my eighth-grade teacher told me and the other
guys, ''You've been hot stuff around here, but you're going
out there with the big boys now.''

And that scared me. I'd done pretty well at Wendell Phil-
lips without having to work that hard. But as I went on, it was
getting tougher and tougher to stay on the straight and nar-
row, because the guys were escalating into other things. Big-
ger things. I think that's what Lovelace saw—that he had to
get us out of that trap.

Leroy Lovelace sat before his freshman English honors class at
Wendell Phillips High School one autumn day in 1965, sweeping the
room with a severe gaze and an invisible inward smile. Phillips was
a depressed area most days, a warehouse overstocked with youngsters
from the surrounding projects, and not, for the most part, the best
and brightest youngsters; they commonly wound up in the trade school
program at Dunbar Vocational, on the theory that only the quicker
learners could be trusted around the fancy shop machinery there. The
leftovers went to Phillips, drifting through its crowded classrooms
and its gang-infested corridors till they graduated or dropped out.
There was an air of despair about the place, so heavy that Lovelace
had almost succumbed to it himself in his first year as a teacher. But
he had endured, a lonely and wintry voice for excellence, and now
he was being rewarded with the means to change—no, *save*—three
young lives.

The magic that had fallen into his hands was a program called A
Better Chance, ABC for short; he had spied the papers on a counselor's desk and snapped them up before anyone else could get at them.
ABC was a by-product of the civil rights movement of the early sixties and the aftershocks of conscience it set off in the boardrooms of

white philanthropy. A consortium of upscale public and private secondary schools in the East and Midwest decided it was time to integrate their mostly white student bodies, and not just with the sons and daughters of the black haute bourgeoisie. Their plan was to scour the ghettos, the barrios, and the reservations for their most promising students. The chosen few would be put through a summer's cram course on a university campus, then sent on to top-of-the-line prep schools and the prospect, if they did well, of a quality college education.

Lovelace knew at firsthand how important it was for a poor black child to escape the undertow of deep material and spiritual need. He had himself been born in poverty, one of seven children of a hard-scrabble Alabama farm couple, and had grown up during the Great Depression. His parents had never had a chance at formal education. In the rural South, in their day, black children were considered too valuable at stoop labor to be wasting their time at book learning.

But the Lovelaces wanted education for *their* children, seeing in it their deliverance from bondage to the land. Lovelace remembered his mother playing spelling games around the dinner table, goading her children to master words she didn't really know herself. They would point to this object or that, and she would spell out its name; she probably got the letters wrong, Lovelace imagined, but she made learning fun, and they responded. Lovelace was furious that an older brother mastered reading before he did, and started school first. He knew the day he went that he wanted to be a teacher, and he couldn't wait to begin.

There were no ABC rescue programs in his boyhood. There wasn't even a public high school for black youngsters in his backwater district outside Mobile; most black children, particularly black boys, graduated from grade school to the fields. Lovelace's parents found a better chance on their own. They put him through a private school run by the Dutch Reformed Church, and he did well enough to win a scholarship to a church college in Michigan, appropriately named Hope.

Lovelace believed, out of his own experience, in the importance of helping hands, but not in pampering his students. He had tried that when he started at Phillips in 1959. It was his first teaching job, and while he had no illusions about schools in the ghetto, he was unprepared for how tough it was going to be. Defeat was part of the landscape, a kind of common ground between faculty and students; it was expected, and those youngsters who wanted to succeed at their studies had to fight through the discouragement of their teachers and the taunts of their peers. Lovelace started out playing nice guy to his classes, inviting their attention instead of commanding it and freely granting second chances when they failed. He nearly drowned in the mediocre work he got back. He considered quitting in frustration but thought better of it. Instead, by conscious plan, he hardened his heart, or, anyway, his classroom manner, as if he were an officer preparing himself for war.

He began with the premise that ghetto children were born with the normal ration of talent and intelligence. Nature, he thought, could not be so cruel or mad as to deny them *that*; it was his duty as a teacher to goad them to use the resources they had. He believed further that it was not necessarily disabling to come from a large or a fatherless family, no matter how many studies you read about the "pathology" of the ghetto. What counted was the measure of motivation a child got at home; a single mother in the projects with an apartment full of youngsters could still push them to succeed and still make plain her disappointment if they did not. Lovelace needed parents like that, parents who cared, with or without benefit of matrimony. He was at war, and they were his allies. He was fighting the environment for the souls of their children, and he meant to win, by any means necessary.

Mr. Nice Guy accordingly died after one academic year. The new Mr. Lovelace was challenging, demanding, even nasty when he had to be. He forgave his students for gaps in what they had learned before he got his hands on them, but not after; they were strictly accountable for anything he taught them. He worked them from bell to bell, and sometimes beyond; we're not through yet, he would say, holding them overtime at their desks so he could bang home one last point. He flunked them for missing so much as a single class without a medical excuse. He drilled them like a marine sergeant in the proprieties of speech and grammar. He made them write every day and read every night. He force-marched them through the classics, from Homer to Hemingway. He assigned them his own favorite, *Moby Dick*, though it was tough going even for his brightest seniors; it was important to him merely to expose them to its mysteries at an early age. He required that they think about what they were reading, not just memorize it and play it back in their tests and recitations. Recall, for Lovelace, was only the beginning of learning.

He developed a ferocious reputation around the school, which precisely suited his purposes. He was neither big nor tough, not by the standards of the street, but his room was a clearing in the forest, a place of silence, order, hard work, and nearly perfect attendance. Being liked no longer counted as much to him as being a *teacher,* whatever the cost in popularity. Though it hurt him sometimes, he would not let himself ease up; you couldn't, and he didn't. He came to be regarded with dread in the corridors, and the freshmen who pitched up in his room were the objects of upper-class pity. You got Lovelace? Sweet Jesus. Poor guy.

He began to see progress, and he felt particularly blessed that autumn by his freshman honors class; he would think of it in future years as the best he had ever had. Only a few of its thirty or thirty-five enrollees were *really* honor students, he knew that. The honor students, the ones who should have been reading the classics and preparing for college, were mostly learning to run lathes and drill presses at vocational school; when they showed up at Phillips, it was usually by accident or by inertia, because it was close to home and their friends were there. The most that could be said for the majority of Lovelace's kids was that they seemed to want to learn and were trying.

But that was a small victory in itself, and a few of the thirteen- and fourteen-year-olds in the class had become quite special to him. There were only openings for three of them in the ABC program, and he had decided that they ought to go to boys. Black families had traditionally favored their daughters with what educational opportunities were available; a boy could always get by on muscle and mother wit, so the supposition went, but a girl without schooling was likely to wind up slaving her life away in Miss Anne's kitchen, if she worked at all. Lovelace had grown up in that tradition and was conscious of it when he chose his nominees. He may have seen something of himself in them, in black boys struggling toward daylight as he had, against the most difficult odds. He thought, in any case, that they merited what some distant white benefactors had chosen to call a better chance—a chance at escape.

His eyes, framed in aviator glasses, roamed over the room and found his nominees.

"Monroe . . . " he intoned.

Vest Monroe was the easy choice, the class intellectual underneath his Trey-nine protective coloration. He was already reading two or three years ahead of his grade level—some of Lovelace's honor students were a year or two behind—and he was devouring the school library at a rate of an author a month. He had good support at home, a strong-willed mother goading him forward, and the respect of his peers as well. Serious students could be pariahs in the projects, but Vest was a popular boy, and even the gang-bangers at the Taylor Homes seemed fond of him. They called him Brainiac, after a character in *Superman;* they hung out at his apartment, enfolded him in their gang and stuck out their own chests a little at his A's, as if some part of their own hopes rode on his making good.

". . . Steward . . . "

Steve Steward was less obvious, less sure a bet. He was part of Vest's old crowd at Prairie Courts, not the tougher Robert Taylor bunch, and was almost as gifted a student—gifted, that is, when he wanted to be. He had a great flair for math in particular; a seventh-grade teacher had spotted it and, trying to be encouraging, wrote in his yearbook, "Good luck being a statistician." His problem was getting serious—about school, which was too easy for him, or a career, which seemed beyond his powers of imagination. He couldn't think of anything he really wanted to do, and his mother was too soft to get after him about it. He was growing up an impish boy, small and baby-faced, with mischief in his heart. A joker, Lovelace thought, and yet the talent was there; it was Steve's compass that needed setting, and maybe ABC could manage it.

". . . Stingley . . . "

Charles Ray Stingley, too, was a student of promise, more than he had yet let himself show. It wasn't so much direction he needed, in Lovelace's view, as a kick start to get him going. Ray came from one of those big ghetto families, dysfunctionally big by the conventions of urban sociology; he was the seventh of twelve children crammed into an apartment at Prairie Courts, sleeping four to a bedroom. But the family was whole, warm, and supportive, and Ray's parents, refugees from rural Mississippi, were strong for education—stronger, it sometimes seemed, than Ray himself. School was a chore for him, a labor of filial duty rather than love, and his lack of enthusiasm showed at first in his work. Lovelace concluded that he was lazy and gave him an F at midterm to get his attention. It worked. Ray knuckled down and started turning in A+ tests and book reports, the quality Lovelace had expected of him all along.

". . . I want to see you after class," Lovelace said.

His voice had that low, razor-edged tone that usually signaled trouble. The three boys stole glances at one another, trying to remember what they had done wrong—there was usually something—and wondering what terrible punishment would be visited on them.

I didn't do it, Ray Stingley was thinking.

The bell rang. The three trudged forward to Lovelace's desk.

He's gonna give me another F, Ray was thinking.

What Lovelace had in mind instead was another life.

He pushed some papers toward the three boys. The logo said "ABC," and the papers were about going somewhere else to school, somewhere rich, white, and far away from Thirty-ninth Street. It wouldn't be a free ride, Lovelace explained; they would have to pass an entrance exam and spend a summer in intensive catch-up study in English and math just to get on the plane. It was a little scary for boys to whom even downtown Chicago was another country inhabited by an alien race. Lovelace made it sound like a ticket to tomorrow, a passport to a world beyond the ghetto. "We've got to get you away from here," Ray remembered him saying. They listened, half happy, half wary. For them, getting away from the ghetto meant leaving home.

Where opportunity revealed itself, a chance for success followed, and in 1969 Vest Monroe was on his way to Harvard after three years at a prestigious Rhode Island boarding school. "I was pleased that I was showing what black boys were capable of," Vest said. "Yet somehow, it seemed, attending St. George's made me a good Negro in their eyes, while those left in Robert Taylor were bad Negroes or, at the very least, inferior Negroes." Coming home had its problems as well, though of a different kind, like when an old friend asked Vest if he was the Man. But Vest had learned that being born black, no matter where he went or what he achieved, there would always be the inescapable fact of his blackness. When he finally went home to Robert Taylor, he knew he had never left.

CONTEMPORARY PHOTOGRAPHS
BY JACQUES CHENET

Roy Johnson had stayed in The Life too long, but from the evidence all around him, that was itself a victory; most of the studs he'd known were now either dead or locked up for life. His career in banditry, begun convincingly in childhood, had until recently been a success; he'd attained local fame, a transient fortune, and, by accident, a religious wife and a house in the suburbs. But encroaching middle age and impending imprisonment had left him wondering whether it had really been worth the risk. He'd been a big player, but on a little stage, and with his midnight reputation as the baddest MF, his options ranged from bad to worse. He was stuck in his history, which was Thirty-ninth Street, and his only letters of transit were from the Illinois Department of Corrections. But going to prison didn't worry Roy. If you came up in Trey-nine, he thought, prison was where you were from.

Billy Harris wasn't on Front Street anymore, but at least he had a past, a brief but tangible record of achievement, and a basketball court was still his domain. He had made it his from the age of eleven, when he announced his intention to be both superstar and provider for his family. But with his first taste of what he later called a vicious business—the white business of college sports, a commodity market trading in black bodies not for sport but for profit—the dream began to sour. His brother Willie (far right) had sensed the harm and dropped out early. Billy stuck with it long enough to achieve some measure of success before he found himself back on Thirty-ninth Street in the cycle of poverty where he started. But he had his friend Tina to make life more bearable, and his mission with the next generation to make his life a success.

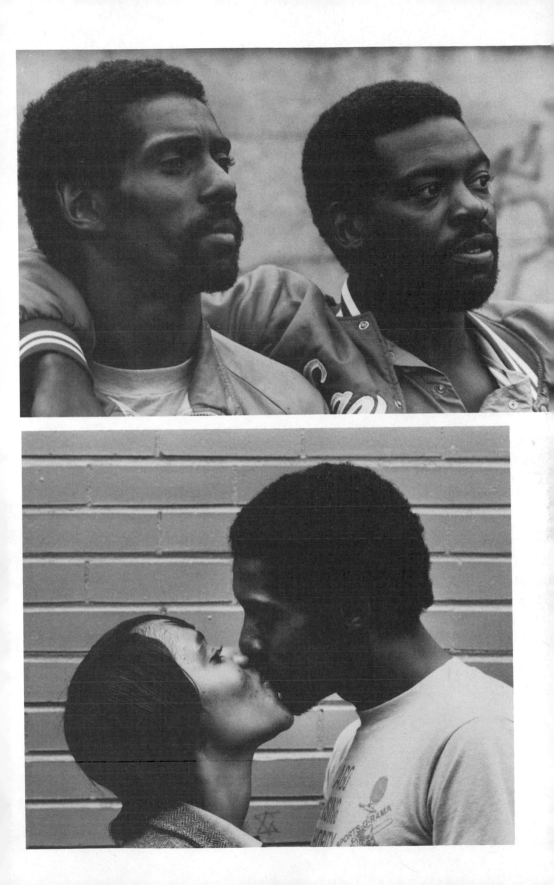

Sonny Spruiell wasn't exactly on Easy Street, but the narcotic smog that strangled him for a time on Thirty-ninth Street had lifted; his down-and-out passage through the dope houses of the South Side was ancient history. There had been a time when Sonny relished the image of being a hope-to-die nigger, but he looked back now and could pinpoint the moment he'd hit rock bottom; it was when he went to visit his mama and found her following him around the apartment, scared that her own son would steal her blind. From the peaceful distance of middle age he could look back in safety with his old friend Moose Harper on their gang-banging youth. He was in control now, and with his family around him his life looked like a Bill Cosby script played by a Trey-nine company (bottom left, left to right, Keita, Sonny, Jean, Nookie).

In his youth, Moose Harper was like a character from a family show who had mistakenly wandered onto the set of a gangster movie. He played his part, sometimes with conviction, but never quite gave up the idea that, deep down, he and his homies were really the good guys. He sold and took drugs, a daily anesthetic against life and his conscience: You did it to feel good, he thought; you could feel good in this ugly place after a trip to the corner drugstore. But his conscience was stronger than his brew of drugs, and when his sense of what was right overtook his vocation for what was wrong, he set out to change his life. He sought his answers in religion and found them. He became a witness for Jehovah and with his new family went out to heal other lives as his had been healed with the word of the Lord. With his wife, Lydia, Moose was finally home.

Pee Wee Fisher had glimpsed the American Dream for a brief time before finding himself back at square one on Thirty-ninth Street. He'd had the house and the lawn and the car, but never much peace. His first journey from Trey-nine had been to Vietnam, and when he came home, it was plain that he'd come home different, his life an extension of the combat zone— a series of skirmishes, some won, some lost. But in his early middle age, Pee Wee knew he wouldn't make the same mistakes again; he had his objective in his sights now, and he was going for it.

If Pee Wee didn't have much in a material way, he at least had his two lady loves, his daughter and his mother. He would have preferred being a part-time son and a full-time father, but for now he would do the best he could. He was, in any case, there for both of them should they need him; they, in turn, were sources of love that would keep his vision clear till he could see his way back up.

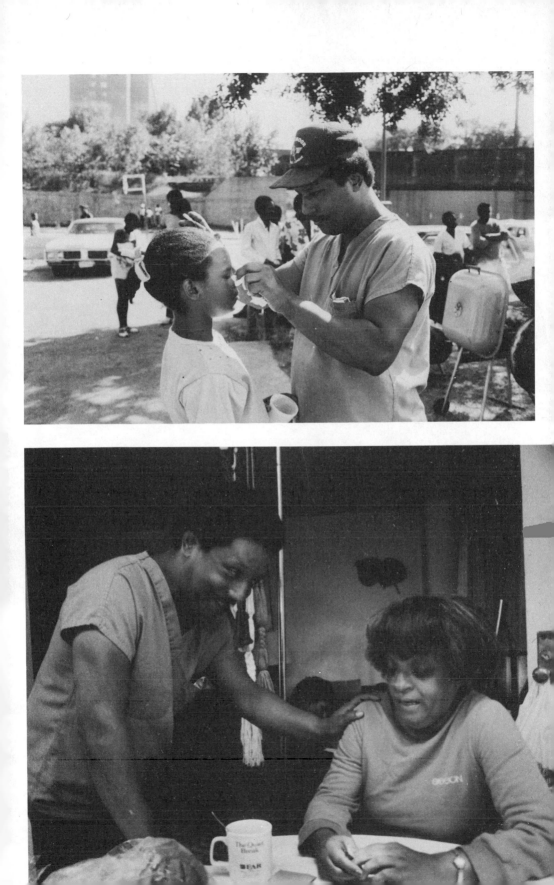

If James Bonner was born to be a one-man gang, it wasn't as clear that he had set out to be a father figure as well to the mostly fatherless boys of Trey-nine; with his murderous eyes and a shotgun named Betsy, his most reliable companion, he bore no outward resemblance to Father Flanagan. But in his own raw way, he taught them right from wrong, caring enough to tell them not to be like him. Society considered him a criminal, but society didn't know him and didn't care when he met his own senseless ghetto death. His Trey-nine family and his daughter Tyrine mourned at his unmarked grave. The obituary notice describing him as a defender of the downtrodden made perfect sense to them.

A VOYAGE TO A FAR GALAXY

I *remember a time,* Vest said, *when Ray and I came home for Christmas vacation—we had been away at school for a year— and we went back to the old neighborhood around Prairie Courts. It was dark out and snowing, and we were sitting on a snowbank, drinking 151 proof Bacardi and chasing it with snow to take away the burn. We were talking about how in our wildest dreams, we would never have imagined going away to two of the best secondary schools in the country, and now people were telling me I could go to* Harvard. *We each took a swig of the rum, and Ray looked at me and said, "Yeah, it's amazing—just a little while ago, we were kids from the projects, and now who knows* what's *going to happen to us? We're gonna beat these MF's in their own game, man. We're gonna get out. We're gonna make it."*

In the fading summer of 1966, just shy of his fifteenth birthday, Ray Stingley sat on a bus bound for a distant galaxy called Indiana and wondered if he could breathe the air there. All he had really wanted to be, growing up at Prairie Courts, was a baseball player; it was one of the short ration of dreams available to black kids in the projects, and he had spend numberless hours on a rubbly lot across the street from home, a solitary boy hitting rocks with a stick, pretending he was belting home runs out of Comiskey Park. He had rarely gone at his lessons with that same furious concentration and had never even thought about college, and yet here he was, watching the miles of highway slide past, headed for someplace named Culver

Military Academy and a future he wasn't sure he could master or even imagine. He asked himself, not for the last time, what the F he was doing it for. The answer was always: for *them*.

Them meant his daddy and mama, J.C. and Cora Mae Stingley; he had no other goal, going off to Culver, than to make them proud. He still remembered the day nearly a year before when he had come home from Mr. Lovelace's class with the news that he had a chance to go away to school.

"Boy, stop lying," his mother had told him. She thought it was a joke.

"My teacher told me to bring this home," he said. He showed her the papers Mr. Lovelace had given him explaining the ABC program.

She studied them. It was true: Her boy would be leaving home. She knew she was going to miss him. She also understood that it was something he had to do. She put her trust in the Lord and was happy for him.

Ray himself considered it a mixed blessing at first. He was not unhappy at Wendell Phillips; the work was mostly undemanding, and all his partners, the boys he had grown up with, were there. He began to get excited about leaving only when he saw what a fuss people were making over him. It was nice hearing his name at assemblies and reading it in the school paper, along with Vest's and Steve's. It was nicer still seeing his mama looking pleased and his daddy puffing his chest out just a little bit.

It was hard to please J.C. Stingley, or so it seemed to his dozen children. He loved his family but had no idea how to show it; Ray was a grown-up the first time his daddy ever hugged him, and by then the old man was dying, slowly, of emphysema. J.C. had lived a lifetime outside the American Dream looking in. The initials were all the name he had—it was as if his parents couldn't afford a whole one—and he had spent his manhood at hard labor, as a sharecropper, a mill hand, and finally a janitor in the projects. Even in good times, he made a precarious living at the edges of the economy, about enough to keep his teeming household clothed and fed on neckbones, grits, and greens. Once, when his plant shut down, he accepted welfare for six months and was miserable. Work was too central to his life, and his pride.

BROTHERS

He gave it so much of himself, his wife reflected in later years, that he had neither time nor emotion left to spend on his children. What pampering Ray got resulted mainly from his being the baby boy in a houseful of older sisters. J.C. Stingley approached parenthood, so far as the children could see, as if it were more a responsibility than a joy; the token of his love was the single unadorned fact that he stayed with them. He didn't take his kids to ball games or go to their graduations; it was a major event for Ray to be allowed to sit up with him watching the Saturday night fights on TV. Any larger displays of warmth, or even approval, were closely budgeted, and a distance opened between father and son as a result. In Ray's make-believe ball games in the sandlot, he was always the White Sox; the enemy was the New York Yankees—they were his daddy's favorite team, and Ray hated them.

It was only later in life, as he sifted his boyhood memories, that Ray came to understand the man inside the granite outer shell. He remembered being home one day, feeling a bit sorry for himself because everyone he knew had a bicycle, even his sisters, and he didn't. He looked out the back window, still brooding, and there as if by magic came his daddy, plodding across the grounds, pushing an old red bike in front of him. He had salvaged it from the junk heap at the Dearborn Homes, the project where he worked. It was aged and battered, but the two of them labored over it, father and son, until they got it working. Ray had his bicycle. He wished long afterward that he had had the right words as well, to break the silence and tell his father he loved him.

His daddy was the provider, his mama the heavy-duty parent to their children. Cora Mae Stingley worked, too, starting when she married at seventeen and continuing between babies through a low-paid lifetime. At various periods she did washing, labored in an ammunition plant, and minded old folks at a nursing home. But the household was her real domain, and she ran it with a strong hand. You could raise children right in the projects, she believed, if you worked at it, if you kept in close touch with them and disciplined them when they got into something bad. Parents in the ghetto today—kids with kids, really—seemed not to have the time or the inclination to try. Ray's mother had the inclination and made the time. It was she who laid down the rules, steering her kids away from bad company and keeping them at their schoolbooks. Her own life was a lesson in hard work and self-control, and her children learned from it. They came of age surrounded by poverty and its consequences, but nobody in her whole outsized brood did time or subsisted on welfare. The Stingleys all grew up accustomed to working and to doing for themselves.

Most of all, Mrs. Stingley believed in education. Neither she nor her husband had much schooling themselves, but they saw in it the means to a better future for their sons and daughters, and she pressed it on them with a nearly religious passion. "I loved school," she told Ray when his own zeal for learning would flag, "but I didn't have a chance to finish 'cause I was out so much. You know, when pickin' time came around, everybody went to the fields to pick the Man's cotton for him." She left no doubt that *he* would finish, or her other children, as practically all of them did. Only her firstborn, Sonny, would drop out of high school, and even he had stayed at Dunbar long enough to learn a negotiable trade. The others would all graduate, and three would go on to earn college diplomas.

It helped that she was rearing her children at Prairie Courts, not one of the bigger, tougher projects like the Taylors. Prairie Courts was a safer, sunnier, and vastly less desperate setting, a mix of high-rise towers and low-rise town houses designed on a human scale; it looked and felt more like an urban village than a poorhouse or a prison, and a bright child like Ray had an easier time falling in with the right crowd. His ace buddies from second grade on were youngsters like Vest, Steve, and Gregory Bronson, all good students and, except for Steve's streak of mischief, all well-behaved boys. He fought when he had to, not caring a S how big or how tough the other guy was; if a MF knows you're going to fight back, win or lose, Ray figured, he's going to think twice about starting something. But he and his partners gave a wide berth to the local gang in residence, the PC (for Prairie Courts) Pimps. His group had other interests. They were on an academic fast track, thanks to a few caring teachers who had seen and nurtured their gifts, and their school day did not end with the last bell; they were seeing faculty advisers, hanging out at the student social center, or puttering with cameras and model airplanes at meetings of an urban-model 4-H Club.

Or reading, hungrily and competitively, till they were racing one another through a book a night. Their tastes in literature tended to Schoolboy Romantic—the *Black Stallion* novels captivated them— but their favorites were a series of childhood biographies, *Thomas Jefferson: Boy Statesman* and *George Carver: Boy Scientist,* exemplary stories of success through creativity and hard work. Only Steve Steward wondered to himself whether the dreams embodied in the stories were meant for children like them. The white people in the illustrations all had faces. The blacks were done in featureless silhouette.

The others had little time or patience then for the metaphysics of race. It was whites who were faceless abstractions in the all-black society of the projects, a people who mostly existed, so far as Ray and his pals could tell, on television or in books. They were accordingly of small interest in the daily lives of boys growing up at Prairie Courts or Trey-nine. The civil rights movement was exploding all around them and ghettos were burning down, but when it was news time on TV, Ray would go outside and play till *Gunsmoke* came on. The day his brother Noonie put him on the bus for Culver Academy, they caught a passing glimpse of Martin Luther King, who had spent the summer in Chicago leading marches against segregation northern style. Noonie was excited. Ray was not. He could tell you who got in a fight at Phillips that day, or who was supposed to have robbed the produce warehouse over on Twenty-sixth Street, but he barely knew who Dr. King was.

He wasn't even scared about going off to live among whites for the first time in his young life; he felt worse saying good-bye to his old friends than he did thinking about making new ones on foreign soil. He, Steve, and Vest had taken the qualifying exam together and had all scored well up in the top 10 percent. But the luck of the draw had sent them down separate ways thereafter, for summer orientation and then for school. Ray was accepted by Culver. Vest would be going to St. George's in Rhode Island. Steve, by chance or design, mislaid his ABC application papers and seemed less than pleased when Ray found them, a week past the deadline, lying forgotten in a folder in a cupboard in French class. His chance at boarding school was lost; he was assigned instead to Hanover High in Hanover, New

Hampshire, a public school on neighborly terms with Dartmouth College. Steve secretly preferred staying home with his mama in the projects. The projects were the only place he felt *safe*.

Ray had no such anxieties when he arrived at Culver. His butterflies had to do with whether he was good enough to handle the work, and his response was to study harder than he had ever had to do. I'm not going to flunk out of this sucker, he told himself, and once he had survived his first quarter, he knew that he could get by. His color was a fact of life he could not change, and so was his isolation as one of only six or eight blacks in a cadet corps of 850. He knew that he was different, that he was black and poor in a world of the white well-to-do. His classmates had grown up in *houses,* with their own rooms, where he had lived in a project and slept with his brother's feet in his face.

The folklore of his boyhood said he should be wary of whites, and for a time he was. A kid in the projects usually had parents or grandparents from the Deep South, fugitives from what was then still the land of Jim Crow, and many of them had strong feelings about white folks; it was the residue of segregation, the bitterness of the dispossessed toward the master race. Their tales of the Man and his wicked ways were part of a ghetto education, the wisdom of the generations passed down to the young. Ray's tutor in matters of race happened to be his grandmother, but everybody had one, and the moral of their stories was usually the same: White folks didn't like black folks and wouldn't do them any way but wrong. Ray accordingly arrived at Culver with a sizable chip on his shoulder, waiting for the first time some white boy would call him nigger and wondering how he would react.

What he didn't want was to let those worries dominate his life. He felt no personal grievance toward white people; he had been talked about and messed over by *brothers* back at Prairie Courts, but nobody white had abused or misused him, at least not out in the open where he could see it. He had always been a quick-tempered boy, aggressive by nature, and he remained primed and ready to fight if anybody put a hand on his body. What people said or felt was their problem, not his. Hey, he thought, scanning the opaque white faces around him, you ain't gotta like me and I ain't gotta like you.

There were bad moments. English class was a torment when they were studying *Huckleberry Finn,* and everybody in the room was going "nigger-nigger-nigger," as if Mark Twain's using the word had made it OK to say. It wasn't OK with Ray. Black people tossed it around freely where he came from, coloring it with their own ironic shadings, but they regarded it as family property, for their use only. For white boys to speak it in Ray's presence was like touching a match to a perilously short fuse. His belly said fight. His will said no; they were going to have to mess with him with something worse than words to make him show he was hurting. F it, he thought. He swallowed his fury and listened.

He had a worse time at mess one day during his plebe year, sitting at a table with several instructors. Two of them were teasing one another, lobbing insults back and forth across the dinner dishes, only the jokes kept getting more personal and less funny as they went along.

"You got some nigger in you," one of them, a guy named Chip, finally told the other, a white southerner. "Your people *all* screwed the slaves down there."

Ray sat quietly, face frozen, blood boiling.

"Hey, Chip," a guy named Griese said at his elbow. "Stingley's at the table."

There was no answer.

"Sir," Stingley said, "I would like to request permission to leave."

The instructor ignored him.

"Hey, Stingley," Griese said. "Just go ahead."

Ray left.

There wasn't much more he could do by way of protest. There weren't enough blacks at Culver to form a clique, let alone a movement, and those he felt closest to were the ghetto brothers, poor broke MF's like himself, just trying to get by. The most militant black there was a wealthy doctor's son, and, Ray figured, he could *afford* to be radical. Ray couldn't. He was a scholarship student scraping along on B's and C's, with a charitable D− for effort in chemistry. He wasn't in any position to demand anything because, he reasoned, I don't have nothing coming. So he set a survivalist course for himself: hit the books, obey the rules, and stay the F out the way.

He did, and to a degree that surprised him afterward, Charles Ray

Stingley, late of Prairie Courts, became a part of Culver. He thought, while he was there, that he hated it. He perceived, or imagined, a bias in favor of the better-off students, white or black, at promotion time; boys who had money behind them seemed to him to rise faster and higher than those who did not. Ray, a have-not, didn't even make sergeant until December of his senior year, a rating he considered too little and too late. He dashed off a huffy letter to the school administration, rejecting his stripes. Fine, the administration wrote back, and Ray graduated back in the ranks.

He saw his protest in later years as childish, a last rebellious act of boyhood. The truth, he came to understand, was that he belonged at Culver and would happily send his own son there if he could. His own discontents had been the standard cadet gripes about chow, reveille, and regimentation, and his involvement in the barracks bitching was a measure of his assimilation. It wasn't until he had graduated and gone on to Albion College in Michigan that he realized how much he missed the academy—the people, the uniform, the routines, even the square-cornered military discipline—and how much it had formed his character.

The realization that he had needed that cornering was the most precious lesson he learned at Culver, or so his sponsor, Leroy Lovelace, thought. Ray was no longer the ghetto underachiever Lovelace had plucked out of the crowd of underachievers at Wendell Phillips High and sent off into the world. Lovelace had watched his progress and was pleased, not so much by Ray's grades, which were only passable by his old mentor's standards, as by the qualities of the man he was becoming. Ray had the strength and the equilibrium to play the game in an arena owned by whites and still keep his dignity and his soul. Ray *was* going to make it, Lovelace thought. Ray knew who he was.

LIFE IN THE PRESENT TENSE

Half Man was my best friend in the projects, Vest said. *I looked up to him. He worked, and while the rest of us were still in school and struggling and penniless, he had some money. He set standards for us as kids in terms of dress and being cool and throwing parties and knowing how to deal with girls.*

But it's a real kind of trap, because that money's not going to grow over the years; the difference between what you make at sixteen and what you make at thirty-six is not going to be very great. So what you've done is cut yourself off from the future by not preparing yourself for it. But when people say that guys like Half Man don't have any sense *of the future, it's not that clear-cut. The future they see is shut off. It's closed. You're afraid to dream for fear of not reaching it, so you don't set up any goals, and that way you don't fail. You just live for now. You get as much as you can today.*

When Edward Carter was a sprout coming up at Trey-nine, answering to Half Man if you said it with a smile, the headiest dream he ever dreamed was driving a 1964 Impala Supersport. His ace friend Vest was going away to school, on an *airplane,* studying to become a big-time writer; Billy Harris was talking about making a million playing ball; even Big Honk knew what he wanted, which was money, no matter how he had to get it. But there was never anything Half Man aspired to *be,* and damn little he ever hungered to have—just a job, a home, a lady, nice clothes, and a luxury ride—that Impala maybe, or later, with changing fashion, a Trans Am or a Firebird. He never wanted big, he mused in later years, and so never dreamed big. It don't even come into my head, he reflected, surveying the bare landscape of his life; I dream simple dreams that can come true.

His ambition from boyhood on was to be a survivor and a provider, that was all. There was no one at home to push him to make more of himself, or to lead him to believe that he could. His parents had met in Georgia and married young and poor—too young and too poor, Half Man always thought, except that his mama was already carrying the first of their five children. She was fourteen years old; his daddy, seventeen. They found their way to Chicago and then to the Taylor Homes, movin' on up like the Jeffersons, Half Man thought, but their lives did not magically improve with their new surroundings. Pete Carter, with raw skills and a third-grade education, was locked into that class known in social science as the working poor and that life-style known in the street as scuffling—making just enough in subsistence jobs and day-off gigs to get by. He was a family man, in his fashion. He stayed home where other men in the projects gave up and fled, and when he finally got decent work with the housing authority, the Carters moved on up a little higher, out of Trey-nine and into a house of their own. They had not arrived in the leisure class with their change of address, and had not wished to. Pete Carter couldn't abide *not* working seven days a week; if there was nothing else, he would knock down the fence around his new house and re-build it, just for something to do. He set a strong example by his labor, and as Half Man grew into his teens, his own life took on a strong family resemblance to his father's—a life wedded to work from his first paper route on. Work was in his blood, he figured, and it didn't even matter what kind. Work was the only thing he could ever remember wanting.

His parents were no more dreamers than he. Their view of their duty to their sons and daughters was to get them what they needed that day, and emotional nourishment was not on the list; it was as if they were too bent down by food and clothing bills to see any further horizon, for their children or themselves. Half Man regretted that in later years; he thought he might even have been a lawyer or something if there had been someone around to tell him, hey, you oughta do this or that. There wasn't. His mother left him some change for carfare and lunch at school every day, but she never asked what he was studying there and did not seem unduly concerned whether he went at all. You ain't gonna go to school, she would tell him, don't be spending my money. Otherwise, he could do whatever he wanted to do. The choice was his, and if he chose wrong, hey, that was on him, not his parents.

His choice was life in the present tense. School was an investment in a future he didn't believe in; there was little evidence around Trey-nine that tomorrow would be any better for young black men, and a lot that it might be worse. There was a fleeting time when he thought he might like to sing for a living—when he imagined he might even be good enough to make it. He and some of the brothers organized a vocal group, Half Man, Honk, Pee Wee, and Moose, and Billy Harris as the lead singer; Billy could sing as good as he could play ball, which was saying some. They practiced every evening, copying their *woo-hoos* and *my-girls* from the Temptations and the Miracles and throwing in some sudden little dance steps of their own just for style. Sometimes they sang nights on the galleries or out front of the building once they got their act tight, and nobody ever booed them off the set. But it was kid stuff, and Half Man drifted off to his other, more grown-up pursuits: work and women. He had neither the time nor the patience to wait around for a daydream to come true.

He had elected today over tomorrow, a get-it-now existence financed by work and bathed in the sweet, cool glow of success. He was still a boy, and undersized at that, but he always had money, and ladies, and leather coats, and Stacy-Adams shoes—the kind with wing tips and white stitching—and easy access to fast cars, the latter usually borrowed from a dude he knew who stole them. He had respect as well, a tough-guy reputation born the first time he got in a fight with a bigger boy—they were *all* bigger than Half Man—and doubled him up with a lucky punch. He had been scared, but nobody knew that, or needed to. What counted was that the little brother with the sleepy eyes and the try-me grin could hit like a baby Ali.

His further claim to recognition was that he could pay for it. Guys like Honk lived cool lives on what they could steal from the shopping center or hustle in the street; they looked good, Half Man thought, but he was the one with the drive. He made money the old-fashioned way: He earned it. He hawked papers. He cut hair, with some fancy clippers and a vinyl loveseat his father bought him; he charged bargain rates, $1.50 for grown-ups, 50 cents for kids, and still made $70 or $80 a weekend. He scrubbed cars at a carwash, grilled kielbasa at a barbecue, drove a forklift in a warehouse, and made blankets in a factory, all in his teens. Half Man always had jobs, and once he was established in a place, he would bring in other boys from Trey-nine behind him, Pee Wee and Vest and Ed Hamilton. It was, he thought, as if he were leading them up the rocky face of a mountain; he'd leave them the lower rocks and find a higher one for himself.

The pay was always low and the work usually unrewarding, but in Half Man's eyes it beat doing time for nothing at Wendell Phillips High. At Dunbar Vocational, you could at least learn a trade. Phillips didn't even have that enticement; it offered what was called a general education, but its demoralized teachers counted it a successful day if they could just keep order in their classrooms. Half Man, having no goals, had nothing to bind him there except the state law requiring his attendance at school until he was sixteen. He got into trouble for his attitude when he went—he wore his hard-guy face to school in self-defense—and was hassled for truancy when he stayed away.

When he quit during his junior year, more or less by invitation, it no longer mattered to him. His approach to life was just going out and doing the chore in front of you. With no longer-term plan than that, he saw no further use for his studies, and no reason to stay at Phillips; the money he was making without a diploma had got next to him, and he had been dropping out on the installment plan anyway, a day or two at a time. He went to continuation classes for a while, then made one last pass at Dunbar Vocational. His reputation had preceded him, and he was placed in a special class for troublemakers. He didn't like getting hollered at, or being poked in the rib cage, or having to endure the constant lectures in deportment. He sat through two weeks of it and left.

A lot of his homies at Trey-nine were dropping out, too, and for a time the Carters' apartment, 803, became their daytime clubhouse, a place where they could hang out, play cards, and fill the empty time with empty talk. Roy Johnson would be there: Big Honk, smart enough to get into Dunbar but too bored and too busy hustling to stay. And Pee Wee Fisher, once so quick in school the other kids called him Professor; he was working now so he could buy his own stuff and lighten the load on his mama. And Moose Harper; he had got more interested in gang-banging than in his lessons, or in his fading boyhood dreams of being a writer. And Ed Hamilton, a loner and a brooder; he dropped out psychically the day he saw his own kid brother fall from an upstairs gallery at Trey-nine, fluttering down like a rag to his death. And Sonny Spruiell, a bright kid who had slid downhill from the smartest room at Attucks School to the lost-cause list at Dunbar; he had got into wine, pills, and petty busts, and by the time the school authorities showed him the door, his file was stamped NO REHABILITATION.

The lazy days were fun, but Half Man had never liked to lie around long, and he had new responsibilities in any case, a man's responsibilities piled on a boy's narrow shoulders. One day in 1968, in a ceremony at City Hall, he married the lady he had been dating since junior high, a Trey-nine girl named Harriet from apartment 1203. It was a source of pride to him that it wasn't no shotgun wedding because of no baby; unlike a lot of child couples around Thirty-ninth Street, they married *before* she got pregnant. It was, for the bride-groom, an act of love and a declaration of independence, his coming out as a grown-up with a job, a woman, and a place of his own. He was seventeen and she was sixteen, almost as young as his father and mother had been when they got married. They needed their parents' signed consent to go through with it. Still, Half Man had, or so he imagined, become a man.

He learned quickly that he hadn't. He had pictured marriage as a kind of tableau including himself, a wife, a house, a car, and a couple of children. But neither he nor Harriet quite fit the picture; they were too young, kids playing house together even as they kept pursuing their separate adolescent pleasures. Half Man was still the gang-banger from the projects, a bad-ass brother with cold eyes, quick hands, and an evil temper. He didn't do reefer then, or 'caine, but he drank hard and gambled badly, sometimes blowing a whole week's pay at the track in a single day. When he came home to Harriet, in his own good time, it was usually with empty pockets, a hundred-proof high, and an attitude. Otherwise, he wasn't paying her much attention—not unless somebody else was.

She was expected to tolerate his vices. He was unforgiving of hers. Her worst, in his eyes, was pitty-pat, a card game she appeared to like better than she played; her losses and his aggravation rose in parallel lines until, in the second spring of their marriage, he—and it—exploded. There was a baby by then, a girl named Sherri, and Half Man wanted to buy her some pretty clothes and a real live rabbit for Easter. He gave Harriet the money, $60 or $70. She lost it on pitty-pat. He found out and went off on her in a drunken rage. She fought back, and suddenly he was out of control, pulling her hair and popping her around the bedroom with his fists.

She fled out onto the gallery. He followed, trying to grab her, and there was Honk's brother, Reginald, Mr. Reg, placing his imposing person between them.

"Excuse me, guy, what's up?" Reg said. "It ain't no sense you beatin' on this woman like that."

"Look, man, this *my* wife," Half Man answered. *"I'm* the one that married her."

Reg didn't budge. Harriet cowered behind him. Half Man cocked his fist and made his play. Reg jumped a step back. A .38 materialized in his hand. Half Man was in full flight toward Reg when he saw it. He stopped himself in midair. He would think of that night years afterward as the start of a long low tide in his fortunes, the first in a lifetime of disappointments. It was as if some curse was hanging over his head, he thought; as if he were getting punished for what he had done. He heard later that Reg had moved in with Harriet somewhere down on Twenty-seventh Street. Sherri was with her. Half Man's heart contracted. He knew he would never love a woman again, not in the same way. His life was starting down, he thought, spoiled before he was out of his teens, and for once he felt powerless to battle back. It was almost like he would be going one-on-one against God.

His world was contracting, too. His old Trey-nine partners were disappearing one by one into the military. Some of them were sitting around one day, drinking Orange Rock and talking about joining, until somebody said, "Well, when we gonna go?" Everyone lost interest then, all except Pee Wee Fisher; Pee Wee's lady was pregnant, he was out of a job, and he enlisted mostly to be doing *something*. He hadn't told anybody his plans; he just materialized on

Dearborn Street, looking sharp in his starched army fatigues, with enough ribbons on his chest to make General Patton blush.

Jaws dropped. "Man, how you get all this mess?" Sonny Spruiell demanded, goggling the decorations. Pee Wee said he had earned them. Sonny suspected, accurately, that they were borrowed. But he was secretly thinking how nice they looked, and in short order he joined up, too.

Sonny went to Germany and got militant. Honk went there, too, and got rich; he came home with a black market bankroll, a Rolex the size of a manhole cover, and a diamond on every finger. Pee Wee and Ed Hamilton wound up in Vietnam, Pee Wee humping a radio in the boonies, Ed sitting twenty miles offshore on a carrier. Moose Harper meant to go to war, figuring he was getting shot at on Thirty-ninth Street anyway and might as well make it worth something to somebody if he got killed. When a guy died gang-banging, his family had to beg door to door for burial money, but a dude in a building went down in 'Nam, and they supposedly gave his mama a check for $10,000. It sounded to Moose like a good deal at the time, and he signed up for it. He was shipped to Korea and then Germany instead and afterward counted himself lucky; only way he'd have come home from 'Nam was in a body bag, he thought, and nobody would have cared.

Half Man never left home at all. His marriage had been his ticket out of the service and what he thought of as the Man's war, not his own. So he stayed in place and went on with his left-behind life, a blues life lived out in the closed world of the ghetto. His days were filled with work, one nondescript job after another; his nights were occupied with crises of love and money, and with his stunted dreams. Once, in the early autumn of 1971, he bumped into Moose, just out of the army and still high on the new black consciousness then bubbling through the American military. Moose had helped organize a group called the Black Scorpions, a GI clone of the Black Panther Party, on his base in Germany; it was a new day for black people, a season of pride and righteous anger, and he was eager to bring the spirit home.

He threw Half Man a clenched-fist salute—*black power!*—and a fraternal "Hello, brother."

"It ain't that way here," Half Man told him. Nothing had changed in Moose's three years away. Life on Thirty-ninth Street was still about today, not tomorrow; you had to be a dreamer to believe in the victory of black people, and Thirty-ninth Street, as Half Man could tell you, was a place where dreams died young.

A STUDY IN BLACK AND WHITE

W*hen we were kids,* Vest said, *we used to have little ditties, little rhymes about race. "If you're white, you're all right. If you're brown, stick around. If you're black, stay back." The sense was that being black meant you were going to get the short end of the stick. Or there were self-effacing rhymes, like the one we had about Thunderbird wine: "What's the price? Thirty twice. Who drinks the most? Colored folks. Who drinks the less? Eliot Ness." You laughed at them, but they all suggested a sort of sense that if you were black, you didn't quite measure up.*

I was lucky. My mother and my grandmother gave me a sense of self-worth, a sense of striving. And it was important, because for a black kid, there was a certain amount of self-doubt. It came at you indirectly. You didn't see any black people on television, you didn't see any black people doing certain things, and you couldn't really rationalize it. I mean, you don't think it out, but you say, "Well, it must mean that white people are better than we are. Smarter, brighter—whatever."

I had that feeling when I went away to school. I didn't know for sure if I could do the work. I got there, and my first semester, when the grades came out just before Christmas, I was about sixth in the class. After that I never worried. But some people always have those self-doubts. And sometimes the pendulum swings back too far the other way, to where you don't say, "I'm as good as everybody else." You say, "I'm better."

Gregory Bronson learned his earliest lessons in the ways of white folks sitting outside a locked bedroom door at Prairie Courts, eavesdropping on his father. His father was not like a lot of the men you saw around the projects, beaten down by a system designed for that purpose. His father was a strong, proud black man, a *warrior*, Greg thought, with a lively mind, a college education, and a fierce commitment to the old values of faith, work, and family. But the white folks he worked for at one of the giant insurance companies buried him for years on the loading dock, a B.A. packing and unpacking supply cartons, and even when they let him have a supervisory job in purchasing fifteen years late, they never quit dogging him. He came home tense and worn, and some nights he disappeared into his bedroom, locking the door behind him. Greg sat outside those evenings and listened. Inside, hidden from the family, his father—his hero—was crying.

Not many kids in the projects had so direct a window on the world outside, or so humiliating a glimpse of how it could punish a man. They had heard all about the perfidy of white people, mainly

from their elders; the Man, it was said, owned everything worth having and wouldn't let black people get in the door. But they practically
never saw a white face except on TV, and the innocent suburban
lives depicted there—on *Ozzie and Harriet,* say, or *Leave It to Bea-
ver*—were as distant from their own as Mars from Earth. Their cityscape was nearly all black, except for a few bureaucrats, teachers,
and cops, and they rarely left it; a trip to the Loop, for most, was a
major expedition. Thirty-ninth Street, that's *your* world, Honk Johnson mused in later years. The rest was *they* world, a white world
with different codes of speech, dress, and conduct. Boys from the
projects were made to feel like trespassers there, alien and, because
they were black, presumptively dangerous.

Their world was enclosed by invisible walls, and the epic political
struggles of the sixties were little more than background noise in their
lives. The Black Panthers did attract favorable notice on Thirty-ninth
Street, with their antiwhite, anticop bravado and their guns. But even
the Panthers were largely a West Side story. The South Side remained the property of what had become the Black P Stone Nation,
the same old Blackstone Ranger gang dressed up with a new name,
a veneer of civic concern, and a treasury swollen by white conscience
money. The mainstream civil rights movement, even when it played
Chicago, seemed as exotic as a medieval morality play. When Martin
Luther King spoke at Stateway Gardens during his Chicago crusade,
Ed Hamilton, practically alone among the Trey-nine boys, bothered
walking across Thirty-ninth Street to see him. Half Man Carter hardly
gave him a thought at all, until he came home one night two years
later and found his mother crying. He asked why. She told him they
had killed Dr. King.

But Greg Bronson's father was rearing *his* children in his own
image: as unyielding as stone on principle and as touchy as a hair
trigger on questions of color. Thomas Earl Bronson had grown up
poor, black, and fatherless in the Great Depression. The experience
left him with a fierce sense of duty to his family, and he expected it
to be repaid with obedience to his autocratic will. His children knew
he cared about them; it was said in the Bronson household that he
would buy a beer for himself only after the icebox was amply stocked
with milk for them. They knew as well that you could not budge him
from his rules or his beliefs.

BROTHERS

The world he saw and described to them was painted in two colors: black and white. He had himself come of age in a time when it was dangerous for a black man to protest too much. He was thrown out of Tuskegee Institute for getting mixed up in racial demonstrations, finishing up at Southern Illinois University instead, and his career with the insurance company was a thirty-four-year trial of his capacity for silent suffering. Work, for a man of his generation with a wife and five children, was often a series of small compromises and forced smiles, and he went along. His tears at home revealed the cost to his spirit, but the Man never saw him cry. It was a matter of pride with Thomas Bronson that nobody white had ever visited his home or dined at his table.

His further revenge was in the education of his children. There was no fair-housing law when the Bronsons lived in the projects and therefore no means of redress when he tried to find a home in the white suburbs north of town, near where he worked. What he could do was drive his family there—Greg was nine or ten years old at the time—and show them where his co-workers lived and sent their children to school. *You* could have lived here, he said. *You* could have gone to this school. *They* wouldn't let you.

Greg Bronson was thus on a running start into angry young manhood when he first encountered the color line on his own. He had been an honor student at Stephen Douglas Middle School, along with Ray, Steve, and Vest, but he didn't want to follow them to Wendell Phillips High. He was smart enough about himself to know that he needed teachers who would push him, hard, and the main way they seemed to push black boys at Phillips was toward the exit. He saw a chance in the permissive-transfer program, a stopgap instituted by the school authorities that year to hold off citywide busing. If your home school was overcrowded, which Phillips was, and if you had the grades, which Greg did, you could apply to go somewhere better.

Greg chose Von Steuben High, a mostly white school and one of the best, academically, in the country; it was home to a tennis team besides, and Greg, like his father, was passionate about tennis. But Von Steuben said no thanks. They had decided against accepting further transfers under the program, Greg was told, and he found himself at Phillips, stuck fast and smoldering. It was the way things worked. They had let him peek through the door, then slammed it in his face. If you're white, you're all right. If you're black, stay back.

He spent two aimless years at Phillips, liking little about it *except* its blackness. He went out for football and track and loved the sense of closeness he felt with his black teammates; loved it even better than the victories and the trophies they regularly brought home. But his schoolwork suffered, as he had sensed it would. The smell of surrender hung in the corridors, mixed occasionally with the scent of gunsmoke. The school had become a kind of day care center for adolescents, many of them the children of two- and three-generation welfare families, and neither parents nor teachers seemed to Greg to be greatly concerned about what they did so long as they showed up and sat still in class.

Some had quit caring even that much. Greg was enrolled in sophomore geometry, but he wasn't getting it, so he regularly played hooky.

"Greg," the teacher told him finally, "we're going to call your father, because you missed class twenty-eight times."

"You won't do that," he sassed back; the rules said you were supposed to be suspended if you cut *three* classes, so how was a teacher going to explain having waited till he had skipped twenty-eight?

He was right; his absenteeism went unpunished. There were caring teachers at Phillips, a hardy few like Leroy Lovelace, and Greg responded to them. He was blessed as well with parents who monitored his report cards and came to school meetings; not all did, or even knew how. But parents like the Bronsons and teachers like the Lovelaces were overmatched at Wendell Phillips, and Greg coasted along, working no harder than he had to. A white school, he imagined, would have *demanded* his best. At Phillips, his best wasn't necessary. His teachers seemed to him mainly interested in drawing paychecks and moving bodies, and he became a partner in the game.

His uninterest showed in his performance, and when Lovelace picked his nominees to go away to school on ABC scholarships, he passed Greg by. Another door had closed, and Greg blamed the system; there would never be room, he supposed, for more than a token few blacks to make it up and out. Lovelace had other reasons. Greg's record wasn't quite strong enough, and neither, Lovelace had begun to suspect, was his temperament. He was bright, handsome, and articulate, a boy with a lot of potential, but he was bitter in his blackness, and Lovelace wasn't sure how well he would survive in an all-white prep school. He had seen others of his students, boys as bright and as angry as Greg, driven literally mad by the color question, confined to institutions because they could no longer function as black people in an inimical white society.

As it developed, the Bronsons bought their own ticket out of the ghetto. Greg's parents were a two-career couple, his father moving up at the insurance company, his mother doing public relations at a mostly black hospital. They had never been a project family, strictly speaking, though they lived in two while Thomas Bronson was waiting for his break at the company. Public housing had always been a way station for them, a port in a storm, and when their means caught up with their middle-class aspirations, they moved out to a house in the suburbs south of the city limits.

The development they bought into was black. Greg's new school, Thornton High, was predominantly white, and he fell into a state of culture shock, an unease he felt from the day he enrolled till the day he graduated. The facilities, in his teenaged eyes, were awesome; the school even had a stadium, with stands and lights, where Phillips's championship track teams ran their indoor meets in the corridor on the third floor. It was the company of whites Greg couldn't get used to, the sense of difference he felt among them. He was like a castaway washed up among a people whose intentions he doubted and whose ways he did not understand. It was hard adjusting to their bleached-out style of life and thought; even the cheers at ball games bored him with their soulless white sound, and he withdrew, psychically, to a secure middle distance. He dropped out of team sports and didn't mix much with his white classmates. He knew, or thought he knew, when he wasn't wanted.

When a break did come his way, his suspicions very nearly spoiled it for him; they were becoming part of the baggage he would carry wherever he went in life. He was chosen during his senior year for a part-time work-study program and was placed in an office job posting stock at a steel plant. He went expecting racism and, expecting it, found it—saw it in the blank white faces all around him, felt it in the way people looked at him, heard it even in their compliments on his work. There was disgust and hatred behind their smiles, he thought, an animus tinctured with jealousy that he had the job and some white kid—their own, maybe—did not.

"You're black and you're lucky," someone told him.

He didn't feel lucky; he felt qualified.

Just doing his daily inventory counts became an adversary proceeding for him, a test of wills in which he pushed for answers and his co-workers seemed to resist giving them. He would inquire about a shipment, then sit smoldering at his desk awaiting a reply; a bureaucratic delay of twenty or thirty minutes became, in his inflamed vision, a racist affront. A teacher would come around every other week to check his progress and would be told, effusively, that Greg was doing just great. Then she would leave, and he could feel the atmosphere clouding over again. They don't want me here, he thought; they want to see me fail.

He endured, as his father had, but without the compromises *or* the smiles. His survival strategy was to be all business all day long. Except as the day's assignment demanded it, he spoke only to the man he reported to. He took his break at 3:30, long after the others, so he wouldn't have to socialize with anyone white. If he felt the need for company at all, he drifted back to the mail room and rapped with the black dude who worked there, the only brother on the office force besides himself.

The low regard his colleagues felt for him was plain, at least to him, and if he could not alter those feelings, he could at least return them in kind. He did his nine months among white people as if it were a penance, but when he graduated from high school, he fired them in his mind and chose a black college. A nationalist had been born, and in the open air of the suburbs, not the shut-in black society of the projects. If the world could close its doors on Greg Bronson, he could close the door on the world.

PART III

Outlaws

*People ask me if I'm not afraid to
go back to Trey-nine,* Vest said.
*I'm not. I feel safe there, and not
just because it's where I grew up.
I married Honk Johnson's oldest
sister. The baddest dudes on the
block are in my family.*

AN ENCOUNTER ON THIRTY-NINTH STREET

The Life had been good to Honk Johnson for twenty years, but the way things had been going lately, he couldn't *buy* no luck. Like the day he was sitting on the back of a parked car out front of Trey-nine, playing chess with some sucker before a knot of admirers. The dude was dead and didn't know it. Honk was fixing to tear his ass up.

"You hip to *en passant*, brother?" he taunted, flanking an enemy pawn with one of his own. "Nigger, if you ain't hip to *en passant*, you in trouble."

But a sudden thunderclap interrupted him, and a hard rain came down, soaking the board and washing out his position. Everybody scampered for cover, and Honk found himself in a fire-engine-red Buick Skylark talking shop with Billy Harris, two longtime players pushing thirty-five and entering what for hustlers and basketball heroes is the portal to old age.

Billy had been sitting there reminiscing with Hot Shot Hanks, once the star of the stable of ladies he had kept for five years after he quit playing ball. She was not quite eighteen when he found her, a beauty bad enough even then, he always said, to pull the same S on Chicago that Cleopatra once pulled on Rome. They had had good and profitable times together, Billy and Shot, till his mama and his own good sense made him get out of the game. They wore fine clothes then, drank Cordon Bleu cognac, and drove a clean ride, a white Cadillac stretch limousine.

All that was gone now, a remembrance of things past. Shot was pouring her cognac from a half-pint flask hidden in a brown paper bag, and Billy, in sneakers and basketball shorts, was sipping Hawaiian Punch out of a bottle. But he wasn't regretting anything. He got out, he was saying, because he had to.

"If I had stayed around," he was saying, "I couldn't walk away from it. I couldn't walk away from this S if I got to look at it every day." He gestured toward Hot Shot in the front seat. She had put on a few pounds since their days together, but she was still a striking woman, the color and warmth of coffee in the morning. "See, the girl," he said, "she's a hell of a MF."

She pouted, remembering how he had vanished from her life one day and she had had to hunt him down on some basketball court somewhere. "I came and I found him," she said. "I had his friend Reg to take me to him. See, 'cause it wasn't no reason for him to up and just leave without telling me anything."

"I was going a mile a minute," Billy was saying when the rain started and Honk dashed over. "I had got *out* there. So I just disappeared."

Honk slid into the back seat beside him, his tailor-mades in a state of meltdown from sharp to soggy. "Where the dope at?" he asked. "F this BS. Where's it at, Bill?"

"I don't know where it's at," Billy said.

"What you got in the bag, baby?" Honk asked Hot Shot.

She tugged the half-pint out of the sack just far enough to expose the label. It said Martell. Old Shot still traveled first-class.

"Naw, baby," Honk said. "I don't F with that."

Billy went on with his soliloquy, lamenting the quality of the younger men coming into The Life. Dumb MF's, he said; he had tried to be an honorable nigger, but these new dudes were bastardizing the game.

Honk was half listening. He fished up a stash from somewhere, rolled a joint, and handed it to Billy. Hot Shot wanted one, too. Billy took a deep drag on his and passed it forward.

"I want a *whole* one," Hot Shot said, pouting again. She wasn't used to begging no Negro for nothing, but she didn't have as much money as she used to with Billy; times were tight in her game, too, and she was on welfare. "I ain't seen no reefer in a week," she said.

"Well, we lucky for this nigger here to give us this," Billy said.

"You ain't gonna see none till you pull them bloomers down," Honk told her, grinning mischievously.

"Hey, nigger," she shot back, "you better bust that out your game."

"You broke now?" Roy teased.

"I'm satisfied," she said. She took a hit on the reefer. Billy was remembering the old times, better times for both of them, 'cause what he had made in The Life, he remarked, he had shared with his ladies. He was built that way. He had been a player, not a pimp, he said, and there was a difference. "See, *pimp* is just a old nasty-ass name that a honky came up with for a MF that's all right with women, 'cause *he* ain't figured it out yet. That S even sounds nasty—*pimp*." He drew out the word, as if it were painful for him to say it. "This S they call the *pimp* game, that's all a—"

"—a demoralizing—" Honk prompted.

"—a demoralizing, fictionalized BS that a honky shot at a nigger through the media and television. Man, that S hurts to see black people want to knock a MF and be reading S into what you're doing and have no knowledge of what the F is going on. Hey, it ain't about no nigger having no certain type of car or none of that. It's about what type of nigger you are, and what amount of charisma God gave you when you came here. There ain't no tricks to this S. That's how John Kennedy became president. He was all-right-looking and knew how to throw that *power* out, and all the bitches in America voted for him."

"Why you got to lock a bitch up because she want to sell her body?" Honk said. "I mean why? Really, if you gonna buy it, it's business. It's selling *her* body."

"Well, they want to control *all* business," Billy said, " 'cause pussy gets sold every day. When a MF goes to buy a marriage license, it's the worst deal a bitch ever makes."

Honk grinned, player to player. They were privileged men; they had had money; they had been around.

"See," Billy said, "the average MF, if he hasn't had the fortune or *misfortune* to have to deal with white society, he don't know whether he's having it hard or not. OK? Now a nigger like me who's tasted some of that pie, they've been around white folks and see how these MF's play it. Live good—''

"Living gooder than a MF," Honk interjected. *"They* livin', boy."

"Now, *we* know what the F a nigger's really missing," Billy said.

"A nigger ain't living down through here," Honk said. He looked out at a dumpster behind the shopping center, overflowing trash and garbage. "You don't see S like that out in the suburbs. Them honkies are *living*. They surviving good."

"But if you ask the average MF that's out here tryin' to get down and have it," Billy said, "that S is like talking to a MF in Japtalian."

"They never had nothing," Honk said. "They never was organized. See, white folks be *born* organized in the world. They already got a channel to go down. But these niggers out here so unorganized—''

"Cause of the limited view that these people got," Billy said.

"See, niggers ain't livin'," Honk said. "They *housing* niggers. That's the big organization down here now—to house niggers. They housing 'em here''—he pointed toward Trey-nine— "and if you F up out here, then they got somewhere else for you. They send you to the *big* house."

"Rent-free," Billy said. He had never done time. Honk had, two and a half years at Pontiac, and was looking at more, the long ride, this time, for armed robbery.

"They just lock you on down," Honk said.

"If you F up and kill a MF," Billy said. "Or too many of 'em."

"You can't kill nothin' but a MF you live around," Honk said. He knew; that was what he had done time for. "You ain't gonna kill no fabulous honky. If you go out there and F with a honky, they gonna give you the chair."

"And for the first time in your life," Billy said, "you get some free electricity. You kill a honky, it's the only time in your life they give you some free electricity without charging your ass."

"You're a celebrity then, when you kill one of them," Honk said. "You ain't a celebrity until you shoot a honky. But you can shoot niggers. You can have a record where you killed ten niggers, and you never hit the news until they kill your MF'ing ass."

But neither man was killing anybody, except maybe himself. Billy was between hustles, and Honk had laid out much of a year trying to beat or bargain down the robbery case pending against him. It wasn't looking good; the state's best offer so far was ten years.

"I can't keep going home broke," he said. "This year's layoff has been *chaos*, 'cause it's hard to be out here without some cash."

"You *know* that's right," Hot Shot put in.

"Hey, man," Billy said, "I was on the topside so long, this S is freakin' me out. We could have been thousandaires."

"It ain't too late," Honk said.

"Naw, it ain't too late," Billy agreed. "This nigger gonna get on down and *get* it. We ain't but thirty-four."

"We just gettin' to be *in* the game, really," Honk said.

"And with the knowledge that we got," Billy said, "whenever we make a breakout, *boom!*—we gonna be running."

But Honk's line of sight into the future was a narrower one, a view obstructed by iron bars. "You can always slip," he said. "You ain't even got to be in this business and you can slip. They got the best MF's slipping."

He knew.

THE CHIEF OF THIS AND THAT

One night in the summer of 1978, back when Honk Johnson *was* the best MF on Thirty-ninth Street, his younger brother Ronnie found him in a saloon near the projects and told him to get the pistols. Honk was fogbound by drugs at the time and not quite sure what was happening—a fight, a stickup, or World War III. But Ronnie was a down

dude, a hell of a nigger just like Honk, and when he said it again—
"Get the pistols!"—Honk slid off his stool and started for his lady's
crib on Forty-eighth Street, where the guns were, without asking
questions.

He should have asked some; it was the night Big Honk slipped,
and before his freefall ended, it had cost him a piece of his leg, a
part of his life, and a chastening glimpse of his own mortality. He
was the merchant prince of vice in the neighborhood then, chief of
this, chief of that; hey, he thought in expansive moments, the baddest
nigger in the world. He had been in the game for ten years and had
been lucky at it. He was carrying .32-caliber slugs in his hip and
thigh, the souvenirs of a shoot-out with a perfect stranger, and a
heroin monkey on his back, a burden of his own making. But he was
still walking and still free, a no-time loser, where other studs he
knew were dying in the street—maybe ten of them a summer—or
laying up in prison for eighty years. He hadn't stopped to think yet
that he was throwing his life at a *dream,* a fantasy of wealth and
power. He was still young in The Life in those days, and he took his
luck for granted, until that summer night in '78 when it ran out.

He sensed it practically as soon as he got to his lady's place and
went for the arsenal—not the pistols but his trusty three-piece, twelve-
gauge shotgun. The gun was the tool of one of his trades, which was
sticking up night spots where dealers and gangsters gathered to drink
and signify. He had his routine tight: He would smuggle the gun in
three parts into the men's room, assemble it in twenty seconds, and
come busting out after the money, and what could all them players
with all that illegal paper do about it—call the *police?*

Only this night, when he found the gun, he discovered to his
horror that one of his rappies—the young brothers from the projects
who followed him—had got the barrel sawed down short. Honk didn't
like sawed-off shotguns, didn't even want to be around one. It was
like carrying a live bomb, and if it blew up in your hands, which
was likely, it could tear you apart. But the gun was what there was,
so he wrapped it in a coat, tucked it up under one arm, and started
back to the saloon.

When he got there, Ronnie came out the door and waved him
away. The game, whatever it had been, was off, and they retired to

the project, Ronnie and another dude up front, Honk trailing behind with the twelve-gauge squeezed tight between his arm and his rib cage. They had started up the gangway to the building when Honk felt the gun slip. He stopped, let it down carefully, and started unwrapping it, meaning to do it up tighter. He was peeling back a layer of cloth when he felt the triggers move. It's going off, he thought, and if he swung it up and away from his leg, the double-O buck would blow the back of Ronnie's head away. He was thinking he couldn't do that to his brother, couldn't *live* with himself if he did, when he heard a boom as loud as a hand grenade and felt his lower leg explode.

He took a step or two, then shuddered and fell in the gangway. He didn't feel much; the heroin dulled the pain, but there was a hole in his ankle big enough to stick his fist in. His foot was connected to his leg, barely, by a thin skein of sinew and fractured bone. Some ricocheting pellets had hit Ronnie. He was out in Forty-eighth Street trying to flag a cab, face all bleeding, and when one driver passed him by, he hailed the next more persuasively, poking a .45 automatic up his nose.

They got Honk to the hospital, but when the doctors there recommended amputating his foot, he shoved the consent papers back at them and said no. He couldn't afford to be no cripple, not out there in the street with these younger hustlers looking to make a reputation by trying his ass. He had seen a lot of MF's out on the concrete gasping for their last breath, and he didn't need to be one of them.

So he stayed in the hospital from August to December while some plastic surgeons improvised a new ankle, transplanting gristle and skin from his side and packing it around what was left of the bone. The reconstruction was ugly to look at, a scarred and ulcerated mess, and the doctors who built it didn't think it would work well enough for Honk to walk on. But when he came out on a Christmas pass, he said F the doctors and the crutches they sent him home with. He could do anything, he said, and on the right brew of drugs he actually believed it. He would get stoned, take a step or two, fall down, get up, and take a step or two more until he began to get mobile again.

He and his rappies had owned Thirty-ninth Street till his accident; they wore tailored clothes, did *el primo* drugs, and threw big parties

for themselves and their admirers in the disco at the Trey-nine shopping center. But their enterprises suffered during Honk's long recu-
peration. You were always fair game in The Life, and with Honk
holed up at his lady's place in the project, his ankle swollen like a
balloon, his challengers were coming out in the open. He could practically hear them telling one another, "Man, we got him now—this
nigger here ain't even got no *foot*."

There was, for one, a dude named Dozier, a hustler who owed
Honk a piece of money and was long overdue paying. Honk would
send his rappies around to collect, but all they ever came back with
was excuses. They were no longer feared without him on the set, and
chumps like Dozier—*kids*—were stealing Honk's action out of their
leaderless hands.

What Dozier didn't know was that Honk was like a wounded
tiger; he had become more, not less, dangerous in his pain. As far as
Honk could see, Dozier didn't understand the rules of play at all. It
was hard out there in The Life, a Darwinian jungle, and you had to
be stone cold to survive. You had to be prepared to *kill* if it came to
that. You had to understand that the police didn't care who killed
who in the ghetto, long as they both black; the police just let the one
on the ground die and bust the one still standing. You had to know
that if you weren't really ready to murder no Negro, you didn't go
out there and fake it, 'cause he wasn't going to give no second thought
to murdering you. You had to realize that at game time, it was better
to be the one headed for the joint than the one laying there dead; if
you kept it in the neighborhood, brother against brother, you weren't
going to do more than five, six years any damn way.

So Honk couldn't believe it the day Dozier himself appeared at
his door, hands jammed in his coat pockets as if he were cradling a
pair of pistols. Some of Honk's rappies were visiting, but they looked
scared, and Dozier pushed inside like they weren't there.

"All y'all get the F up outa my way," he said. "I just want to
talk to Honk."

The rappies parted like the Red Sea. The two men stood face to
face, Honk leaning on his crutch, Dozier keeping his hands buried in
his coat.

"You got my money, man?" Honk demanded.

Dozier said he didn't. He started some jive story about why not, debts to other dudes and this and that, only Honk had tuned him out. Joker been messin' with the rappies and figure we something to F with, Honk was thinking. Joker don't know I'm the spark plug. He don't know he's in the lion's den, talking wacky like that.

"You don't have nothin' more to say to me," Honk told him.

Dozier stood fast, hands still hidden.

Honk lunged at him, grabbed his wrists, and yanked down hard, ripping away both coat pockets.

They were empty. Dozier was bluffing. He had no guns, and no respect either, walking in with that attitude and nothing to back his play. You don't walk in unless you got a way back out, Honk was thinking, 'cause if you don't have a way out, you ain't gonna see daylight no more. The dude might as well have jumped out the window and saved Honk the trouble, which Honk in fact invited him to do. That he declined the invitation didn't matter; when he came in the door, he had killed himself.

Honk wouldn't have had to take him all the way out the game, he reflected afterward, if it hadn't been for his bad leg. They could have fought it out, shake-and-baked all night if the dude wanted, and settled their differences fair and square. But Dozier had tried to take advantage of him. He had run off with Honk's money and then come around talking trash, when Honk could barely stand on his two feet. OK, my man, Honk thought, tightening his grip on his crutch. The dude's ass was *grass*.

"I know you, Honk," Dozier was saying when Honk hit him the first time, bringing the crutch down hard on his head.

Dozier staggered.

Honk skulled him again and then again, the crutch rising and falling like a sledgehammer driving spikes. He could hear one of his rappies, a stud named Midnight, yelling, "Stop him, stop him," but Honk was too deranged on drugs and rage to be stopped. He had fallen on top of Dozier, still flailing away, and when they finally pried him loose, the dude was dead.

The police came and surrounded the building, but Honk hobbled down four flights of stairs in the bedlam and persuaded a homeboy living on the eleventh floor to give him shelter. He held out there for a day while the cops made a floor-by-floor search. On the second day, they found him and led him away, manacled and limping on his ruined leg. He had caught cases before, and had always managed to beg, bargain, or buy his way out of trouble. This time there was, inconveniently, a body, and the only thing that meliorated Honk's situation was that he and it were black. The killing of one black person by another was known around the criminal courts as a nigger disorderly, a crime as common and as trivial as disorderly conduct, and Honk was punished accordingly. He was sentenced to five years in prison. He served two and a half.

The course of his life changed during his years away, though not because of anything the penitentiary did to or for him. Prison wasn't no thing for Honk; in all his years on the street, it had been less a deterrent than a constantly pending due bill, the ante you had to pay sooner or later if you wanted to sit at the table with the other players. You know the rules, man, he told himself; you *got* to get caught, and when he did, he was ready. Doing time was not a troubling event in his world, or even terribly newsworthy. A brother would disappear from the street, and people would say, "Aw, the ol' boy's in jail," as matter-of-factly as if he were away visiting his maiden aunt in Mississippi.

What did change for Honk was his solitude, the loneliness of a life in which one's friends are at least as dangerous as one's enemies. He was laid up in the hospital awaiting trial when a lady appeared at his bedside, a born-again Christian sister visiting the sick and shut-in as a matter of holy obligation. Her name was Anne Pinkins, and she was an attractive woman with flowing hair, a sad smile, and, given her religious vocation, surprisingly knowing eyes. She had come to Chicago from the Delta in her teens, yet another country girl answering the lure of the big city, and had lived in the semi-fast lane for a time. She married once at seventeen, got a divorce, and lived with another man for nine years. But with her conversion experience, she changed everything, her life-style as well as her life. She gave away her worldly goods—her car, her television, her stylish clothes—and consecrated her being to her Lord.

Women were objects of pleasure and sometimes commerce in Honk's world, but there was something different about Anne, something cleansing. He found himself drawn to her, talking to her in an almost confessional way about his life and asking her to help him change it. She wasn't interested at first, but Roy—he was Roy, not Honk, to her—was insistent, and she prayed to the Lord for guidance.

"Anne, I want you to marry Roy," God told her.

"This gangster?" she said. "No way. I can't do that."

"Anne, it's going to cost you a great deal," God said, knowing Honk; still, He put it in her mind and her heart that it was her Christian duty to help him. They had nothing in common, she knew that, and as much as told Honk so. Whatever she was doing in his behalf, she said, was her *work,* her sacrifice to God. But she finally gave in, and a year after they met they married. The bride wore white. The groom dressed in blue—his Pontiac state penitentiary fatigues.

Anne visited him every week in prison, and after he came out she made a home for him, a place in the northern suburbs far distant, so she hoped, from the temptations of Thirty-ninth Street. She didn't approve of Honk's business ventures and wasn't drawn by his money. She didn't need it; she had her own good job, on the graveyard shift at 3-M, and her community work with the aged filled her days. Honk was her reclamation project, her witness against sin, and she undertook it more out of duty than of hope or love. He made it difficult. Marriage in his view was utilitarian, an arrangement of convenience more than love; it gave him a place to go home to, and someone to see to his needs when he got there. Anne in turn was a willing servant, believing it was God's wish. She prayed for Honk's recovery from his wound, and it ultimately healed—her one unambiguous victory. She prayed for his deliverance from evil and was regularly disappointed; the most she could say was that he was not as bad as he had been.

Sometimes she was angry at him for his disobedience to God's will. Sometimes, when he strayed, she would lock him out of the house and ask herself how long she could go on; there was not much in the union for her *except* sacrifice, not even Honk's dependable companionship, which was all she ever asked of him in return. God would talk to her when she thought those thoughts and bring her through her despair. In the end, as she knew she would, she always forgave Roy one more time.

If her prayers could not redeem him, she believed at least that they sheltered him from harm when all his friends were dying. She knew *he* wasn't living for the Lord, but the Bible taught that an unbeliever was sanctified by a believing wife; that meant God was protecting Honk through her. There was, for example, the time Honk's main man of the moment, Big Ed, got killed trying to stick up a dope house. Honk should have been with him, but he wasn't. The Lord, in Anne's pious eyes, had seen to that.

Honk, more worldly, thought it was Mammon's doing, though the bottom line came out the same. He and Big Ed had just made a sizable score together, except Big Ed had run off with all the profits, maybe $40,000 or $50,000. That wasn't really no money, not to Honk, but Big Ed was a slow, semiliterate kid who wasn't old enough or smart enough to spell c-a-t when he first went to jail, let alone count to 50,000. Big Ed had spent most of his youth locked up and all of it hungry. Nigger ain't never had nothing, Honk mused; nigger never even had a chance to wear *suits* before, and he thought $50,000 was rich.

Honk didn't even think $50,000 was worth killing Big Ed about. They broke up their partnership instead, and Big Ed took someone else along on the dope-house job. Both men got blown away, Big Ed and the dude who could have been Honk. Their demise was discovered when Big Ed's blood came dripping though the ceiling onto the table in the poolroom downstairs. He was twenty-seven years old.

Honk was past thirty then and aging in The Life, tiring of getting shot at and sleeping in cars and trying to outrun the law of averages. Sometimes it scared him just thinking about all the S he had been through; sometimes he wondered why he kept gambling his life on dreams of fortune and fame. His town house in the suburbs was a comfortable place, done up by Anne in chrome, glass, and soft browns with color TV's upstairs and down. The sounds at night were the calls of children at play, not the gunfire and the sirens he had grown up with at Trey-nine. There were days when Honk thought he could live there broke and happy with Anne and her two sons from her previous life; days when he laid aside his iceman scowl like an article of costume and pedaled around the neighborhood on his ten-speed, Honk the unnoticeable-ass nigger, smiling pacifically at the suburbanites in their Toyotas and Trans Ams. He felt ready, those days, to give peace a chance. He didn't need to be chasing the good life anymore. Anne had created it around him.

"Man, why you even want to come to the city?" a homeboy visiting from Thirty-ninth Street asked him one day, seeing Honk at his ease in the suburbs.

Honk didn't have a very good answer, except that the city was where he was from and where his family still lived. He was lounging on the hood of a car on Dearborn Street one afternoon in his last summer on the block when the State Street bus rolled up and deposited a middle-aged black woman on the curb across the way. She was weighted down with purchases, and Honk, seeing her, smiled and shook his head. "My mama," he said. "Been shopping again." He was the prince of the city, but somewhere under the big Borsalino and the expensive tailor-mades, he was still Ernestine Johnson's wayward son. He took off after her at a rolling jog, eased the bags out of her hands, and walked her into Trey-nine. So long as she was there, it was still his home.

It was his place of business as well, or had been in his prime; mostly, on his regular day trips to Thirty-ninth Street, he was like a ring-worn fighter hanging out at the gym because he wasn't sure where else to go. So he kept on going and kept getting into *stuff,* except it was tougher and tougher staying ahead of the game. If you were into drugs, it was tough just staying even. Making money was no problem. Keeping it was. Honk and everyone around him was doing 'caine, and it broke you overnight, took every dime you made and your franchise with it; you couldn't get no product to sell anymore, 'cause you'd be labeled that you used it instead.

The competition was getting scarier as well, a new generation of kids coming up in the projects with no respect and no morals, not even the samurai code of the street; to Honk, it looked like whoever get a gun that night figure he got a license to kill anybody he feel like. He had affiliated with the Disciples when he came home from the army and still wore their pin sometimes, a gold six-pointed star with a G for "Gangster" in the middle. The emblem told the world that you were a hell of a nigger without your having to prove it in combat all the time. But some of these younger bloods didn't know no better than to try you anyway.

One of them had shown up on the corner on a summer day in the middle 1980's, a kid in a sharp black jumpsuit with a crimson stripe, putting out word that he and *his* rappies ran the drug scene on Thirty-ninth Street now. Honk was losing interest in the game and the territory, but he couldn't brook the open challenge; couldn't no MF come around Honk's corner, some *new* MF, and say he the chief. You F with the wrong people, you get killed, Honk told the kid, and when the sucker went for the trunk of his car, Honk came up on him with his own piece, fixing to burn him.

"Uh, man—I don't want no thang," the kid stammered. "I wanna make sure it's over."

"It ain't *never* over!" Honk screamed at his retreating back.

It would never be over, not for Honk. He was trying to ease on out of The Life, but he had cut off all his options, at least partly because he had never seen any he could believe in. Whoever made the world put whites in charge, he thought, and *they* weren't going to let no niggers live the way they show on TV. The ghetto was their place, and if you had to live there, you just as well have money and fun. Honk wasn't going to be one of them sorry MF's stuck in the projects, one more trifling stud living off some young girl's welfare check. He had his pride and his pleasures, and he couldn't turn them loose; he had become as much a prisoner of the game as a player at it.

He *had* got in it for money and fun, but the money was gone and the fun was going. He sat in a car one day trading bits of street wisdom with his protégé Ronnie Boy, ten years younger than himself, one in the long succession of rappies he had raised in The Life. Ronnie Boy had lately disappeared from the street for a few days, locked up in Cook County Jail on a wrong case, and Honk had been amused by his difficulty scaring up $300 to make bail. Damn, he thought, a nigger in bad shape, he can't get nobody to raise $300. As it developed, Ronnie Boy found somebody good for it and re-appeared on Thirty-ninth Street in a couple of days as sharp as ever, dressed clean in a blue and white jumpsuit; a rakish black Borse rode back on his head like a halo, and a wispy bit of mustache tried bravely to make him look older than he was. Jail hadn't wiped the smile off his cherubic face. He was just what his nickname said, a boy, too young to be combat-fatigued.

Honk was not, and there was a heaviness on his side of their conversation. Kids like Ronnie Boy made him feel his years, all thirty-four of them. Studs who played the game as long as he had knew in their hearts that jail wasn't the problem. *They* were; they got to be so *bad*—such do-anything, don't-F-with-him dudes—that they scared one another.

"Feuding took a lot of dudes out," Honk was saying, still the teacher. "That's the biggest threat, 'cause you don't worry about the enemy—you got to worry about your friend. You get into it with him and y'all shooting each other."

"You sitting up in your work joint"—a drug house—"and you holding *pistols*, looking at each other," Ronnie Boy said. "We used to carry two pistols, hands on both handles at all times."

"Gangsters do that," Honk said. "They get to fighting over who gonna be this or that. Next thing you know, they go to killing each other, and that brings the police in, and that makes it bad for every-body."

And there were the specialty stickup men, hustlers preying on hustlers; Honk had played that game, too, but the younger bloods out there frightened him. "The stickup man is more dangerous than the police," he told Ronnie Boy, " 'cause he gonna *pop* that pistol. Police just gonna throw down on you—you got a chance to give up. Stickup man isn't taking any chances. You give up and he guns your ass down anyway. A lot of niggers died for what they had."

A lot died, period, Honk was thinking. It was a *lot* of dead MF's out there, most of the niggers he had come up with; if they weren't dead, they were doing time, and if they weren't doing time, they done went crazy, and if they weren't dead *or* crazy, it was only 'cause they had had the good sense to come in off the street. Not many of them made thirty-four. He felt his age catching up with him, and his notoriety, and, lately, the law. He had been up for some type of case all his hustling life and had known he couldn't stay out of jail forever. If it's got to be, it's got to be, he always figured, and now it looked like his number was coming up.

"It ain't like the end of the world, y'know," he told Ronnie Boy, rationalizing in advance. "You might get there and make some money. It betters you for the street life. You got to look at it from the advantage point. I can't look at it like, 'Man, they *got* me.' So they got me.''

"If I coulda-woulda-shoulda," Ronnie Boy said, mocking those suckers who couldn't take it when it came. Being cool meant never saying you were sorry.

"In that jail, studs get just as much money as they get on the street," Honk said. "Get *more*."

"Send money home," Ronnie Boy said, nodding.

Honk's calm was at least partly for show, an act of noblesse oblige for the prince of players. Dues time was at hand, and his regrets were compounded by the knowledge that he had contributed to his own fall. As times tightened, he had been taking more chances and paying less attention to the level of danger or the quality of the partners he was running with. He had never thought of hustling as particularly risky, and his success at dancing a step ahead of the law had made him overconfident.

His luck ran out one afternoon in the summer of '85, in his fifth year back on the street; his luck, that is, and his good sense. A chicken shack at Forty-forth and Cottage Grove had been robbed in broad daylight, and a police patrol spotted Honk and two of his rappies an hour later, sitting in a parked two-door a few blocks away.

"Man, *drive* this MF," Honk told the wheel man. The cops were almost in their laps.

The dude froze; he wouldn't start, wouldn't even turn the key, and Honk sat in the backseat, trapped and helpless. There was a .38 in his hand when the first cops got there, and another in the car. The guns fit the eyewitness accounts of the stickup. So did the license number on the car. So did Honk and one of his partners, a dude named Marvin. "Man, I never been there in my life," Honk protested, but the chicken-shack people picked him and Marvin out of a lineup that same day and said they did it.

They were sinking fast when Marvin came into their cell at five in the morning, looking sheepish.

"Man, I just told them I did everything," he said.

"*What?*" Honk demanded.

Don't worry, Marvin said, he had only talked about himself, not Honk. Of course, he *had* mentioned that Honk was at the scene, he said, and it turned out the wheel man had confessed, too.

Honk could feel the walls closing in. A sense of sadness stole over him, a feeling of defeat made sharper by his own complicity in it. Here he had survived twenty years in The Life, he thought, and still got mixed up with two deranged young niggers who didn't have no better sense than to confess. They might have beat the case, their word against the witnesses, but the state's attorney came at Marvin with the old okey-doke about the advantages of coming clean, and Marvin went for it. Nigger too young to understand them people didn't give a F about him as no *person*, Honk thought; he was just another nigger to them, and Marvin gonna lay there and admit doing it. How you going to beat something after you tell on *yourself*?

Doing time didn't scare Honk; it wasn't much worse than living in the projects, and in the joint, unlike the street, they fed you free. What he mainly felt, staring at Marvin, was old.

"Man, man, man," he said, shaking his head. Honk's luck had run out at last. The ol' boy was going off for the long ride.

TO AN EARLY GRAVE

When people at Trey-nine told the tale afterward, they said that James Bonner, too, had broken one of the iron rules of the outlaw life: the one that said it was your friends you had to worry about, not your enemies, 'cause your enemies couldn't get close enough to do you no harm. James Bonner knew that. He had survived thirty-seven years on the street with his guard up, looking out for himself and the building. But his daddy, Mose Bonner Sr., had just died in Mississippi in the waning winter of 1983, and James Bonner, helping with the funeral arrangements, had grown incautious in his need and his grief.

He was staying on the sixteenth floor at Trey-nine then, keeping an apartment for a lady who was away, and he in turn had taken in his old buddy Rabbit Wells and Rabbit's girlfriend as boarders. People said *that* afterward, too—that James Bonner had always been too generous; he never made big money on his odd jobs or his petty hustles, but if he had food in the kitchen or a roof over his head, you were welcome to share it. Rabbit and his lady, as it happened, were paying guests, or were supposed to be; they had fallen behind in their share of the rent, and James Bonner was tight for cash, so tight that he had to borrow a black suit for his own father's funeral. He found himself in the unwelcome position of having to dun Rabbit to pay up.

What about it, he asked Rabbit.

Later, Rabbit told him. He had been drinking.

I need it for the rent, James Bonner said. He knew Rabbit had the money; he had just got his income-tax refund.

Rabbit said he couldn't have it now, he would have to wait.

"Forget it," James Bonner said finally. "We ain't gonna talk about it until you get sober."

Rabbit stalked out of the apartment, then reappeared a few minutes later. "I'm fixin' to get my clothes outa here," he said.

"Naw, Rabbit, whyn't you go on, man?" James Bonner said. "You're drunk. I ain't gonna let you take nothin' outa here until you pay your share of the rent."

"Oh, so you takin' my stuff, huh?" Rabbit said.

He walked out again, then came back, full of 86-proof courage. James Bonner shooed him away. It had been like a schoolboy game till then, bluff and counterbluff, but when Rabbit appeared a third time, he was carrying a long, serrated kitchen knife.

James Bonner was thunderstruck. *Nobody* did him that way; his friends had better sense, and his enemies wouldn't dare.

"You call yourself goin' to get a MF'ing knife at me, man?" he demanded. "You gonna hurt me with a knife?"

He came partway out the door; James Bonner always moved forward. Rabbit backed off a step. "Naw, man," he said, "I don't have no knife for you."

James Bonner stood fast, holding the door. His eyes were a dare.

Rabbit stopped retreating. "F you!" he shouted.

James Bonner stared at him. Rabbit was eight years younger than he was, and nearly as big, but it wasn't youth or strength talking, it was whiskey.

"Yeah, I got it for you," Rabbit was saying, showing the knife. "What you think, I'm scared or something?"

James Bonner let the door swing shut and stepped out onto the gallery.

"Yeah, come on, MF," Rabbit teased.

James Bonner feinted toward him. Rabbit edged back. The knife flashed through the space between the two men, a short, swift underhand flick.

James Bonner's eyes widened. His shirtfront turned red. He wheeled and lumbered down the gallery. Rabbit stumbled after him, then ducked into an open apartment.

James Bonner disappeared through the door to the stairwell and started down. A few minutes dragged by. A little boy came out. Honk Johnson's brother Weasel was standing there; he had seen the whole thing, except that Rabbit's knife had moved quicker than Weasel's eye, and Weasel didn't think anything serious had happened.

"That man, James Bonner," the little boy said, "He's laying down there in the hallway."

He was one floor down, sprawled on the concrete gallery opposite the door to 1501. The word was already flying through the building, and a thicket of people clustered around, wanting to help. James Bonner had always preached that, caring for one another, except when *he* was the one who needed help, it came too late. There was a small slit near his heart. His lung had been punctured. He was fighting for breath, his chest heaving with the effort. Blood bubbled out. The elevators weren't working, a common occurrence in the building. James Bonner was still alive, but only barely, when the police finally labored up the fifteen floors to get to him. All anyone could do was watch him die.

His body lay side by side with his father's at the funeral four days later, on what would have been James Bonner's thirty-eighth birthday. The church, a big, converted movie theater, was crowded with family, friends, and not a few old adversaries, street dudes come out as if to reassure themselves that the baddest brother on the block was really dead. Society considered him a criminal. The obituary notes distributed at the funeral described him more nearly the way his neighbors saw him, as a defender of the downtrodden. He was buried in the poor folks' section of a black cemetery, a field carpeted with weeds and brush and crosshatched by ruts from tractor tires; even the plot number was missing from his unmarked grave. His six-year-old daughter, Tyrine, and his ten brothers and sisters mourned him. So did Trey-nine.

But people there were curiously forgiving of Rabbit Wells, and of the light hand of the law in his case. He served less than a year in prison for killing James Bonner; the charge was involuntary manslaughter, which was about the way Trey-nine saw it. Rabbit hadn't *meant* to kill James Bonner, people said; if he had, he would have been the one got buried. Rabbit had probably been scared, people said, as anybody with good sense would be if James Bonner was coming at him with that tombstone look in his eye. Even sudden death can be banal in the ghetto, which has seen too much of it, and James Bonner's seemed as empty of meaning or of volition as an accident on the highway. It was one of those things that happen, people said, and by the evidence of their lives, they were right.

COOL IN THE GAME

It was only a playground basketball game, blue shirts against green, two teams from the projects paired off in a summer tournament named for a child who had wandered too close to a gang fight and gotten killed by a stray bullet. There were no bright lights for Billy Harris this time, no writers or cameras, no pro scouts waiting to assay every fake move he put on his man and every jumper he buried from twenty feet out. Billy wasn't on Front Street anymore. But a basketball court was still his domain, and from the moment he crossed its boundaries, flashy in his yellow headband and his Air Jordan sneakers, he was like landed gentry moving among the tenants on his own estate. He had the gallery high-fiving with a couple of indolent dunks during the warm-ups, and when he got the the ball at cardiac time in the game, one second to go and his team two points behind, it was like it used to be; it was as if the whole world centered on this rectangle of concrete at this moment in time.

Billy had dominated the esthetic of the game till then, his body flying and his shot falling as if he were twenty-two years old instead of thirty-four. What he could not do was win it by himself. His team-mates in green kept dropping the ball as if it were stolen property and the police were looking, and it was well along in the second half before they finally got their S together and started crawling back out of a ten-point hole. They tied the game twice in the closing minutes, but the blues hit a pair of free throws for a 52–50 lead. The clock showed twelve seconds left, and eleven of those had oozed away when the greens got one last possession out of bounds.

The inbounds pass found Billy near midcourt, deep in that long-distance artillery range where a basket counts for three points instead of the usual two. You had to be a desperado or a dreamer to shoot from as far out as he was and think you could make it, but Billy had some of each in him, and this was his moment; he could feel it. There were blue shirts all around him as he started his ascent, one dude hanging on his arm and two more poking their hands up in his face. It didn't matter. He was airborne, and it was as if he were alone, flying outside time, space, and the possibility of failure, launching his shot toward the basket with a cool eye and an almost elegant hauteur. The ball was in flight when the buzzer sounded. It dropped through the hoop, making the net snap and dance. Score three for Billy, and a one-point victory for the greens.

The kids from the projects mobbed him, yelling and slapping hands, and homies with longer memories were telling him he hadn't lost a thing—it was just like the old days. Billy knew better. He received the acclaim as his due, his face as gaunt and solemn as the likeness of a saint in a Gothic cathedral, but he understood that the ball thing was a part of his past now—just some moments of pleasure and years of pain he had had to pass through, he thought, to get wherever it was he was going.

At least he *had* a past, he thought, a brief but tangible record of achievement. The ball thing—basketball—had given him that; it had brought him a notoriety that had long outlived his days as an active player. You could measure his present by his threadbare wardrobe—there were three pairs of jeans, one pair of street shoes, and one pair of gym shoes in his closet—and the future was as unreliable to him as to any of the brothers you saw hanging out around Thirty-ninth Street waiting for something to happen. But Billy, unlike them, knew who he was, or anyway who he had been. You could pull out your scrapbook and *see* your past, he thought, memories of glory frozen forever in newsprint and pictures.

His history was in those pages, and his identity, his proof to the world that he really existed. Otherwise, like a lot of black dudes around the projects, he would have disappeared down the cracks in the society with hardly a trace. His number wasn't in the computers, and there wasn't much on paper besides his clippings. He had no college diploma, no job résumé, no lease with his name on it, not even a rap sheet for the years he had spent in The Life; he had been such a master of the game that on his retirement there wasn't a single conviction on his record. With his scrapbook, Billy Harris was a celebrity. Without it, he might have been just another invisible man.

His visibility—his definition—rested precariously on five years in big-time ball, four in college and one in the pros. He had been a hot property coming out of Dunbar High, a six-three wraith of a kid with a game as slick as satin and high PSAT scores besides. The bids came in from flesh markets everywhere, from the Ivy League on one coast to the PAC-8 on the other, some bearing the strong scent of money; and Kansas, in the middle, courted him as if they were the lost tribe and he the messiah. The head coach himself came to Trey-nine to see his mama, and when Billy went to look at the campus, he was borne through the streets of Lawrence in a motorcade, a poor black teenager from the projects riding in splendor past banners and posters that said WELCOME BILLY HARRIS.

But his coaches steered him to Northern Illinois University instead, delivering him, or so he suspected, as a kind of bonus for accepting other Dunbar graduates with less negotiable records and skills. It was a choice he later regretted, a further piece of evidence, in his eyes, that he was no more than a piece of black merchandise in the white business of college sports. A *vicious* business, he came to believe when he had been around a little longer; a commodity market trading in black bodies not for sport but for profit. His own brother Willie got a bellyful and walked away after an honorable-mention all-America season in junior college. He got a scholarship offer from Pepperdine University in California; the deal looked good, and his bags were already packed the day he told Billy he wasn't going.

Billy was stunned. He was seventeen, and he still thought basketball was a game; he hadn't yet peeped what it was *really* about, which was money and flesh and how many years they could bleed you before you burned out. He was staring at Willie, wondering where the nigger was coming from to turn down a chance like that.

Willie met Billy's gaze. His eyes were older than the two-year difference in their ages. "I'm through with this shit," he said. He was tired of the game and the gaming. He had a couple of kids and a living to earn. He was staying home.

Billy went away, pursuing his dream. He enjoyed Northern, enjoyed the ball, the people, and the learning experience; it was, he thought, like being hungry for a week and suddenly walking into a smorgasbord of good things. Sometimes he looked up at the stands, packed with paying customers, and wondered where all those dollars were going. But he was getting something in return for his pound of flesh, the natural high of status and privilege that went with being a major-college athlete. The normal money and perks were there, and the soft phys ed curriculum. His quick mind went largely unchallenged. You could be *brilliant*, he thought, and nobody would give a damn; if you were sticking twenty-five points a game, your coach didn't want you majoring in physics or something, he wanted your ass eligible to play.

His regret was having said no to Kansas; the coach there told him he was making a terrible mistake, and Billy came to agree. Kansas was an established basketball power, a major purveyor of talent to the pro leagues. Northern was not; its basketball program was a young one, only just making its claim to serious notice. They had collected a good coach and a lot of talent, three live pro possibilities including Billy, and they were ready to crack into the national rankings for the first time. But Billy began to wonder if he had chosen the right showcase for his gifts and his hopes. His all-America mentions didn't seem to help, or his twenty-four-point average, up there among the top twenty in the country, or the thirty-five points he scored in front of a platoon of pro scouts in Madison Square Garden. It was the dudes at the blue-chip schools who seemed to get all the press and the big pro contracts.

Still, there was speculation in the papers that Billy would be a first-round choice in the National Basketball Association's annual draft of college players. The brothers at Trey-nine mistook the guess for prophecy: This nigger about to get a million dollars, they were saying, as if the money were already in the bank waiting to be drawn down. Billy himself believed it—believed he had earned it—and began spending it in his mind, buying stuff for his mama and his friends.

But the buzz around the NBA was that he hadn't had quite the senior season he should have had, and he was chosen on the seventh round of the draft, not the first. His million-dollar dream dissipated like smoke on the air. It was about as likely for a seventh-rounder to win the lottery as to make it in pro ball, even at the minimum wage, and for Billy the odds were even longer. The Chicago Bulls, who chose him, were already overstocked with quality players at guard, which happened to be his position.

In his gloom, Billy concluded that he was beaten before he began. The last thing the Bulls wanted to show their white fans, he figured, was a black athlete from their own racially fractured hometown; being from Chicago in those days was something a black player had to live down before he even got a look. He went to camp determined to give it his best anyway, ready, he thought, to run through a MF'ing *wall* to stay in the league. He practiced hard, volunteered for everything, and ran sprints on his own after everyone else had dressed and gone. The older players were encouraging, and the coach, Dick Motta, told him a time or two, "You can make this team, Harris. You can make this team."

But Billy's suspicions gnawed at him from day one. "Hey, man," he told his brother Willie early on, "this white dude is gonna pull some S with me."

"Man, he can't," Willie said. "Nigger, you're *bad*. You're killing these MF's."

Billy thought so. The management didn't. The official book on him was that he wasn't quite good enough to be an NBA guard, at least not on a team as talent-rich as the Bulls. The private appraisal was that he had an attitude; the moody kid from the projects lacked a certain maturity about the way things worked. BS, said Billy when the rumors reached him; they had to give up some type of reason for cutting a player of his caliber, so they made a head case out of him. His defense was too little too late. His rep was made, and neither his sweat nor his skill was enough to overcome it.

"This is one of the hardest things I've ever had to do," Motta told him just before the Bulls broke camp.

The dude was staring down at the floor. Billy knew what was coming. They're crossing me out of my future, he was thinking, and the man isn't even looking at me.

"We just can't use you," Motta told the floor.

Billy, for once, was silent. He said good-bye to a couple of the veterans who had befriended him. They told him not to worry, he was sure to catch on somewhere. He knew better. It was too late to get a tryout, let alone a job; he hadn't had enough playing time in preseason exhibition games to impress anybody, and the regular season was about to begin. He packed his gear and went home to Treynine, still silent, but when he saw his mother, he started to cry.

"Mama," he said, "all those things I wanted to get you—now I won't be able to."

"Billy," she said, "I'm here and I still love you. Your family still loves you, and they're with you. Whatever we have, we'll share."

She prayed. He disappeared for a time on a trip, a retreat in the urban wilderness; it was, he said long afterward, a matter of backing up and licking his wounds. Then he reappeared on Thirty-ninth Street, hurting inside, hardened outside, too proud to show the brothers there what he felt. He had discovered how much he had wanted that success, 'cause if he had become a million-dollar bonus baby, then everyone around him would have, too. Whatever he had was theirs, he thought, even his stardom if he had achieved it; they looked on him as the one who would lead them out, and now he had let them down. Only he didn't run and hide, like most of these MF's that reach the top, however briefly, and then take that fall. The average nigger would have gone crazy, he guessed. He didn't; he went back and faced them all, friends and enemies, the embarrassed smiles and the know-it-all smirks. Take your best shot, MF, he was thinking. I'm still Bill and I'll tear your ass up.

"I told you, nigger, you wasn't S," a dude on the corner said to him.

"Yeah, you right, MF," Billy answered, "so what does that make *you*?"

His bitterness was his refuge, a layer of callus encrusting his soul. It was a bad patch in his life, a vicious time, he thought years later. He was discovering the loneliness of defeat. He followed the fortunes of the Bulls in the papers and was secretly pleased when they got knocked out of the playoffs; the sons of bitches might have gone all the way, he thought, if they had had an off-guard who could shoot it like he could. On the street, he turned cold, Billy the outlaw nigger, his gaze as warm as dry ice; some people out there felt the chill in his eyes and his mirthless laugh and figured he *had* gone crazy.

At home he withdrew into silence and prayer, shutting even his family out of his interior life.

"Billy, you don't get anyplace by being like that," his mother told him. "You have to let that go and just have a lot of love, and you'll make it. Sometimes what we want, we don't get. We have to pick up the pieces and go from there."

"I know, Mama," Billy said. "It just looks like everybody's against me or something."

"Maybe it doesn't mean they're against you," she said. "Maybe they're trying to see what's *to* you, you know. Testing you out to see what you're *about*."

Billy was unpersuaded. In his view, basketball was what he was about, and the test had been rigged to ensure his failure.

He did get one more shot, after two high-scoring summers in the semipros. A letter arrived one day from the San Diego Conquistadors of the American Basketball Association, inviting Billy to try out. It wasn't the NBA; the Conquistadors—the Q's to their fans—were a dying team in a moribund rival league, but Billy went for the chance as if he were an early Christian martyr in training for the lions. He spent a muggy Chicago August playing ball all day every day, that and running, five miles downtown and five miles back in sweats and combat boots. Nigger done lost his mind, the brothers on Thirty-ninth Street were saying. They didn't realize he was fighting for his life.

He showed up ready for battle, the coldest he had ever been, and this time he got the job at $60,000 a year. The Q's didn't know he would happily have played for nothing. He was only a backup shooting guard, a sixteen-minute-a-night relief man for a dude named Bo Lamar. Billy was sure he could outgun Lamar, though their stats were roughly even, and he got three chances to prove it when Lamar hurt his leg. Billy responded, with nineteen-, twenty-four-, and twenty-eight-point games on successive nights. Lamar's leg got better fast, and Billy went back to the bench, a sub again.

He loved the pro life anyway, and the playground ambience of the ABA. The league was blacker in spirit than the NBA, more ghettoish in its style and soul. There were some has-beens and never-wases, MF's who couldn't play *dead* with a knife stuck in their back; they were there, Billy figured, because someone in power wanted them there. But all the renegade niggers in pro ball were there, too, hellacious players who had got jammed somewhere along the line just like he had. The league, to that degree, was like a road show company out of Trey-nine. It hurt Billy to be sitting. Still, just being there, he was home.

It was a sweet trip for the single season it lasted, and when he came back to Thirty-ninth Street this time, he came in triumph. He didn't have to be there; he had a place on the lake now, along with a Cadillac, a closetful of clothes, and a retinue of ladies chasing his ass. But he liked being back with his homies, liked busting a hundred-dollar bill and spreading fives and tens around the street like Rockefeller distributing dimes.

"Hey, nigger," someone would say, "give me twenty or thirty of them dollars?"

"Here, nigger, I got *thousands* of these MF's. That's all you want? Here."

"Bill, give me your ride?"

"Here, take the MF," he would say, handing over his car keys; that was the kind of stud he was.

But some of the brothers who had celebrated his failure seemed to resent his success, and Billy's wariness deepened. He thought of himself as a shy and insecure man, inside the light show of his celebrity, and when he saw how people reacted to him, saw that there were dudes out there who didn't dig your ass because of this little success you had, he hardened himself against them. He built, or rather completed, a wall around himself, a facade of toughness, and hid behind it. You couldn't survive in the street if people peeped that you had a heart; you didn't want *everybody* to know you were righteous, 'cause if the niggers knew that, they wouldn't think twice about F'ing with you. So Billy became, by an act of will, a mean MF. You don't like me? Cool. F you.

He needed his new demeanor where he was going. His contract with the Q's was extended, with a rich raise to $130,000, but before he could cash in, the team folded, and then the whole league. He got a couple of gigs thereafter playing in Asia and South America, one more dude in the foreign legion of scratched-out stateside athletes working abroad and waiting to be rediscovered. The money was OK. The future was not. The bright lights were out for Billy Harris; his body and his talent had always been articles of commerce, commodities to be bought and sold, and there was no market for them anymore.

He had already explored the legitimate job market, after the Bulls dropped him, to discouraging effect. He had nothing to sell except basketball and, like too many ghetto rent-a-stars, he had left college shy of graduating when his eligibility ran out. The Man owned everything, he thought, and if you didn't have that piece of paper with his signature and his seal of approval on it, you might as well not even apply. He knew. He had gone after all types of jobs, manual S that any dumb son of a bitch could do, without success. He was fifteen hours shy of a college degree and he couldn't even get work as a janitor in the projects.

So Billy withdrew from what white people were pleased to call legitimate society. He had begun *thinking*, which was, he supposed,

turned them out to walk the streets, and constantly encouraged them to use their earnings and their contacts to better themselves. He in turn was pleased when one of them would walk away and say of him that the nigger sure was sweet; it was his certification to himself and his unquiet conscience that he had not really done them wrong.

Hot Shot was his favorite, the power behind his game. He had found her one night at Al's Disco, a dim night spot in the shopping center across the street from Trey-nine. Shot was working there as a barmaid, but when she went switching by in a purple dress, an outfit sexy enough to hang in the booty hall of fame, Billy knew he had to have her for his stable and for himself. There was one small inconvenience, a dude she had been dating off and on. The dude was hard-timing her over a gold chain of hers; he had taken it, and she wanted it back. He's one of them gorilla pimp-type niggers, Billy thought, watching them bicker. Nigger got a million-dollar thoroughbred over there and act like he's F'ing with a watermelon-wagon horse or something.

When he had seen enough, Billy patted his pistol and walked over to them.

"Is this your woman?" he asked the dude.

"Naw, I ain't his woman," Hot Shot broke in.

"Is this your man?"

"Naw," she said. "He's just a friend."

"Does she owe you any money?"

"No!" Shot said.

"Well, go on about your business and leave this lady alone," Billy said.

The dude looked into his eyes. They said leave. The dude muttered something and disappeared into the night, out of Hot Shot's life. When she got off work, Billy showed her to his stretch Cadillac. She was impressed. He was a sweet-looking nigger, she thought. He wasn't one of them flashy, peacock-type of players; he was riding around in a big limo in his gym shoes. She liked that, too.

They drove to his place in Hyde Park. He poured them each a Cordon Bleu.

"You the power, baby," he told her. "You a bad MF. You so

bad I'll attack Russia with your ass. I get you into Khrushchev's bedroom, I'll be *runnin'* Russia."

Her glass was empty. He filled it again.

"With the natural charisma you got, baby," he said, "you can go to the MF'in' moon. Don't need a penny, and go first class."

She turned up her glass. He poured another drink. She spent the night and wound up staying with Billy, his main lady, for five years. He had been attracted by her looks, but it was her game, her personality, that bound him to her; you could take her to the Waldorf-Astoria, he thought, and these MF's would think she was a college graduate. There was nothing exploitive about their relationship, he told himself; hey, she was in love, and he was her mentor, ten years older and wiser in The Life, helping her take her game to a higher level. He slapped her around some when she got out of place, but he always went for her bottom, never her face. Mostly, he gave her what she needed, money and love, and eventually got her started toward a legitimate life, learning computers.

She in turn was Billy's backbone in The Life; she had as much of a game as any nigger, he thought, but she wasn't about anything except making sure *his* game was strong. He realized the depths of her devotion to him when she walked into his crib on his birthday one year with a pretty young girl trailing behind her.

"What you bring me for my birthday, baby?" Billy asked.

"What you think this is?" she said, gesturing toward the girl. "This is Sunshine, and she's for you."

"For me, baby?"

"Yeah," Shot said. "Happy birthday."

Sunshine stayed with Billy for six months. Shot seemed not to mind. She had set out to make it a memorable birthday—the best a nigger ever had, she thought—and so far as Billy was concerned, she succeeded.

But her tolerance for his vagrant way with women finally gave out when he took up with a pair of twins named Tina and Tracey. She had just come home from a trip when she found out about it; Billy came around to his place in his fancy ride, and all three of them got out, Billy and his new matched set of ladies. I don't want to see all that, Shot was thinking, but the threesome became a regular sight.

She told Billy finally that Tracey was all right but Tina was not; Tina, she said, was trouble. Billy ignored the warning and kept gaming on both women. This man don't know *which* one he wants, Shot thought, her own patience nearly gone.

It ran out only when Tina got pregnant with Billy's child, one of the six he would father and leave behind in the projects. Shot ended their affair then; wasn't nothing else she could do *but* end it, with that baby in the picture binding Billy to Tina. She had no regrets. Her years with Billy had been beautiful times, she thought, a season of love that flowered and faded. For her, at least, it never quite died.

The Life was exacting its price on Billy anyway, fraying his nerves and what was left of his conscience. He was dealing cocaine as well as ladies, geometrically increasing the risks of the game along with the profits. He had been Billy the Kid for a long time, living off the land like the outlaws of old. You had to be a bad son of a bitch to do that, he thought, with all the technology available to the Man; you had to get out there and *take* what you needed, and somehow stay out of that Graybar Hotel. But the pressure kept rising, and Billy wondered how much more he could take—how long he could outrun the law, the competition, and his own nagging conscience.

He had always had a strong sixth sense for danger, only now it was going off on him constantly, like a burglar alarm echoing down an empty street in the night. One time he was idling with his new lady, Tina, in a launderette on Thirty-ninth Street, waiting to make a delivery to his street pushers, when some police cars pulled outside. Billy's back was to the door. He didn't see the cops coming. Tina did.

"Be still," she whispered. "There's some detectives out there. They look like they're coming in here. Where's the pistol?"

"Right in front," Billy said. He was carrying a gun every day, just like the police.

Tina eased close to him. He kept his back to the door. She pulled his jacket back a bit, tugged up his shirt, and eased his snub-nose out from under his belt.

"Where's the coke?" she murmured.

"In my inside pocket," he told her.

She reached in and fished up the packets of 'caine. Then she unhooked the beeper from his belt; it was a tool of the contemporary drug trade, a cold giveaway if you got caught with it. When he was clean, Tina turned away, burying the evidence in her wash. Billy walked out to his limousine, past the detectives coming in. He was home free that time, thanks to his lady. But his escape only sharpened his feeling that he was heading for the big fall, that every day he woke up in The Life was one more day spent throwing bricks at the penitentiary door.

He had to watch his back as well. If you were as good at the game as he was, there was always some envious MF coming up behind you, some dude looking to take you out for what you had. Finesse was what Billy had always been about, on the court and in The Life. He wasn't out to hurt nobody, but he had become a target out in the street, and he no longer felt dressed without a pipe—a pistol—stuck in the front of his pants; wasn't nobody going to hurt *him* either. He was at his place one night with a partner, an old homie from Stateway Gardens, when a customer phoned to arrange a buy. Billy's partner took the call. Billy's nerve ends tingled. He had his man tell the dude to come alone. Still, his inner alarm system said something wasn't right.

When the dude knocked a few minutes later, Billy picked up his .357 Magnum and hid behind the door. He signaled his partner to open it.

The buyer was there. He had brought company, two monstrous dudes who looked like they were under contract to a needy undertaker to create some business.

Billy cocked the Mag and stepped out where they could see him. He said nothing.

"Hey, man," the buyer said, staring into the gun, "what's *that* for?"

"You were supposed to come alone," Billy answered. "What's with these two gorilla niggers?"

"Aw, man," the dude said, "they OK."

"Naw, they ain't OK," Billy said. "Now get the F out of here."

The three backed out. Billy's partner closed the door. Billy uncocked the pistol and sighed a deep sigh. Hey, nigger, he was thinking; he knew then that he could have killed someone, and he wasn't sure he liked his self-discovery.

He knew, too, that he was running too hard. He kept three apartments, but even then he had to disappear into a room at the Hilton now and again just to heal his synapses and catch his breath. He was out near the end of his string when his mama called him in the small hours one morning. Guys on the block had been talking about him, jealous niggers, he thought, trying to get at him through her. Billy done gone crazy, they were telling her. Doin' this, doin' that. When she came on the phone, she was crying.

"I hear you're pimpin'," she said. "Got these girls whoring. I hear you're out there selling drugs. Boy, I didn't raise you like this." She wasn't accepting his help anymore; he couldn't pay for anything, because his money wasn't coming right.

Billy was in torment. She had a heart condition, and he couldn't bear hearing her cry. "Mama," he said, "I'm not going to do that anymore."

He took the promise to heart, halfway; he vanished underground for a time, and when he reappeared on Thirty-ninth Street, he had retired from pimping. But he was still dealing drugs, and in his frayed state he was losing his half-step edge on the law. The Feds caught him and his partner in a narcotics sting one day in 1985; it cost them $25,000 to beat the charge, and $13,000 more to replace the lost drugs, and Billy found himself at the bottom of a deep hole looking up. He had only just begun climbing out the following spring when the Feds struck again, this time at his lady's place. Someone, purportedly a customer, had called ahead wanting to make a buy. Billy's lady, at his instruction, said he was indisposed. The narcs came anyway and, according to his own inventory, cleaned him out—took his clothes, his car, his $15,000 in rainy-day money, and his last four ounces of 'caine. Billy was gone. The only thing they didn't get was him.

His string had run out; he was back on Thirty-ninth Street, back in the cycle of poverty where he started, with not much more than his scrapbook to prove he had almost made it out. He was known for his ball and his gift of gab; otherwise, he thought, he *had* become one more invisible man among invisible men. He had no permanent address, just a series of compliant ladies in the project willing to take him in; he would stay with one until they got on each other's nerves, then drift on to the next. He had no money either, for a long time, not even a welfare check. When he worked at all, it was usually in some sports program for kids, trying to teach them a little about basketball and a little about survival in a society he believed was organized for their destruction.

He did get a steady job finally, chauffeuring the director of the Chicago Housing Authority. But he sometimes thought that God had made him for a larger mission, that his disappointments in basketball and his successes on the street had all been a kind of education for a new life as a leader of his people. His hero, Malcolm X, had been a pimp once, and a drug dealer, and had been in prison; he had climbed up out of a deeper hole than Billy's and fired the hearts and minds of black people everywhere. The need was there, a generation of little brothers growing up vicious in the projects with no one to guide them. The Man had crossed them out at birth, Billy told Vest Monroe one day, and hey—when they crossed out those kids, they were crossing out the future of black America. 'Cause within the midst of those cats, he said, there's another you. There's another me.

Billy knew he could reach them; he was still Bill, still the baddest, still a hero on Thirty-ninth Street because he had never really left home. He wasn't precisely sure how to go about it, or how to pay his own way back into the straight-up world. You might find him out there hustling again, he thought, plying the only trade he knew, but with a purpose this time: preparing himself to be a trailblazer for those kids. He wanted it said of him that you could count on that nigger. He wanted it said that in the clutch, Billy Harris was *down* for his people. He had a recurring dream set sometime in the future in a stately home in a nice part of town. A Ferrari pulls up in the driveway, and a young man steps out, Billy's grandson, with a pretty lady on his arm. She pauses inside to admire a painting, the portrait of an important-looking black patriarch, and asks who it is.

"Well, that's my grandfather, Billy Harris," the young man answers. "That's the nigger that started all this S. He was just a nigger. But he was a *hell* of a nigger."

GOOD-BYE TO A BOSS DUDE

It was time for the long good-bye, and Honk Johnson was dressed up prettier than a *GQ* picture when Billy Harris found him on a lot outside the Taylor Homes one afternoon in the fall of 1986, waiting for the action to begin. The puzzlement, to Billy, was why the ol' boy was going off to the joint so quietly—why, indeed, he was going at all.

Honk had run the last time, when he caught his murder case. He had made the Man come and find him, but this time it was like he was sailing to Europe on a long vacation. Printed invitations were fluttering up and down Thirty-ninth Street—*GOOD-BYE PARTY FOR A BOSS DUDE: ROY*—and the day-shift players were already getting into the Chivas at Cigar's Lounge. And here was the guest of honor, out in a parking lot, with a rappie named Barksdale at his elbow running down how much *gusto* old Honk used to have for The Life and how fair he had been to his partners—"fair when he was on the top," Barksdale was saying, "and fair when he hit rock bottom." The ol' boy wasn't even gone yet, and they were talking about him in the past tense. They were treating Big Honk like he was history.

"Man," Billy told him, "I can't believe you're givin' in to 'em. I been saying, 'Big Honk's gonna be out here somewhere kickin' back when the day to go to jail comes.' "

Honk shook his head. Ain't no sense in going nowhere, he was thinking, not no more; you jumped bail in this day and time, you'd be looking at the thirty-year max for armed robbery instead of the eight he got. But he was stuck inside his legend—known dealer, known killer, don't F with him—and people expected him to live up to it. They thought he led a charmed life, with all the bullets he had dodged for twenty years. Aw, man, you ain't goin' nowhere, they told him, and when it looked like he might have to, they simply assumed he would run.

"Honk, why you doing it, man?" Billy was saying.

"The deal was too sweet," Honk answered sadly.

He had in fact hoped for something sweeter, seven years maybe, or even the minimum six in exchange for his plea of guilty. But he knew when he was beaten. There was that homicide on his record, and they had him dirty in the robbery case. His own rappies had talked. The witnesses were persuasively sure that he was the one; how, Honk wondered, were they going to forget someone sticking a pistol in their faces with a wild and crazy look in his eye? He had scouted the judge besides, during a series of court appearances, and he hadn't liked what he had seen; all the dude did was bang that gavel and go, "Lock 'im up," time after time after time. "Boy boy boy boy boy," Honk murmured, waiting his turn in the gallery one day. The man was *raw*.

You couldn't reason with him, and you couldn't buy judges anymore, either. There had been a time when, if you did catch a case, it wasn't no big thing; you'd get the right lawyer to visit the right judge with the right money and walk away free. It was a racket, of course; even if you hadn't done nothing, Honk remarked to Billy Harris, they'd say, "Make him pay some money. If he don't, give him some time." But that way out was closed now. Honk hadn't stacked any money, a serious oversight for a hustler, and even if he had, a wave of courthouse scandals had everybody running scared.

"They bustin' the *judges*," Honk lamented to Billy, "so how bad you think it is on *us* now? They won't even take our money no more. They used to take our money and let us come on back out here."

"We used to be able to buy a case," Billy agreed. "We can't do that anymore. Our money ain't no good anymore."

"That's bad for niggers," Honk said. "I feel for the judges they're bustin', 'cause they was helping niggers."

Nobody was helping *nobody* now. Honk had worked his way out from under a lot of times, but everything was cracking, all the rules of the game he had grown up with and mastered. You especially couldn't buy an armed-robbery case, even if you had the money. If you were an ex-con and got caught, you were looking at up to thirty years, and it was like slavery time, Honk thought; your freedom was not for sale anymore. So he found himself with no choice except to deal, his plea in exchange for short time. All that remained to be settled was the price. He turned down the state's attorney's first offer, which was ten years. But when his public defender came to him one morning after a year and a quarter of maneuvering and whispered, "I can get you eight today," Honk figured he'd better snatch it.

He scheduled one last weekend of partying, a round of revels so strenuous that he had to check into a hotel and take a nap before he ever got to the official send-off at Cigar's. He showed up fashionably late, at ten in the evening, dressed cleaner than the Board of Health. Dudes were buying him screwdrivers—Honk winced in something like pain at every sip—and pressing tens and twenties into his hand, a little paper to buy him something with before he went in. After a while, everybody adjourned thirteen blocks south to a place called Rudy's, where the family was waiting. A buffet dinner had been set out, and "Saturday Love" was playing on the sound system, but Honk remained the center of interest. His friends couldn't believe he had got caught that way, his own partners telling on him.

Honk said it was true.

"Messin' with marks," a brother said. It was a given in the street that a mark—an untested kid—might punk out on you at crunch time.

Honk said he *knew* Marvin, the kid who cracked, was a mark. He had tried to school Marvin in The Life, he said. He thought he had taught the nigger better than that.

"You always did do that," a dude said. "Trying to teach a lame MF something."

"You gonna take him out?" someone else asked.

No, Honk said, wasn't any sense killing anybody now. The thing now was to deal with what he had to deal with.

The party, as it turned out, was premature; Honk, with the help of his lawyer, ducked and dodged for another month before his string ran out the Tuesday before Thanksgiving. He had entered his plea by then and had come to court dressed in traveling clothes: cords, boots, and a leather jacket, with a couple of sandwiches and a couple of cartons of juice stuffed in the pockets for the ride. His processed hair had been cut short; you didn't want to go to court *or* prison looking too pretty. He toyed with the idea of asking for a few more days, but his resolve began to melt with the first cases of the day.

A probation violator came forward with an unconvincing story.

"Lock 'im up," the judge said.

"Is he *cold?*" Honk whispered in the third row, shaking his head. "Don't let him catch you in *no* kind of BS."

The Robert Taylor Homes had been open only three years when Vest and his friends Greg Bronson, Ray Stingley, and Steve Steward graduated from the Stephen A. Douglas Middle School in 1965. The gangs with their comic-book names were not yet pandemic, the drugs not yet lethal, and the underclass not yet labeled "permanent." They

were children growing up in the want and isolation of the ghetto, but they were also the children of the sixties, and their chance for success never seemed brighter (top row, Greg is third from left, Vest is fourth; second row, Ray is fourth from left, Steve is second from right).

To meet the people of Trey-nine through newspaper headlines or sociology texts is to miss much of their lives; indeed, it is to barely meet them at all. Disguised in poverty, the habits of Middle America are regularly played out in the ghetto, the connecting threads to a more prosperous nation, and to find the soul in a community better known for its heartlessness, one need only watch Sonny and Jean Spruiell playing to the folks at a neighborhood barbecue on Labor Day, or witness the varsity crowd on their concrete playing fields. To meet the school kids, hooked on learning by Leroy Lovelace, is to see a future where, according to the statistics, there isn't supposed to be one.

From the upper stories, the invisible men of Trey-nine could see the spires of downtown Chicago. They seemed distant and unreal and, without benefit of signs, as unwelcoming as an all-white lunch counter in the Mississippi of Jim Crow. For Sonny and Ed (bottom left) and Pee Wee (below), the most striking single fact of the world they grew up in was its encapsulation, its remove from the world of possibilities open to whites; to venture out was to risk one's manhood with menial labor and wary glances. Downtown, the danger to one's psyche was as great as the danger to one's person on Thirty-ninth Street; Big Honk's entreprenurial skills counted for nothing there, but at his corner office on the South Side (top), he worked as hard, and often as profitably, as his white counterpart at the Chicago Board of Trade.

In 1962, when Robert Taylor opened its doors, Ed Hamilton and Pee Wee Fisher moved in and became best friends for life. The Hamiltons had come from a tenement so raggedy that it had been ordered torn down; for Ed, Trey-nine was a place where life began. It was an innocent time for him and others who believed that you could deliver the poor from poverty with the dream of public housing. In fact, such places were built in those parts of town where blacks already lived; they were designed as independent townships—insular and dependent—and the only deliverance was for nearby white neighborhoods. "A nigger ain't living down here," Big Honk once lectured. "They just housing 'em here." A boy stepping out his door in the morning saw downtown Chicago through a barrier of steel mesh; if its purpose was to protect the tenants, its effect as to seal them in.

Another young probationer stood before the bench. The judge had ordered him back to school as a condition of his freedom. He hadn't gone.

"I told you to do that," the judge said. "Lock 'im up."

Honk grinned a gallows grin. "I know I ain't got a prayer," he said. "Judge gonna look at *me* and say lock 'im up."

Yet another miscreant took his turn with yet another customized tale of woe.

"You'd better watch yourself," the judge said. "You dropped through the cracks this time. Next time you're going to slip in the county jail."

"Cold man," Honk said, and then, before he was quite ready, it was his turn; the judge was calling on his lawyer, asking him what he had, and his lawyer answered, "Sentencing. Roy Johnson."

"Oh, Lord," Honk said under his breath. It was almost a moan. He stepped forward, past the bulletproof shield between the spectators and the judge, and stood before the bench.

The judge checked his plea and his sheet. "Is there anything you wish to say for yourself?" he asked.

Honk forgot his speech about the extra days and said no. His voice was barely audible. The game was over.

"Eight years," the judge was saying. The bailiffs closed in. Honk retrieved his coat, waved good-bye to Anne, and was gone.

· He went to Joliet first for processing and then downstate to the Shawnee Correctional Center in Vienna, Illinois, 400 miles from Thirty-ninth Street, to do his time. It was *only* time, Honk told himself, and if you had to do it, Shawnee wasn't bad. It was new, one of those modern joints with one-man cells and shower stalls, and gym three times a day; you could have your own TV, and Honk soon did. The fact that prison was still prison didn't perturb him that much, not so much that he was letting anyone know it; it was too important to him to be cool. He had done what he thought he had to do to survive, and when you F up, he told people, hey—you got to pay your dues. Doing time might even do him some good, he said; get his mind back to basics, where it all start at.

He had been in tougher places than prison in any case. There were no tigers there for him anymore, he thought, no dangers lurking in the shadows that he hadn't seen and dealt with before. All he had to do was survive and stay out of trouble and, his lawyer told him, he could be back on the block in three and a half years instead of eight. In the meantime, he saw nothing you had outside and didn't have inside except women and freedom. The ghetto and the Graybar Hotel, his new address, were otherwise pretty much the same.

Yet time, in another sense, was his enemy. He would be close to forty coming out of prison, an old man in The Life. He spoke sometimes of getting all the way out of it, maybe taking a straight-up job, maybe opening a store in the shopping center across from Trey-nine. There was something unpersuasive about these musings, even to himself; just picturing himself as a shopkeeper—BIG HONK'S GROCERIES—made him laugh. But he wasn't sure he was up to being the baddest nigger on the block anymore. He would have to prove to a whole new generation of bloods that he was not to be F'd with. He would be a marked man at the police station, a known hustler with two X's on his rap sheet; get that third and you wind up in the joint for the rest of your life. He didn't know if his game would still be tight. He didn't know if Anne would be waiting for him, helping him find a way out, and she wasn't sure either; she only knew she couldn't live the rest of her life as she had lived it with Honk thus far.

His problem, he mused once in an introspective moment, was that he had never wanted to stop being a kid. There had been a time, a long time, when he had made it pay, when he was getting rich off the pleasure principle and the dude out there working for a living couldn't buy his shoes. But the dude with the job was the boss now, and Big Honk wasn't *nobody*, not no more. He was Inmate N01760 now. He had stayed at the table too long and had lost everything he owned, even his name.

the most dangerous bag in which society could put a renegade nigger like him; it was dangerous because what he was thinking was that the system, the world of work and hope, was pure orchestrated BS for a young black man. His mother, working as a teacher's aide, approached him one day about doing talks to young kids on the worth of staying at their books. He refused. He would become part of the lie, he said; he wasn't going to sit up there and co-sign the American Dream where the only guys living it in the ghetto—the guys with money and honor—were the dealers and pimps.

He had become an outlaw in search of a hustle, something, he thought, as close to legal as he could find, and he didn't need to look farther than Thirty-ninth Street to find it; an old-time player put it right in his hands. "There's things about you that *you* ain't even hip to," the dude told him. His power over women, for one thing— "Hey, only thing they can't put you in jail for is that. There's no law against a lady givin' you all their money. You ain't got to tell them to do S to *get* it—just require them to give you some if they're gonna F with you."

Billy tried it—got to do *something*, Jack, he told himself—and for several years made it work. At the peak of his game, he had five ladies each bringing him $300 to $500 a day, all love offerings so far as the law was concerned. His prime asset was himself; he was as smooth with women as he was with an open jumper from the key. His major liability was his sense of right and wrong, a dangerous burden for a hustler. It was of his mother's making; he was doing S that went against everything she had taught him, everything he had absorbed at her knee. The case for the defense, that he was doing what he thought he had to do to survive, did not fully anesthetize his feelings of guilt. It was a MF to be doing wrong and knowing it, and he had to rationalize himself into a kind of inner-city Sundance Kid, the hard guy with a heart of gold.

He saw, or came to see, that there was no way to make it work, no way to be that shining knight out there when you were in fact doing the lowest S on the planet. Still, he tried, playing the game by his own chivalric code; it was as if he were a boy again and his mother were still watching. It became a point of pride with him that he was fair with his ladies—that he always split the money, never

PART IV

Scufflers

I think the first thing that happened with guys like Half Man and Ed Hamilton and Pee Wee is that they didn't get the breaks, Vest said. They're very smart guys, and they really didn't get the breaks. And the second thing was education. They were very bright, but they just didn't get the right kind of education. They looked ahead and they just didn't see any promise, so they lived for now, and they're still waiting for that break—some one-time big break where they'll make a lot of money. And generally that means hoping to hit the lottery. The lottery has become, for these guys, the American Dream.

A BLUES LIFE

A friend once asked Half Man Carter to name something, anything, that would make him happy, and his imagination
shorted out. He didn't say $4 million or $5 million like Big Honk
might, or Billy. He didn't even say hitting the number, or owning a
boat or a Cadillac Eldorado. He said he might *pray* for $20,000, but
he would settle for $500 and would naturally expect to have to work
to get it.

Half Man had never given his dreams much running room; he
didn't believe in them, and in his middle thirties, he had drawn, or
accepted, a tight line around his existence. It was a boundary inside
which he had found a form of contentment, the peace that flows from
the absence of hunger or risk. He was not, he thought, where he was
supposed to be; he was working two jobs and was still out there
dancing a half step ahead of a pack of bill collectors holding IOU's
on the free-range days of his past. But he had a decent place to stay
and a lady who loved him enough to put up with his moods and
attitudes, and if his life was a roller-coaster ride above and below the
poverty line, at least he was *working* poor. He didn't have to borrow
a dollar or beg for his beer.

Except at love, in fact, he counted himself lucky. He had never
not worked, not even when he was adrift between steady jobs for
eleven or twelve months one time; he did day labor as a temporary
for the minimum wage and hustled housepainting gigs on the side.
He considered any job better than welfare and two jobs better than
one, no matter what kind of work at what kind of money. Sometimes
when he was between jobs, he would fill out an application form

someplace and scare people off with the sheer length and variety of his past work record. "You're at the wrong place, we're only paying five dollars an hour here," the Man would tell him, to which Half Man would reply, "I'll take it." White people wouldn't work for $5. Half Man would if he had to.

He had lately been doing a good deal better than that. His course, up and down for most of his thirty-six years, seemed to him to be going steady up. He was working days in a paint factory, filling cans on an assembly line that might have been designed by Charlie Chaplin, and moonlighting as a janitor in the three-building apartment complex where he lived. The wage at the plant was as good as he had ever made, nearly $10 an hour, and his basement flat was rent-free. If he had managed his finances better, he thought, he could have been living pretty medium, the only phrase he could think of to describe his minimalist hopes. He could have had steak any day he felt like it, he thought. He didn't need or want caviar every night.

But he had handled his money about as carelessly as he ran his life. His days had been spent hopscotching from moment to moment without much regard for the lessons of the past, which seemed best forgotten, or the needs of the future, which was a blank. He could not in fact be sure there *was* a future. Sudden death is a sad commonplace in the ghetto, and two of his own brothers had died young. One, Wilbert, had had a stroke at nineteen. The other, Waddell, had come home from Vietnam at twenty-four with his mind all messed up by the war. Waddell was dealing drugs on Thirty-ninth Street, in partnership with Moose Harper, except some of Waddell's heroin was going into his own arm. No one in the family knew it or wanted to confront it, not till he shot up in the bathroom at the Carters' house one night and hit the floor with a loud thud. Moose and one of the Carter brothers splintered the door. Waddell was lying on the tile, the needle still stuck in his arm.

They hauled him to his feet and walked him out of trouble, that time. A sister, trying to save him, set him up with a job, an apartment, and a car in Milwaukee. But he was still doing H, and one day he just disappeared. The mail was overflowing his mailbox and parking tickets were wadding up on his windshield when the police finally got curious. They checked out his place and found him, alone this time and dead of an overdose at twenty-five.

Half Man's parents sought solace in religion, as Jehovah's Witnesses. Half Man found his in motion, the aimless journey of a rolling stone. He seemed to have a hard time making lasting connections; he had about him the air of a man constantly reckoning the odds on the profitability of human relationships. Twenty years after the collapse of his first marriage, he was still haunted by the feeling that he had blown it all emotionally then and there—that his life had been damaged beyond repair. He drifted from bed to bed for years thereafter, his attachments as impermanent as his jobs and his bankroll. He liked women but felt he could not love them anymore, not in the old way. Instead, he used them; he had a power over them, a promise in his deep-set eyes and his awkward smile, and they came easily under his spell. He fathered a daughter by one lady and a son by another, five months apart, and moved on. The mothers got to be friends with one another; the well-known unreliability of men was something they had vividly in common.

Half Man did try marriage a second time, fourteen years after the first. He was working part-time as an attendant in a launderette, trying to pay the bills during the winter-layoff season in the construction trade. She was a customer, a lady named Barbara with two kids of her own. He was attentive. She responded; she began bringing in her wash three times a week, and lunch for Half Man besides. He shut down early one day and met her at the lakefront. Lights flashed. They started seeing each other. He was broke; he had a place on South Shore Drive, a nice place in a middle-class neighborhood, but he was having a hard time keeping up with the bills. His phone had been disconnected. He couldn't even buy groceries.

She was sympathetic. "You payin' that high rent and tryin' to make it, too," she said. "Whyn't you give up South Shore, honey, and come live with me?"

He did, and for a time he didn't *need* money. She paid the rent, stocked the kitchen, and put some coin in his pockets for walking-around expenses; she even bought the sticker for his car. But when they married after three or four years together, she changed her ways and wanted him to change his. He was suddenly the man of the house, the breadwinner for her and her children, responsible for this and that. She was piling on the burdens, more than he could handle right then. He had been fired from one job as a tool salesman. Another, as a carpenter, folded under him. The mother of one of his own kids had the law on him for child support. He couldn't produce what Barbara was demanding, and she wouldn't ease off. She picked fights with him, loud battles with a lot of broken china and torn sateen, and then called the police on *him,* telling them *he* gone crazy.

The time finally came when Half Man could no longer live with her nagging and his own failure as provider. He moved out, and the marriage split, one more casualty of the oppressive home economics of the ghetto. They stayed man and wife, nominally, and saw each other sometimes, until the Saturday morning Half Man came by in his father's pickup truck to collect his painting gear for a job. He walked in the back door and found her with another man. Her children—his stepchildren—were in the house. She should have went out to a hotel, he thought. She should have had more respect.

He walked out hurt and angry, gathered up his gear, and left.

"What you do then?" his parents asked when he told them the story.

"Went on and finished paintin'," he said. "Made that money and kept on pushin'."

He might have been summing up his life. He had spent it at a succession of unskilled and semiskilled jobs, most of them vulnerable to the cycles of the seasons and the economy and none very rewarding except for the money. It struck him that that there were guys out there who had been working their way up, while he had just been working. His job at the paint company, for example, filling those cans and smashing on the lids at about two seconds per can—it was nothing but elbow-and-ass work, he thought, like most of the jobs he had had.

He owned a mind, too, and wished he could use it, but they didn't pay him for that. They didn't pay *blacks* for that, he told himself, 'cause white folks always think they smarter; they never think you got any sense, and they hate for you to show them you do. He didn't even like to give them suggestions, 'cause if you give them a suggestion and it *work*, they ain't even gonna act like they appreciate it. You would see them do something wrong around the plant, try to put a part on backwards or some such foolishness, and you couldn't say anything—you just had to sit there, even though it hurt you, and wait until they figured it out. So Half Man eased silently on through his days, doing what he got paid for, smiling all the time. They thought he was dumb, he guessed, but they were going to think that any damn way. He knew what time it was, and what color he was. He knew how far he could go.

It wasn't that he didn't like white people, or couldn't get along with them. He could; he wasn't prejudiced. You could come around to his crib and check out his record collection, just for instance; he could throw on a couple of Elvises, or some Elton Johns, or a Cyndi Lauper, or even an old Walter Brennan side, "Mama Sang a Song." He sometimes thought that he disliked more black people than white. Blacks on the job would get on him for talking to white folks, and he would answer, "Man, these white folks speak to me, I speak to them. What you all want to be—ignorant?" He didn't even care if they spoke back or not. It was about him being a man, too, just like them, and if they wanted to be ignorant, it didn't mean he had to be.

It was whites who had helped him at work, he mused, and blacks who had tried to hold him back; one of them almost slit his damn throat. He had been assistant foreman on one of his early jobs and had had a hard time getting his way with his black workers. When the white man came around and told them to do something, they grinned and smiled and did it, but when he tried, they wanted to act the fool and call him an Uncle Tom. He shrugged it off as jealousy; didn't nobody like to see nobody else black get ahead. He got in a fight at a company picnic with a guy who had been hard-timing him on the job. They were both drunk, and when the guy came around looking for trouble, Half Man didn't give him no play; he was still a hot-tempered kid then, and he just went off on the guy, started in whupping his tail without a word of warning. The dude came back on him with a knife, going for the throat. Half Man jumped back. The flick missed his neck, narrowly, and laid open his face instead. It was a black guy tried to kill him and a white guy who drove him to the hospital to get sewn up. The repair took thirty-five stitches.

Half Man had grown up in the ghetto, and he remained in some measure prey to its deep, wounding undercurrents of self-doubt, the suspicion that if white people owned the world, there must be a reason. He was pleased when a black man, Harold Washington, became mayor of Chicago in the 1980s, but it did not seem to improve the conditions of life materially down in the street, where the brothers were, and he guessed that the entire city, *the whole MF,* would burn down if black people were put all the way in charge. Sometimes he thought the white man *should* go on ahead and run things, 'cause they the ones trained, he said. It was a lot of things black people had accomplished that they don't put in the books, he believed, but everybody know who made the electricity and the telephone; it was the white man.

Half Man wasn't the kind, in any case, to blame white people alone for the way his life had got dead-ended. It was true, he thought, that white folks run things and that they don't cut black folks no breaks. But he saw his own complicity in what had become of him. He regretted that he hadn't stayed in school and that he had thrown away his money on the pleasures of the moment instead of making it work for him, buying a little piece of real estate or something. He had got caught in a trap, he knew that, and it was at least partly of his own making. He and Vest Monroe had been best friends at Trey-nine, but he had chosen one course and Vest had taken another when they were still boys. It was Vest who got over; he had gone away to college and *Newsweek,* and when he came home sharp in his down-town clothes, the brothers weren't calling him Brainiac anymore; they were calling him Big-Time Vest Monroe.

"I was very lucky," Vest told Half Man one day twenty years later, when their separate paths crossed again.

"Well, you wasn't *lucky,* you know," Half Man said. "You worked for it, you went to school for it. That ain't lucky."

"You've been working all your life," Vest said.

"But see, that's different," Half Man said. "That's *all* I've been doing is working."

Working, he added, and partying; the money had disappeared, and the years, and he wasn't much ahead of where he had been when Vest went away. He wasn't faulting the Man for that, not entirely. Opportunities had begun opening up a little bit for black people back when he was still young enough to seize them; things weren't all the way straightened out yet, he thought, but at least you didn't have to sit in the back of the bus no more. He realized that life was inherently hard for a man living on the margin as he did. You caught so much hell just surviving that you couldn't tell where it was coming from. Is it racist or is it straight up? Is it BS or not? You could never know for sure; if some honky ain't hiring you, Half Man thought, you don't know whether it's because you black or because he don't need help.

So he lived inside his personal age of limits, seeing no way out and no higher destiny to pursue even if he could. It was still a blues life, still straitened by short money and demanding women. His wages were garnisheed in the winter of 1985–86 to satisfy a bad note he had co-signed, and he had had to pawn his color TV to get his car repaired. The paint plant shut down for part of the winter season, and except for his janitoring, he had no work at all. His three children were all in their teens. He provided what he could for them and tried to show a fatherly interest in what they were doing—more interest, anyway, than he remembered his parents having shown in him. But he was an absentee daddy to his two thirteen-year-olds living in town, Muneerah and Edward, and his first and favorite child, Sherri, at seventeen was in St. Louis somewhere with her mother or her grandmother; he had lost track of which. She was never far from Half Man's mind; still, he reckoned he hadn't seen her more than once in two years.

What had changed in his life was its tempo; inside its narrow ambit, he felt nearer than he had ever been to repose. The anchor of his days was his third wife, Matilda, a quiet woman with a lot of gold on her fingers and in her smile. It was like she *colored* gold, he thought, she was that cute. She was nice, too, real nice by his revised criteria. In his rambling days, he had had ladies with two or three children, raising them as his own as long as he was around, but no more. He wanted his woman working, not sitting at home with a bunch of kids and a jealous attitude, and Matilda fit the specifications. She had a job and didn't mind going every day, earning her own money instead of constantly wanting his; he couldn't get her to stay home even when she was sick. She had no kids, no extravagances, no obvious desire in life except to please him. He gave her a hundred-dollar bill once and asked about it several days later. "I ain't cashed it yet," she told him. She was saving up to buy him a diamond watch for his birthday, which was the way she was; give the woman money and she spend it back on you.

The day they met was like a smile from Lady Luck, the first Half Man had known since his teenage marriage broke up. He was seeing someone else then, and so was she; her old man in those days was a guy Half Man drank beer with, and for a time the two couples went out together. But Half Man and his woman got in a fight one night, a spasm of rage that began with him calling her bitch and ended with her throwing his belongings out the window into the street. Matilda's old man happened by, wandering into the hailstorm of clothes and shoes flying out the house. He helped pick up afterward and hauled Half Man's gear, along with Half Man, to his own place.

"Man, you can let your stuff stay here," he said. "If you don't have nowhere to go, you can spend the night. Sleep on the couch."

The overnight guest became a boarder, at $40 a week. The arrangement suited Matilda's old man just fine at first. He was skin-popping heroin in those days, injecting it under the skin instead of into the vein, and he needed the money to support his habit; he had just come out of prison and didn't have a job. The longer Half Man stayed, the better that $40 looked to the dude. He would take it and vanish for a night or a weekend, disappearing into his drugs and sometimes into the arms of another woman who lived just down the street.

Matilda barely saw him anymore; she would be off to work when he slipped in in the morning to change his clothes, and he was frequently gone when she got back at night. In his lengthening absences, she got lonely. She began wanting Half Man to sit up nights talking with her, and some of the things she was saying were a little—he searched for the word—aggressive. He felt caught in the middle, and he held back at first, wondering what was with this chick; *she* was cutting in on *him* instead of the other way around, which was the way it usually worked. And then one day her old man was gone; there had been an angry last scene, and she had kicked him out of the house.

"Well, I guess I ought to leave," Half Man told her. He had been her old man's guest.

"This *my* house," she said, and she invited Half Man to share it.

Half Man insisted on going to her old man first and telling him what time it was, up front, before he found them together.

"Don't do *that*," Matilda pleaded. The guy was bigger than Half Man. She was scared.

"Yeah, but I gotta do it," Half Man said, " 'cause he gonna be crazy as a dog if he walk up and catch us. I think we might have a chance if I break it to him."

He did lay in a pint of brand-name gin and a six-pack of Coors as a precaution, and he kept it flowing while he was running it down to the dude about him and Matilda. The guy wasn't used to nothing but cheap wine, and the good stuff seemed to ease whatever pain he felt, if any. They both got high, and everything was cool between them. They stayed friends, and when Half Man and Matilda found their new apartment, her old old man helped them move in.

Half Man felt settled there, the underground man, living in his basement flat out of sight of the larger world. He didn't like *outside* too much; there was too much happening out there, he thought, and nothing much he felt he needed anymore—nothing, that is, except work. He began his days at four in the morning, cleaning his buildings for his keep, and when the paint plant was open, he had to be out the door by 6:15 to get there in time. His evenings were mostly spent at home. He almost never went downtown and only infrequently visited his old friends on Thirty-ninth Street. He and Matilda had married in the winter of 1986–87, and the street had lost a lot of its appeal for him. He much preferred the safety of his place, Half Man sitting in the half light with a cold beer and a warm smoke and the glow of the TV playing over the bare wood floor.

There remained trace elements of regret in his life, but he wasn't crying. There were, he thought, a lot of people worse off than he was. He had learned, in his thirty-six years, that you can't have everything you want; he had learned not to mistake his dreams for anything *but* dreams that vanish in the first light of day. If the impossible happened, he thought, it was going to have to come to him; he was too busy getting by to go chasing after it. He had made his choices and was making the best of them, and while he couldn't honestly say he was happy, he thought he might be, sometime soon.

A NEW MAN IN THE KINGDOM

There was a time, in his twenties, when Moose Harper thought he was happy, or at least free of pain. He could get through a day wired on 'caine or speed and believe he was somebody, not just another lost soul blowing away his life on the corner two lines at a time. He was dealing drugs then, anything you wanted from reefer to smack, and trying to shut out the little interior voice telling him that what he really was selling was death—that some dude lying cold on a gurney somewhere with that spike still in his arm might have been shooting Moose's product. He wasn't ready to hear that. He wanted what every stud on Thirty-ninth Street wanted: money, women, clothes, cars, prestige, and high times. His handicap was that he also wanted to be good, and when his sense of what was right overtook his vocation for what was wrong, he found out what being happy really meant for him.

The journey took eight years or, more accurately, twenty-eight, from birth to rebirth. The pity, as he understood only afterward, was that he had wasted so much of that time. He was born the love child of Jake Hull, a Mississippi construction laborer, and Everlena Harper, Jake's lady. They moved to Chicago before Moose started kindergarten; he and a houseful of siblings, nine in all, were growing up in a flat upstairs from an illegal gaming casino before Trey-nine opened up in 1962. Jake worked there and was impressed by the quality of its early tenant rolls, a list that included policemen, firemen, and teachers. It looked like a safe and decent place to raise a family, and he moved his brood in when Moose was in the fourth grade.

Moose seemed a promising boy in spite of the odds, with a particular flair for writing. A fifth-grade teacher was encouraging, or tried to be, and so was Moose's pal, Vest Monroe. As boys, they dreamed of the stories they would write together, and when Vest went off to St. George's, they still shared their hopes by mail. "I'm glad to hear you're in the spirit for writing," Vest said in one letter. "You see, I have this idea for a story about two friends from the ghetto. One of them makes it and goes to a good school and becomes successful, and the other is less fortunate and doesn't make it. The core of the story is that the boy who makes it always feels guilty because he doesn't go back and help his brothers. From there, I think with your ideas and my knowledge of how to construct a story, we'll have something worthwhile.''

The boys were both sixteen then; their lives were taking form, and while Vest did not wholly appreciate it at the time, his idea was prophetic as to how things would turn out. Vest wasn't no ordinary project dude, Moose thought in retrospect; he had support systems, a demanding mother at home and a favored academic track at school, and when the ABC program delivered him his big break, he was ready. It was partly that—a break, Moose believed; the system, and the white people who ran it, were always going to let a *few* people through the door just to be able to say they were doing something. But Vest was smart, and he had worked hard to prepare himself for his opportunity. He was homesick at St. George's, and he wrote Moose, urging him to apply. Moose might have, if he hadn't peeped the entrance exam. "Do you think you could pass this?" Vest asked in his covering note. Moose took one look and thought: definitely not.

Moose had already given up by then and was sliding beyond help, Vest's or anyone else's. There was no one to push him, no one to see that he mastered the words and the skills he would need if he were ever to set his stories to paper. His teachers were mostly too caught in their common despair to help him, and his parents didn't know how; they were short on schooling and slow of speech, and to Jake Hull particularly, education seemed less important than plain hard work. He put a roof over his children's heads, clothes on their backs, and food on their plates, dining last himself to be sure that everyone else had had enough to eat. Everlena Harper surrounded them with her love. As parents they had no other resources, Moose thought, nothing else they could give him, and he went on his own rudderless way.

He didn't blame them; you couldn't expect nothing from a glass of water, he mused, except a glass of water. If Jake had told him to stay in school, Moose would have obeyed, partly out of fear, partly because he would have done anything for some sign of his father's love. But Jake was silent on the subject, and Moose, left to his own devices, was losing interest in his lessons; it was too dangerous crossing enemy territory to get to school and back, and his mind was on gang-banging anyway, not parsing sentences or solving equations. When he finally drifted out of Dunbar High in the tenth grade, not long after Vest left for St. George's, no one objected. His daddy's only reaction was: Get a job.

Even Moose's conscience was fashioned more by television than by teachers, preachers, and parents combined. He spent part of his adolescence out there in the streets gang-banging with Sonny and Crazy Horse and them, busting heads and bibbing MD (for Mogen David) 20-20 wine. But when he came home and plopped down in front of the TV, a different world unfolded before him, a world of white hats and black hats, good guys and bad. The Lone Ranger and the Cisco Kid were his tutors in the codes of chivalry and justice. Spencer Tracy in *Boys Town* taught him compassion and clean living. Lucy and Ricky Ricardo were his models of what family life and love were supposed to be; it did not escape his boyish eye that even though they were married, they slept in separate beds.

Moose never doubted that he and his friends around Trey-nine belonged among the good guys of the world. But with his coming of age, he strayed a long way from his small-screen vision of right and wrong. His army years introduced him to the prejudices of white people—his only enemies in the all-black world of Thirty-ninth Street had been the Disciples—and to harder drugs than codeine syrup and Twister wine. In his boyhood a joint was still a rare and forbidden pleasure at Trey-nine. In Korea, where he did some of his service time, they came in packs of twenty just like regular cigarettes. You bought a pack at one of the back-alley clubs that catered to black GI's, pulled you a square of four for yourself, and left the rest on the table for anyone else who came by.

Moose's taste became a habit with his return and his mother's slow death from cancer. They had been particularly close, he and she, like a lot of ghetto boys and their mamas. His daddy was at home, but Jake Hull's natural habitat was silence, and the more Moose hungered for his love, the less of it he saw. It was Everlena Harper who had had to fill in the emotional blanks in his life, and her illness made a desert of his soul.

He was just back from the service when she took sick, and by the time the doctors found the malignant growth in her uterus, it was beyond treatment. In the single year left to her, she was in and out of the hospital, her pain severe and constant. When she was out, she could no longer cook, and Moose learned how, following her instructions. When she was in, she became an object, almost a victim, of modern medical technology. Once, she had been black as onyx and beautiful as a Benin sculpture. The last time Moose visited her, she looked ninety years old, a withered shadow of a woman kept alive, barely, by machines and medications. Moose cried, knowing then that she was dying. He could not stand to see her again and could not share his sorrow with anyone, not even his family. When they buried her, at fifty-three, he came and left alone.

He felt torn loose from whatever moorings were left in his life. He had enrolled in a YMCA community college, hoping to be a medical technician. It made his mother proud in her dying days, and she told everyone her boy was going to college. But he got into academic trouble as soon as the science courses began. He stayed thereafter mainly for the GI benefit checks, which came to $300 a month, and even that lost its attraction measured against the easier riches available out in the street. A psychology teacher finally advised him to lay aside his studies and go concentrate on what he really seemed interested in. "Go get the money, go get the car," the dude said, "and if they don't bring you satisfaction, come back."

Moose tried it. The money didn't bring him satisfaction, not really, but it did keep him in drugs, and he Novocained his heart against the reality of what his life was becoming. He was smoking reefer, snorting coke and heroin, and dropping strawberries, a street name for amphetamine diet pills. He was too squeamish about needles to shoot H, which saved him from becoming a junkie, but his use of speed progressed from recreation to dependency, a daily anesthetic against life and its sorrows. You did it to feel good, he thought; in this ugly place, you could feel good, and if the doses and the prices kept going up every time you came down, the payoff—the escape from ugliness—seemed worth it.

He had felt that hunger enough in his own belly to recognize it in others, and before long he was servicing it, scoring drugs from a connection on the West Side and dealing them on Thirty-ninth Street. He was not really built for the amorality of The Life, but he was moving with dudes who were; he was a sheep in wolf's clothing, a bad guy with a good guy inside praying to get out. He liked the money a lot and the respect even more, that passage into a twilight zone where the fact of success counted more than the way you achieved it. Moose was running at the edge of the fast lane, hanging with a big-time heroine dealer. He wasn't much more than a gofer, really, but he was close enough to bask in his patron's reflected radiance. There were drugs around, and money, and all kinds of women, and the excitement of it drew him like a moth to flame.

He was in fact being played for a chump, but he only caught on the day he and the dealer went out to score some more drugs. They took Moose's car, at the dealer's insistence, except he wanted to drive. They were good-timing across town together, laughing and talking, when the dealer suddenly handed Moose two big packages of smack.

"Look, I want you to hide this for me," the dude said.

Moose was holding the goods, still talking and still laughing, when a sixth sense told him to look out the window on the passenger side.

A Chicago cop was looking back at him, his white face staring out of a patrol car alongside their ride.

The dealer had seen them coming. Only street instinct made Moose keep on laughing, like it was a couple of pounds of sugar he was holding instead of two Baggies of skag.

"Look you son of a bitch," he muttered to his ex-friend the dealer, "if they stop us, I'm throwin' out this stuff and jumpin' out. Just pull ahead of them."

The dealer did, and the police let them go on unmolested. But Moose felt betrayed. If they would have busted us, he was thinking, who was going to jail? He knew the answer; it would have been him, not the dealer, and he didn't much like it.

He wasn't much liking the whole drug scene anymore. There was no joy left in it, no glitter, no satisfaction; there was only the misery he saw all around him, and his own negative vibes at the center of it. Guys he knew, *good* guys as he supposed himself to be, were getting strung out on the stuff he and his fellow traffickers were selling. You'd see them on the block shooting up, then popping that rubber from around their arms and passing out from the rush; you'd see them waste away, collapse in on themselves as if drugs were devouring them from the inside out. Guys were falling out, their lives ruined and maybe over, and the worst of it for Moose was seeing his own guilty part in it.

Sonny Spruiell, once his main man at Trey-nine, was hooked. So was his partner Waddell Carter, Half Man's brother and one of Moose's closest friends. They had bought their supplies of reefer, coke, and smack from the same West Side supplier and hawked them on Thirty-ninth Street, two traders in human souls. Moose guessed that Waddell, like himself, might be taking a little recreational snort of heroin now and then, but nothing more, nothing serious. Both their lives seemed to Moose at the time to be salvageable; it was Moose's back-to-school period, and he had been trying to talk Waddell into joining him. It wasn't till the night they busted down the bathroom door at the Carters' and found Waddell with the spike in his arm that Moose realized how bad his habit had got. By then it was too late for Waddell to turn things around; his death from an overdose was only a matter of time and, for Moose, crushing sorrow.

It got still worse for him, or, anyway, closer to home. His own kid brother Donnie, his junior by four years, was mainlining heroin and hiding it with a junkie's guile. The Harpers didn't see it, or didn't want to, not at first. People didn't like admitting even to themselves that there was a junkie in the family; it was too much like a judgment of God. They would find splashes of blood from Donnie's ruined veins on the bathroom walls, and things would turn up missing from around the house when he was around: watches, radios, tools, a camera, a guitar, a gun, even meat from the freezer. But no one caught him thieving, he was that slick, and no one confronted him with his habit till they had almost lost him—twice by overdoses, once when he tore up a vein in his buttock so badly that he nearly bled to death.

Moose watched it all, the sudden death and the slow dying, until he could no longer live with his guilt. He was smothering in it. In his own mind he was still the good guy, still the Cisco Kid come to Thirty-ninth Street, and yet here he was doing evil and knowing it. He was out on the corner *hurting* people, trading in misery, and if he stayed, he thought, he would be there forever. There were guys around like that, dudes who had hung out there for what seemed like a generation or two, styling out on the corner as if they were rooted to the concrete. Moose felt himself becoming one of them, one in the crowd he had followed too long. He felt himself starting down, down, down, and if he didn't yell *whoa*, he thought, he wouldn't stop until he hit bottom.

He sought his answers in religion, wandering among the settled churches and the holiness storefronts like a pilgrim in the desert. All of them promised eternal happiness. None of them satisfied his longing for a new life, a personal resurrection. He saw people filled with the Spirit on Sunday, shouting amen and speaking in tongues, and there was no repercussion behind what they were doing; they would *still* go out and sin again on Monday morning. He wanted something that would affect him, that would help him change his life. He kept looking and kept being disappointed. His quest seemed to be getting nowhere when the answers came to him, in the unlikely person of a lady named Mrs. Jackson from the Jehovah's Witnesses.

The Witnesses had been as welcome as lepers in the projects during Moose's growing-up years; people hanging on the galleries at Trey-nine would see them coming and flee into their apartments to escape their relentless piety. He was more open now, but when a first deputation came calling, his sales resistance remained high; they were Hispanic, and if they had the answers he thirsted for, they were lost behind the language barrier between him and them. When Mrs. Jackson appeared at the door to his father's house, Moose agreed to see her only out of embarrassment. She had actually come to visit with his sister Cathy, who had once incautiously expressed interest in studying the Bible. Mrs. Jackson, taking her at her word, had come back, and Cathy had run upstairs to her room, pretending not to be at home.

Moose's hopes were modest when he received Mrs. Jackson instead; he presumed there would be nothing in it for him except the satisfaction of doing an older woman a kindness. But as they sat talking about God and death and good and evil, he found himself drawn to the certainties she offered and to the style of thought as well, the understanding that one's actions have consequences for oneself and for others. Her method was Socratic, posing questions, only she appeared to have the answers where the other faiths he had sampled did not. He saw her again, and began studying the Bible with her. His conversion was not immediate. She was a preachy woman, as persistent as a sore tooth or an unquiet conscience, and for a time Moose ran when she hove into view. Still, she kept coming; wasn't *no* getting away from the lady, and before long a new witness for Jehovah—*Herman* Harper now—appeared among the believers in Kingdom Hall.

He met a young woman named Lydia there, and love flowered between them, a clean, spiritual love. They married in 1979, and a year later she bore a son, Armond, a variant on the French for "Herman." Moose worked nights as manager of security and janitorial services at the Rehabilitation Institute of Chicago, and he and his father-in-law had a little industrial-janitorial business on the side. But his days, and his family's, were ordered around their faith, witnessing for Jehovah. Moose had left his old friends and his old values back on Thirty-ninth Street, where they belonged. He understood that he was engaged now in a daily tug-of-war, with his own soul at stake. If you hung with people who were going in another direction, you were in constant danger of their convincing you to go with them.

He knew where he was going now, and if it cost him a few friends, that was a small price for his deliverance. A new discipline had entered his life, a self-control that had been wanting before he had returned to God's word. His purpose was to serve Him and to love his neighbor, nothing more. He and Lydia were the missionaries now, preaching door-to-door as Jesus did, for five or six hours at a stretch, and if people ran and hid as Moose himself once had, it did not weaken his conviction or his resolve. *He* knew he hadn't come to rob anybody, or steal what they had, or swindle them out of something. He had come to bring them some good news about the Lord. Circumstances might change, he thought. People might listen. You had to keep trying and not take it personal when you were rejected. Jesus and the disciples had been rejected, too.

The slammed doors counted for little in any case against the sense of completeness Moose felt in his life. He had a home, a family, a job and, enveloping it all, his faith in the promise of a paradise on earth for God's children; there was nothing more he needed, nothing he hungered after any longer. His life was directed by God's word set forth in the Bible, not by the whim of the crowd. You couldn't walk up to the new Moose Harper and just say, "Let's go," without his asking, "Let's go where?"

He was sitting on the couch at his place one day, a chunky man with a wide, strong face made gentle by belief, when Armond came skipping into his arms. Moose hugged him and patted his head. Armond, then six, was to speak at Kingdom Hall in several weeks' time, and Moose asked him to recite his talk for a visitor. The boy smiled brightly, revealing the gap up front where two baby teeth had fallen out.

"Hello, my name is Armond," he said. "Today, friends, we're going to talk about Job . . ."

The recitation was singsong and dutiful, but Moose beamed proudly at all of it, smiling what believers call that Kingdom smile. He had hopes for Armond, and plans. There would be school, of course, a rigorous grounding in the basics. He wouldn't need college; the three R's apart, he was learning everything he had to know from the Witnesses, and nothing in the world as revealed to them was going to change, ever. Moose's hope, in fact, was that Armond would one day become a full minister in the faith. He would in any case grow up with what it had taken his father twenty-eight years and numberless wrong turns to discover: a sense of where he was going in the world and how to get there by faith instead of hard drugs and fast money.

HOME FROM THE WARS

It had been Pee Wee Fisher's idea to hold the party, a birthday gathering for his mama, but in the small hours of the morning, when he became the principal topic of conversation, he looked as if he were beginning to regret the whole thing. Maybe a dozen hard-core friends of Mayten Fisher—Fish, they called her—had settled around the kitchen table at her place in Trey-nine for a last laugh or two, old acquaintances held in place by the toss of her head and the kittenish twinkle in her eyes. The radio was playing Motown oldies. Some of her guests sipped beers. Some poured straight shots of Canadian Club. The remains of the chicken and greens that Pee Wee had fixed sat out on the stove, where people could help themselves to seconds and thirds. They did, regularly and appreciatively; Pee Wee was a good cook. In fact, Fish was saying, she had always told him he ought to open a restaurant, only—the twinkle was gone now—"he's lost his motivation."

She was starting up again, all about how he had hurt her. Pee Wee was himself a world-class talker, quick and slick as a TV pitchman, and he had managed to deflect Fish till then by changing the subject. But she wouldn't stay turned off. Pee Wee looked unhappy.

"He went and got married," Fish was saying. "Twice. Once to a woman who already had kids. Then he decided he was going to be like Rambo or something. He went through a period of adjustment from being in Vietnam, and he'd go around beating his chest, shouting, ' 'Nam, 'Nam, Vietnam!' and all this stuff. We thought he was a living time bomb," she was saying, "and he still might be."

Pee Wee was fingering a beer can. Way she was talking about him, it was like he wasn't in the room.

"I don't know what he might do now," Fish was saying, "but at one time I didn't like him. I hit him in the head with broomsticks, and I've barred him out of my apartment. I had him arrested. My own son—I had him arrested. I couldn't accept the way he was acting. I didn't raise him that way. I work, my daughters work, so *he* was supposed to work and support himself, too."

"I *cut* my damn self!" Pee Wee yowled suddenly, yanking his hand away from the can. "Look at that—sitting here listening to you, I cut my damn self. I'm bleeding. I cut my finger."

No one seemed interested. Fish still held the stage. "He doesn't do Vietnam anymore," she was saying. "He'd say, ' 'Nam, 'Nam,' and that used to bug me. I'd say, 'What you *talking* about, boy?' And he'd say, 'Mama, you don't understand.' "

"You *still* don't understand," Pee Wee shouted. He was at the sink, running cold water over his damaged hand.

"But you know why?" she said. "He never told me. We never interacted with one another. At first I thought he was doing it to try to upset me."

"Unh-unh," Pee Wee said, still bathing his wound.

"I thought that's why he was doing it. I thought it was personal. He'd knock holes in the wall and all this stuff, and as his mother I took it personally. See, he never told me . . . ."

"There is no *way* you'da understood," Pee Wee said, softly now. "You woulda never understood."

"But he's acting better now," Fish said. It was armistice time. "He's beginning to find himself," she said. "I don't think it would have ever happened if he hadn't been to Vietnam."

What happened to Pee Wee in Vietnam remained a blank space in his biography, at least in that part of it he was willing to tell. He had joined the army young, mostly to provide for his girl, Angie, and the son she was carrying at the time. He didn't have a job or a high school diploma. The only money he had coming in, apart from some his parents gave him, was earned playing softball and putting down three- and four-dollar bets on the side. I got to *do* something, he figured, and while he was underage at seventeen, the military looked like the last, best recourse open to him. Fish was unhappy, and she refused at first to sign the consent papers. "No, you're my baby," she told him. But his stepfather sided with him, and in the late summer of 1968, he became Private Everette Fisher of the United States Army.

He was a rebellious soldier almost from the jump, with a record of going AWOL every time he got within sight of Thirty-ninth Street. He didn't see where he was doing anything wrong by disappearing; it was just a feeling that *damn*, he didn't belong in the service, he should be a civilian again. The army had other plans for his future, and his run was extended so often as punishment that it took him five years to finish his three-year hitch. He spent thirteen months of that time in 'Nam in 1969–70, when the American war effort was starting to go terminally sour. All he would say about his tour there was that he had been in combat just a while, not the whole time, as a radio operator, and that he had got into further disciplinary jams. Otherwise, he didn't like to talk about it, not even to his mama; not even when she threw him out of her home in her terror of his demons.

What was plain was that Pee Wee had come home different, his life an extension of the combat zone he had left behind in Southeast Asia. He had married Angie, his childhood sweetheart, during a leave and had left her in the care of Ed Hamilton while he was away. Ed was his main man among the Trey-nine brothers; their families had moved in the week the building opened, Pee Wee's on the ninth floor, Ed's on the first, and the two boys became fast friends the moment they met. The tightest friendships can be as impermanent as love or money in the ghetto, easy come, easy go, but Ed's and Pee Wee's seemed to survive everything, even their periodic knockdown brawls with each other. They learned the pleasures of drink together, starting with a twenty-nine-cent pint of Twister wine out back of Trey-nine; they fought side by side in the Ranger territorial wars; they stalked girls together in Ed's father's 1962 Chevy before either of them had come of driving age. They were more like *brothers* than friends, Pee Wee thought. If one needed something, an arm, a leg, anything, he'd get it, no questions asked. There was nothing they wouldn't do for one another, each of them knew that. Pee Wee even trusted Ed with his wife.

The trusteeship made sense at the time. Ed had known Angie as long as Pee Wee had; they had in fact been together the evening Pee Wee and Angie met. Ed was wrestling Moose Harper in the grass outside the building, with Pee Wee refereeing. Night was falling when Angie happened by, on her way home.

"Wait a minute," Pee Wee called after her.

She paused. They chatted. He walked her upstairs to her place on sixteen. They began seeing each other, often double-dating with Ed and his girlfriend of the moment. Pee Wee had been into quick scores till then, the kind that might not last longer than a couple of weeks. Angie was different. Angie, he thought, could be forever. He felt a permanence with her, the conviction that this is mine; I got me a woman of my own. Most of the brothers were hooking up with Trey-nine ladies, in part for self-preservation against the enemy gangs all around them; it was too dangerous having your best girl or your best friend in another 'hood, even if it was no farther than the other side of Thirty-ninth Street. But Pee Wee found more than peace with Angie. He was, or believed he was, in love.

He had no qualms about asking Ed to watch out for her, and the arrangement worked well for a time. Ed was seeing Angie's best friend in those days, and they became a threesome in Pee Wee's absence, partying and drinking wine together. But Angie had a fall ing-out with Ed's lady, and she went out alone one night with Ed. She was a beauty, a Trey-nine girl who had grown up into a fair facsimile of Diana Ross. He was handsome and human. It was late when they got back to her place. Angie invited Ed to come in. They sat up talking and laughing like two kids in the dark till things started happening between them, grown-up things.

"Angie, girl, be cool, be cool," Ed protested feebly, but she was a sweet lady, and they were past the point of no return, too far along to stop.

The night stretched out into an affair, and they cared for each other too much to bother hiding it. When Pee Wee came home on his next leave, he walked in the door and surprised them in bed together. He never said a word to Ed about it; the friendship somehow outlived the discovery, and so, for a time, did the marriage. But the virus destroying his tie to Angie had been there from the beginning, long before Ed moved into the picture and Pee Wee came home from 'Nam with his ghosts. He and Angie had been children, eighteen and sixteen, the day they exchanged vows, with no money, no tradable skills, and no prospects—nothing to their names except Pee Wee's army pay and their four-month-old son. They had neither the material means nor the inner resources to make a go of it, and nowhere to look for help. They were one more doomed ghetto family, one more case study for scholars of the culture of poverty to pore over and say we told you so.

Their final disintegration as a family took only a year after Pee Wee's homecoming. His service had built him up physically; he had gone away the runt of the brothers at Trey-nine, an undersized and underfed-looking boy, and had come home a good-looking and well-muscled man. He had hoped that the army would put him on his feet financially as well, that he would return to what the grunts in 'Nam called the World with enough in his pockets to put some down on a house and maybe open that restaurant he had always dreamed about. It didn't work out that way. Times were tight; he couldn't even find a factory job, so he wound up back at Sally's, the barbecue joint where he, Ed, and Half Man had worked as kids. The money was short and the hours were late. He and Angie had two more kids, both boys, but the marriage was coming unglued.

Pee Wee was falling out of love anyway. He felt that he had outgrown Angie. He was a reader and a talker. She was neither; her taste in literature appeared to him to begin and end with *TV Guide*, and there was nothing she wanted to talk *about* except who was going where this weekend or when Pee Wee was going to find a serious job.

He considered suggesting that they both go back to school and learn something. But he dropped the idea without actually having proposed it; Angie, he figured, had had five years to do it on her own and had shown no interest in anything he was aware of except partying. He responded by spending more of his own time in the streets, disappearing for days at a time. There were ladies in the bars who could talk about something other than some damn soap opera, and Pee Wee went looking for them, losing himself in conversation for hours at a stretch. His theory was that Angie was leading her life, so he would lead his, a sort of second adolescence for two people who had missed their first by marrying too young.

But he *was* a walking time bomb in those days, and he went off the night he came home to an empty bed one time more than he and his pride could stand. It was late on a muggy August evening in 1974; he remembered the date in later years because it was the week President Nixon resigned, and he missed it. He had stopped on the way to his and Angie's place for a couple of shots with a couple of friends on Thirty-fifth Street. Then he continued on home, walked in, and found the kids asleep by themselves. Angie was gone. He went back out into the street looking for her. His first guess was right: She was at a girlfriend's place where she liked to hang out.

Ed was there, too. He and Angie were going out openly then, no sneaking to it. Pee Wee went off on him. Ed split, and Pee Wee turned his fury on Angie. Things got ugly.

"Come on home," he commanded. She had been drinking. So had he.

"OK, I'm coming," she said.

He was on his way out, thinking she was following along behind, when a knife flashed, three times, and Pee Wee didn't even know what was happening until he saw a fountain of blood—*his* blood— gushing from his open jugular. Angie was standing there, the knife still in her hand. He snatched it away and broke it. Then he hit her, hard, and knocked her down. There was blood everywhere. He staggered to a neighbor's door and got a ride to the hospital. *Damn,* she almost killed me, he was thinking, but he didn't really know how badly he had been hurt till he was lying on a gurney in the emergency room, waiting to go into surgery.

"Lay still and be quiet," a nurse told him, "because you're dying. You're bleeding to death."

He survived. The marriage did not. There were no charges against Angie; she moved out with the kids, and it was Christmas before Pee Wee next saw her. He was back with his mother at Trey-nine, mending his body and his life. Angie was a memory. Forever was over.

Pee Wee tried love again, on the rebound, with a lady named Marian, a postal worker with a couple of kids of her own. They met fighting one another for a taxicab on Thirty-fifth Street. They wound up sharing it instead and discovered on the way to her place that they liked each other. They traded phone numbers that day and began going out. Within a few months, he had moved in with her, and in 1976, two years after the stabbing, they married.

The union started well. They bought a house and had a baby girl, and for a brief time Pee Wee lived in the center of the picture he had always imagined the good life to be: a home, a family, a lawn out front, a yard in back, a car in the garage, and a two-income budget, her Federal paycheck plus his wage as a school security guard.

The picture was called the American Dream, but it soon cracked for him and broke in pieces, like a painting on glass. Marian was careless managing their money, and he was reckless spending it, as if, he used to think, he were printing it himself. Bills were piling up faster than he could or she would pay them. He ran away from them instead, staying out all night sipping vodka with his partners for four or five nights on end. Sometimes they would pile into his car at one in the morning and drive across the state line to Gary, Indiana, knowing the whole town was closed for the night; just riding around the deserted streets in the dark seemed to him preferable to the emptiness he felt at home.

The dream was dying slowly, of want and neglect; they had got behind in their payments on it, and it was being reclaimed. He and Marian lost the house and bounced downward through a series of apartments, each seedier than the last. His morale sank with the fall of their fortunes and the rising sum of their misdemeanors, his *and* hers. You got to stop this, he thought. It's not worth it. It's not working.

He left Marian and lost his job, and in the winter of 1986–87 the downward spiral of his life and luck was complete. After some brief interludes with other women, he was living at Trey-nine again, shuttling between his mama's apartment and his latest lady's a few flights upstairs. Pee Wee was a worker, but jobs were scarce, and for a while he found himself hanging out with the other unemployed brothers out front of the building, guys who wanted to work, mostly, and felt blocked out of the market as he did. They gathered there by ritual, asking one another what was popping. Nothing ever was.

What paper Pee Wee did make came mostly from going out with his man Ed Hamilton on Ed's pickup truck, doing building, decorating, and scavenging jobs. It was as if nothing had happened between them, or so Pee Wee chose to believe. Ed was in fact still wary of Pee Wee, still kept an eye on him when they were together. But to Pee Wee they were still best friends; whatever hurt he might have felt over Ed's interlude with Angie lay buried somewhere in the bottom of his mind, down in those deep recesses where he kept his memories of the war.

His feelings of loss were sharpened by the fact that he had become another part-time father. He had wanted to do better, but he didn't know how, not by example, in any case. His parents had separated when he was a boy, and he had seen his father maybe once every six months or so thereafter; he would materialize suddenly, give each of the kids $5 or $10, and disappear for five or six months more. Pee Wee was angry at him for his absence and only began to understand him when he had grown up and fathered children of his own. By then, his daddy was dead, and Pee Wee's own children were scattered, his three sons with Angie, his daughter with Marian. He consoled himself that they at least knew who he was; he saw them when he could and hoped they understood between visits that he was there for them—in their corner, he told himself, with whatever I got.

He didn't have much in a material way. He knew the day he moved back to his mother's place at Trey-nine, back into the daily presence of his disappointment, that he had failed somewhere along the line. The projects were supposed to be a taking-off point, a station on the journey up from the tenements to a better life beyond the ghetto. He had made it out, however briefly, and because he had, his return to square one was more poignant for him. He mostly blamed himself for it. He was a child of the sixties, when opportunities had begun opening up for black people. Vest Monroe had grabbed his and succeeded. Pee Wee had not; he hadn't had that motivation, and no one at home had pushed him, so *his* big break never came—not near enough for him to reach out and seize it. He had gotten over just long enough to taste the good life, and now he was back on Thirty-ninth Street again, one more brother scuffling to survive. The only thing left for him to do, he figured, was to kick that beat-up feeling in the ass. He had to get himself back together and make his second thirty-five years better than his first had been.

The prodigal son wasn't happy coming home. Trey-nine *was* still home, a place of refuge for him. It had the sheltered feeling of a fortified medieval town stacked on end; everyone inside the walls knew everyone else, and anyone coming in from outside was closely and suspiciously watched. Pee Wee's mother was welcoming—he was still, after everything, her baby—and his woman, Sadie, was undemanding of him at a point in his life when he didn't want to think about marriage. But if he felt safe at Trey-nine, he felt hungry as well. He knew life could be better for him. He had been up there once, living the dream, and he wanted it back, all of it, better even than the first time. He had worked for it then, and he would again, only this time there was no way he would do something stupid and lose it. No, he thought, not me; no way. He knew his mistakes now. He just had to say to himself, hey—I did the best I can; I'm back; I'ma start all over again.

He made a small beginning when, after half a year of hunting, he found work as a kitchen helper in a restaurant at O'Hare Airport. The job put some change in his pocket. The psychic income from it was limited; it was almost a parody of his dream of owning a little restaurant someday. He still thought he might—nothing big, nothing fancy, just a *place*—but on the dry ground of his life, even his fantasies were borrowed from somebody else. He would be sitting around over cocktails with his main man, Ed, and Ed would always say that if he ever catch the lottery on a Wednesday or Sunday, when the money's big and good, Pee Wee would have his restaurant. Yeah—first thing Ed was gonna do with his Lotto millions was open Pee Wee's Place.

THE PAPER MAN

Long before the state lottery, before the Man made his own numbers game legal, Ed Hamilton hungered after the big hit, that one golden score that could keep you in bread and dream dust forever. He had hustled reefer in his time, and kept the books for a holdup gang, and watched out for some ladies, but that was mostly to supplement his day wages with a little discretionary income; the ghetto was full of sidelines like that, the night differential between poverty and survival. Only once did he really get next to his dream, so close he thought he had it. For a glorious season he was the Paper Man, a walking money machine with his own private tap line into a bank, and it was like standing under an open spigot catching cash in a bucket.

He was Dillinger without the guns for that magic time, which suited him just fine; he had always preferred finesse to muscle as a means of turning that extra dollar. It wasn't that he was frightened of a fight——no way. He called himself being a hard dude in a hard world; his game face out in the streets was a cold gravedigger scowl, and he carried a straight razor in his pocket to back up the danger signals in his eyes. There had been a passage in his life when he thought of himself as flat-out crooked, a dude in need feeding what was then a $300-a-day heroin habit by any means necessary. Drugs could do that to a man, he thought after he had broken their hold on him; drugs ran you if you let them, kept you scurrying from nowhere to nowhere. But even when he was strung out, he always kept a straight-up job, and he never liked no rough hustle, that crazy stuff that could put you away in the state penitentiary for serious time.

He *had* taken some chances in his twenties, when he was younger and life was harder. He had been through a mismatched teenage marriage by then; its low point, in his memory, was the day his wife bore their first child and went into the delivery room crying out for her mother instead of him. Ain't this a damn shame, he was thinking; here I am, her husband, damn near tore the car up gettin' her to the hospital, and she calling for her damn *mama*. Wasn't no sense missing a day off work for that, he was thinking, so he walked off without even waiting to see if their baby came into the world all right or whether his wife had survived its birth.

A second child followed, Ed's by another woman, and then a mutinous hitch in the navy. The sea was not exactly a calling for him, though the idea of it appealed to him more than humping a 40-pound rucksack in the infantry; he couldn't even swim at the time. His decision was a matter of simple necessity. He and a friend were in a jam over a hit-and-run auto accident, and they figured they had better join *something* before the law caught up with them. So they flipped a coin—heads, army; tails, navy. The toss came up tails.

Ed did some time on his carrier at sea off Vietnam and some in the brig, which he did not find appreciably worse than the war. His offense was refusing, after his tour in combat, to do anything more for his country. "No duties, no *nothin'*," he announced to his superiors one day. "Y'all can do whatever you want to me, I'm not doin' S."

They locked him up.

"Hey—are you going to do right?" an officer asked him when he had been on ice for a while.

"Do right as far as what?" Ed inquired.

"Doing your duty at the base."

"I'm not doin' S for y'all. Naw. F you. F that."

He went back to the brig, for forty days that time, and when he continued his civil disobedience he did sixty more. He still wouldn't bend, and a navy lawyer finally came around to see him.

"Look, Hamilton," the lawyer said, "you want out?"

"S, man," Ed said. "That's what I been trying to *tell* y'all."

The navy gave him his papers and his freedom, and Ed found himself back on Thirty-ninth Street, scuffling up a livelihood any way he could. He dealt reefer and did heroin; his homeboys Honk and Sonny traded him his first H for a half pound of weed, and *damn*— he liked it, too well. He progressed from dabbler to addict, another lost brother with a life in pawn to narcotics. He needed money, a lot of it every day, and for a time in the early 1970's he got deeply and recklessly crooked to raise it.

His friend Piggy from Trey-nine was running a little robbery gang in those days, knocking over dope houses among other targets; straight money was fleeing the ghetto at an accelerating rate, and hustlers found themselves reduced more and more to preying on one another. Ed fell in with the game, only one time it touched too close to home, too near the heart of the man he imagined himself to be. They were sitting around his place at Sixty-second and Winchester one day when someone said, "Look, Ed, there's a drug dealer right around the corner."

"Yeah?" Ed asked warily. "So what?"

"*We* can't get in," the guy said, "but they don't know you. Maybe if you go down there, you can get through the door."

Ed hesitated.

"Look," the dude said, "you help us out and we'll give you five hundred dollars."

Mmmm, Ed thought, admiring the roundness of the number, and against his better judgment, he said yeah. He had to cop a piece first, a .38 revolver; then he presented himself at the dope-house door, while his partners, Piggy, Calvin, and Bozo, lay back out of sight and watched. He was alone in the bull's-eye, and he didn't much dig it. This ain't gonna work, an inner voice kept telling him; we ain't gonna carry it out.

Still, he made himself ring the bell.

The door opened a crack.

Ed started talking, fast, a steady stream of this-that-this-that, until he had negotiated his way inside. His eyes swept the room. Like a lot of work houses, it was a family affair, the men seated around a table mixing drugs, their women and children scattered over the set. Ed still didn't like the looks of it, but he yanked the door wide and *boom*—his partners piled through, all packing their own .38's.

The game went according to plan, at first anyway. They put the women and children against the wall, made the men lie on the floor, and scooped up whatever drugs and money were visible. But the haul wasn't as big as they had figured on. They knew there had to be more reefer in the house, and while his partners held the grown-ups at gunpoint, Ed went looking for it upstairs.

It wasn't there.

Ed came back and grabbed one of the children, a little girl.

"Y'all MF's don't tell me where the S is," he told the room, "I'm gonna shoot the kids."

Nobody said S. The thing was *crazy*, Ed was thinking. The MF's were forcing his hand.

"F this," he heard himself saying. "I'ma *drown* the bitch if you don't give that dope up."

He dragged the girl into the bathroom. The dealers watched him, measuring how far he would go. He had to show them. He turned on the water; it was splashing into the sink when they finally surrendered their stash. Ed breathed again. He had never really meant to drown the girl; that wasn't him. But he was silently grateful then that they hadn't called his bluff, and the scene still haunted him ten years afterward, a bad dream played endlessly in rerun in his mind.

He was happy, in any case, when Piggy took him aside one day and told him, "Ed, man, you too smart for this. Whyn't you just kinda stay here while *we* do the stickups and be like an accountant—watch the money and drugs and S?" He did for a while, profitably, and then Piggy died. Piggy had got drunk on his success and his treachery, to a point where he figured *he* was the baddest brother at Trey-nine. It was then that he made his fatal decision to go up against James Bonner and, more foolishly still, let his intentions be known around the building. Ed had just left Piggy's apartment when James

Bonner came busting in with his shotgun, firing first and taking names later. Only the barest chance saved Ed's life; if he had lingered longer at Piggy's place, he figured afterward, he would have been killed, too.

Ed was built for the solo life in any case. He didn't like hanging with a crowd, didn't like following no type or trend along with everyone else, and if people sometimes asked what's wrong with Ed, it didn't trouble him; it was the way he was, which was lonely. He didn't know why, exactly. It could have had something to do with the winter day when he was a kid out slip-sliding on the ice and saw a form falling from an upstairs gallery, drifting weightlessly downward, like an empty coat on the air; then he was running toward it, a small boy pounding across the frozen ground, and when he got there, the coat turned out to be his brother Grover and he was dying. Ed had had a serious siege of depression after that, and the memory still lay like a scar on his soul a quarter century later. He grew up feeling distanced from the world, even from his friends. The ice in his deep-set eyes seemed to say that life owed him one.

What he wanted from life was that jackpot, that one El Dorado score, and he was still chasing it when fortune put the keys to the bank in his hand. He was on his second marriage at the time—the first had long since folded—and he and his wife, Jennette, were spending maybe $500 a day between them on heroin, far more than they were making on their jobs. But luck suddenly smiled on them, or, more accurately, leered. Jennette came home from work one day complaining about the chief teller at the bank where she cashed her paychecks. He was a white boy, she said, and he kept propositioning her every time she went in. She was scared of him.

"Tell ya what, baby," Ed said. "When you get paid on Thursday, I go over there with you and put this dude in check."

He did, standing behind Jennette in line as if they didn't know each other. Sure enough, the teller started coming on to her.

Ed stepped forward, his broad face as murderous as the kind you see on post office walls.

"Hey, man," he said, "let me tell you one thing—you F'ing with my wife. I don't want you messin' with her no more."

The teller blanched. He was sorry, he stammered; he hadn't known; he would never do it again.

"I ought to drag you from around the counter and kick your ass," Ed told him. "I ought to beat the S out of you."

"No, no, no," the dude said. Ed was street-smart; reading people was his business, and he could see the man was scared. "Sir, sir— don't do that," he was saying. "I'll do anything I can for you. Anything."

Ed left, but that frightened white face and that strangled "anything" lingered in his mind, the sight and sound of opportunity presenting itself at his door. This MF *scared,* he was thinking, real scared, and a scared MF in charge of all that money was a chance just waiting to be taken.

He was still thinking about it when maybe a month later one of his partners came to him with a couple of stolen government checks, a common item of contraband around the projects.

"Ed, man," the dude said, "I wish I knew of a way to bust this paper."

Ed smiled.

He took the checks to his wife's bank, where his new friend was, and waited in line till they were once again face to face. The teller looked at him. Ed stared back, his eyes evil.

"How're you doing, Mr. Hamilton?" the teller said. The fear still showed in his face.

Ed pushed the two checks across the counter. Neither had his name on it. The teller studied them for a long moment, then looked up and studied Ed.

"Mr. Hamilton," he said finally, "can I see you endorse these, please?"

Ed signed them. The teller handed over the cash. Ed pocketed it and ambled out, his good mood accentuating the little bop dip in his walk. A business was born; he had become Hamilton the Paper Man, the hustlers' banker, the dude to see if you were holding a hot check and needed it busted. Sometimes he wrote his own; sometimes he cashed welfare and Social Security checks stolen from mailboxes in the projects. He didn't even have to steal them himself, which would have crossed the line into rough hustles. He had his finesse game now; as word of his connection spread, guys just brought their paper around, and Ed, for a cut, would present it to his personal banker.

The take had reached $45,000 and looked like it might keep

climbing forever when the Feds finally began making inquiries. The pace of their investigation was slow, and Ed did not wait around for the denouement; instead, he and Jennette headed south to Mississippi, where his parents were from, and came to rest in Jackson. They were happy for a time at the slower pace of life there; it seemed to Ed that he had found something like peace. Jennette teased a job out of the owner of a chicken joint, graduating quickly to night bartender. Ed got work at the state liquor-control commission and, with it, a new sideline, appropriating a few half pints each day and retailing them around Jennette's café for $3 a bottle.

They had a house and two cars, and everything was cool until the day their next-door neighbor got it in his mind that Ed was messing with his wife. The lady in question was a white woman and no big deal, not to Ed; she wasn't the type he would even look at seriously. His neighbor didn't believe him. Ed came home from work one day and found the dude waiting to meet him, feeding shells into a shotgun.

Ed had been drinking, but he still had his reflexes. He lunged at the dude, grabbed him, and wrestled him to the ground. The cat bounced back up, swinging the shotgun like it was a baseball bat and Ed's head was a fat pitch in Comiskey Park. Ed threw up his arms for protection. His hands and wrists took most of the punishment; the blows were still raining down when the police came and took him away.

He felt affronted, considering himself the victim, not the aggressor. But when Jennette showed up downtown with bail money, the cops told him, "You can't go." They had run a check on his record and discovered that he and Jennette were both wanted back in Chicago, a little matter of all that bad paper they had busted at her bank. She stayed behind long enough to sell their house and settle their affairs. He was returned to Illinois to answer the charges against him.

He had a little money left, enough to make bond. His first stop, once he was out, was the bank.

"Look, I'm not going to jail by myself," he said. "I'll pay back the money if you drop the charges."

"How are you going to get the money?" a guy with the bank asked him.

"Same way I got it before," he said mildly.

"No," the guy answered, "we can't take any more bad checks."

Ed was out of ideas. Jennette came back to Chicago, gave herself up, and got off with three months. Ed took a bigger hit, a year in Federal prison, but apart from the fact that it *was* prison, he didn't much mind being there. It wasn't no *hard* time, like you might do at a state joint like Pontiac or Joliet or in Cook County Jail. Places like that, Ed thought, you got thrown together with a bunch of street gorillas, dudes with nothing but trouble on their minds. In Federal prison, his neighbors on the tier were mostly upscale white people doing penance for white-collar crimes. He was Ed Hamilton from Trey-nine talking and playing cards with top-flight people—doctors, lawyers, bankers, businessmen, even a few cops. They were a higher class of felon than he was used to, and he felt flattered just to be in their company.

His year inside was a learning experience. His days when he came out seemed doom-haunted. He and his wife, the one lasting love in his life, talked about moving back to Jackson with the kids and picked a date on the calendar to head south. But they had always had an open relationship, the kind where one of them could go live with someone else for four or five months and the other would still be waiting at home when passion died; everything was that cool between them. It was therefore not a breach of faith or custom that Ed happened to be occupied elsewhere at moving time. The appointed day came and went. Jennette waited. He didn't show. He heard three days later that she had been killed in a car wreck, on her way to get her brother out of jail. If Ed had called for her, he thought afterward, she would still be alive, and so would the part of him that she had occupied.

He was still grieving when he hooked up with another lady, named Carolyn. They were a good match, though she came encumbered with eight children; they stayed together for five years, and then he lost her, too, slowly and painfully, to cancer. "Look, baby," she told him when she found out how sick she was, "I don't want to hold you back or nothin', so I'm gonna leave and go up to Milwaukee." Milwaukee was her hometown. Her mother was there and would take care of her.

"Naw, baby," Ed protested, "I ain't gonna let you go like that."

"Naw, baby," she said. "I gotta do this my myself. I gonna go."

She gathered up the children and left. She was near the end the last time Ed saw her, so wasted that he barely recognized her. She knew she was dying, she told him. She didn't have much time.

"Baby, you want me to stay with you?" he asked her.

"Naw," she said, "but I want you to know I love you."

"I love you, too," Ed said. The words were all he had left to give her, and he went home. Three weeks later she was gone.

He found a new woman in the middle 1980's, a receptionist named Theresa; they hit it off instantly and moved in together the day they met. But there remained empty spaces in his life. He had a long, hard time finding a steady job, though he had always preferred an honest dollar to an illicit one. He *had* to be working; it had been a source of pride and strength for him, the baseline of his life even in his hustling days. He put out résumés all over town and shopped the help-wanted ads in the *Tribune* every Sunday, looking for signs and presentiments of hope like a roulette player placing his bets. He finally did land something, a little gig at a box company. Till then, he had had to get by on what jobs he could promote with his pickup and maybe a little soft hustle on the side.

He lived in a triplex basement apartment, dark and sparse, with the faint musty scent of worn furniture and stalemated lives. Sometimes his days began there with a vodka, a smoke, and a jazz record wailing cool and low on the stereo. His three children were staying with his mother. He told himself that he had neither forgotten nor abandoned them, and he regularly dropped off money for their support. But he knew he had neglected their upbringing, and it caused him pangs of conscience when he thought about them. *Damn*—what am I doin' to my kids?

He refused to blame anyone but himself for what had been a lifetime of unrealized possibilities. Yeah, the Man held all the keys, but Ed wasn't the kind to holler race-race-race like some brothers did to explain away everything bad that happened to him. There had been opportunities, and he had let them slide by. He had dropped out of school and gone for that quick dollar, that big score. It hadn't worked out, and who, he wondered, was he supposed to blame for that—white folks?

He had made his own way through life, a solitary path with turnings inside and outside the law, and he felt responsible for the choices he had made. The first, the one from which everything else flowed, had been survival, and if you called it that—if you saw your existence as a suspenseful daily struggle between life and death—the means you used to sustain life didn't greatly matter. Ed accordingly operated by his own code of honor and law, his own definition of what was right and what was wrong. Stealing, for example—if you took something from someone behind his back, and he asked you, ''Where's my S?'' and you said you didn't know, that would be dishonest; that, by Ed's lights, was stealing. But if you just grabbed whatever it was and told the guy straight up front, ''I'm *takin'* this S,'' you couldn't call *that* stealing. That was simple need asserting itself, appropriating whatever a man had to have to get by; you tried to get it the right way, but if you had to get it the wrong way, Ed thought, that was all right, too.

It was a hustler's ethic, and it required a certain toughness, a measure of stone in the face one presented to the world. Ed's bearing in a crowd said don't F with me; he moved through the busy life of the street with the grace and guile of an alley cat on the prowl, and some of its aura of danger. He was walking through the 'hood one winter evening, cruising fast against that icy lakeshore wind known deferentially among the brothers as the Hawk, when a junkie he had seen hanging out on the block loomed up in his face. The dude was F'd up on drugs and woofing loudly, shouting some S about Ed owing him money, which he didn't. Spittle was flying at Ed like April rain. Ed tried to step around the guy, just walk on away from trouble before it happened. That's my thang, he was thinking; he liked to ease his way out of situations, preferring talk to combat.

But the dude grabbed the back of his coat collar, calling his hand, and it was bottom-line time for Ed. Naw, baby, you get off me quick, he was thinking, only there was no longer time for the sucker *to* get off. Ed wheeled, razor in hand. The blade flew open, glimmering in the reflected street light. It drew a red line down the dude's face and neck; the cut was so clean that it took a few seconds—minutes, in

Ed's mind—for the blood to start spurting. Ed didn't stop to watch. He kept moving, never once breaking stride or looking back. He heard only later that the dude had survived, and it was a matter of abstract interest to him. You grab me, he thought, what you *expect* me to do? You couldn't just let people F over you out here on these streets, not if you wanted to survive. *Naw,* baby. Not here. Not me.

But Ed thought of himself as dangerous only if provoked, and he tried to stay out of provocation's way. He was hard when he had to be, which was when he was out in the world; there were too many MF's out there, he thought, who didn't care S about him, crazy cats like that junkie looking to go upside his head. At home, with his old lady or his children, he turned soft and caring. He remained an introspective man, a loner who preferred his own company and his woman's to the society of relatives and friends or the hurly-burly of the street. Time had made him a homebody. His old lady was always wanting to eat out, places like the Red Lobster or some hotel restaurant. Ed went along to please her and sipped a beer while she ate. Given his own way, he didn't care if he ever went out at all.

He had come to like his life private, *real* private. He felt out of his element even at family gatherings and so avoided them; he had nieces and nephews he wouldn't know if they jumped up in his lap. He preferred wandering a museum or a gallery alone to sitting in some cocktail lounge somewhere in a crowd. There were times when he didn't want anyone around at all, and there were places he favored for their solitude—a certain rock on the lakeshore, a certain willow rising stubbornly out of the asphalt and concrete of the South Side. For years they had been his retreats, his islands in the stream, and he would seek them out when he wanted to be alone and think about things.

What he had been thinking lately was that his life wasn't so bad. Its foundation seemed to him rock solid. He had a good woman with her own income. His relationship with his kids was better. He had tamed his drug habit; drugs couldn't run you, as they once had run him, if you cared enough about other things. He was working again, making that honest dollar, though if he had to stray outside the law now and again to get by, well, he thought, that was his life-style; it wasn't up to nobody else to judge him for it. The moonlight hustle was widely accepted among ghetto men, stuck for life at subsistence work and unemployment windows. It was thought of almost as a right, like self-defense, and if you didn't hurt nobody, Ed believed, it wasn't no crime.

Like a lot of dreamers in the ghetto, he was still looking for that big hit, in the lottery this time instead of in The Life. But he was smart enough to know it was a dream, and in the meantime he reckoned he had a lot to be happy about. He felt less like a loser than like a ball player in a batting slump. His luck was going to turn, he told himself. If you kept on keeping on, it *had* to turn; a man couldn't be unsuccessful all his life.

MAN IN THE HOUSE

He wasn't exactly Rockefeller, shoving a food trolley around a VA hospital, but Sonny Spruiell had climbed far enough out of the lower depths of his life to see how low he had been. He was strung out on heroin not so long ago, another trader on the Thirty-ninth Street pharmaceutical market who got too enthusiastic about his product and was shooting it up instead of selling it. It was zombie time for Sonny, a down-and-out passage through the dope houses of the South Side and the S you had to do to pay your way in the door. He couldn't see it then, through his narcotic smog, but he knows now precisely when he touched rock bottom. It was when he visited his people and they started hiding things when he came in the door; it was when he went to see his mama and found her following him around the apartment, room to room, scared that her own son would steal her blind to support his habit.

Effie Spruiell hadn't raised her five children that way. She had in fact seen it as a step up out of the toils and snares of the ghetto when the family first moved into Trey-nine in 1962. Sonny—Ulysses on his birth certificate—was still a schoolboy then, and just thinking about leaving his friends behind made him homesick. "Why we gotta move, Mama?" he had asked. "What's wrong with this?"

"We're going someplace better," she had told him, and when Sonny laid eyes on Trey-nine, with its fresh paint and its working fixtures, he came to agree. In those unspoiled early days, the project even smelled new.

But the street held temptations stronger than Mrs. Spruiell's will. First an older son succumbed to drugs and petty crime, and then Sonny started downhill, too, coming on down the line with the same MF'ing thing. His grades had been good enough to qualify him for the tough admission standards at Dunbar High; he was, by his own adult recollection, a real brain when he let himself be. His problem was that he didn't want to be out in that spotlight looking *serious* in front of his friends. School was Vest's game, not Sonny's. Vest was *supposed* to be smart. Sonny preferred being cool. *His* school was Thirty-ninth Street; he was running with the Satan's Saints and fooling with various legal and illegal chemicals, beginner's stuff like codeine syrup, trees—amphetamines—and Wild Irish Rose wine.

The more formal curriculum offered at Dunbar was not on Sonny's agenda. The only place he let himself excel was in gym. He could dunk a basketball before anyone, before *Billy,* even, when he was still just five feet seven; the other boys took to calling him Frog in awe of his soaring vertical leap. Nothing else at Dunbar held his wandering attention. His mother was regularly advised that he was a student in name only, that his interests during school hours seemed limited to gambling and comic books. Sonny found the reports flattering to his image. He regularly gave F'd up answers in class, failing on purpose, 'cause, he thought then, it looked like tough S to play dumb. Sometimes a teacher would call on him, and he wouldn't respond at all. By tenth grade he quit going entirely. Later for school, he figured; he was F'd up on pills and Rose, and he no longer gave a F about getting what passed for an education.

The feeling at Dunbar was mutual. It was a given that boys dropped out, the accepted human cost of doing business; the school authorities did little to discourage them and sometimes seemed to *want* them gone, out of sight and out of mind. Sonny's mother alone seemed to care if he stayed or not, and she had to sell him on the idea first.

"Why don't you try to get back in school?" she asked him one day.

She looked upset, which troubled Sonny, and he was bored besides; time stood still when you had nothing to do. So he allowed his mama to march him back to Dunbar to see if they would have him.

They were shown into the imposing presence of a woman guidance counselor, large, white, and unsympathetic. Sonny's records were spread out on the desk in front of her. She scanned them with an icy eye, then looked up.

"There's no hope for him," she told Mrs. Spruiell. Her recommendation instead was that Sonny be finally and formally dismissed, not reinstated, and that he be reassigned to an alternative program for dropouts.

Sonny received the news without surprise. The big bitch was trying to make *all* blacks dumb, he was thinking. She wasn't dealing second chances; if you found yourself in her office, it meant someone had decided that there wasn't any saving you.

His mother kept trying anyway; she found a teacher named Mrs. Moore, who felt kindly toward Sonny, and with her help got the school to take him back. The catch was that he would have to start from scratch, a freshman again at seventeen. Sonny didn't like the deal and wasn't in position to take it even if he were interested. His mother told him about it on the telephone. He was calling from a recruiting station. He had just joined the army.

The military was Sonny's adult education, with a curriculum they didn't offer at a ghetto high school. Sonny had never been farther from home than downtown Chicago to the north and Ninety-fifth Street to the south and so had never lived in close company with white people. The experience was not uplifting. He trained in the Deep South, in Georgia and South Carolina, at a time when they had not yet got over the civil rights movement, and the racial folkways of the countryside seemed to infect the base. Black GI's got a disproportionately large share of the scut work, or thought they did, and once Sonny came close to thundering on a white soldier who called him nigger; the joker was one wink away from a horizontal butt stroke, stopping fourteen pounds of rifle with his face. Sonny kept control of himself that time, figuring if he hit the guy once, he might not stop. He resolved instead never to take nothing off another honky, and he didn't.

He was never a happy soldier, anyway. When he showed up on Thirty-ninth Street on home leave, his lady Jean remembered, you had to damn near kick his ass onto the airplane to get him back to his base. He didn't always make it on time, even with a little help from his friends. Once, he and his main man, Honk, overstayed their furloughs, Sonny by twenty-nine days, Honk by twenty-three. The brothers from the 'hood finally saw them to the bus, uniforms wrinkled and heads bad from a marathon good-bye party. They didn't have a dime more than the fare and might not have survived across country at all if it hadn't been for Honk's Midas hands. "Don't worry about it," he told Sonny; he descended from their Greyhound at every rest stop and *killed* the MF's—picked the snack bars and the gift counters clean.

The two of them shipped out to Germany together; there the army split them up, and they went their separate ways, Honk into his hustles, Sonny into reefer, hash, and black consciousness. By the numbers, the army was one of the most integrated institutions in our national life. In fact, it was an arbitrary community of young men living at close quarters by command, not choice, and the racial tensions of the larger American society of the late 1960's were, if anything, magnified among them. Sonny had barely arrived at his new command the first time one of his bunkmates called him nigger. He let that pass. But when his sergeant ordered him to police the hallways when it was some white dude's turn, he rebelled. "I ain't sweepin' S," he said, and when the sergeant hauled him before the CO, Sonny won.

The incident nevertheless confirmed, in his mind, what he had suspected from the get-go: that the army was irredeemably racist. He marched from the CO's office to a club on the base where black GI's hung out, fuming about how the brothers got all the S details and how they ought to start raising hell about it. Nobody said much; the only cause most of them subscribed to was doing their time and getting the hell out. But Sonny kept agitating, and he found his way into the company of men who felt the same way, righteous bloods who called each other brother and meant it. Sonny found a togetherness among them he had never felt on Thirty-ninth Street, a fellowship that began with the color of their skin and their wakening pride in it. It wasn't no gangs and all this S, he thought, nobody living in fear. They trusted one another with their belongings and their lives; they were black men watching each other's backs against the common white enemy for once, instead of choosing up sides and going to war with one another.

They were a brotherhood without a name, but their style and their politics borrowed heavily from the guns-and-leather machismo of the Black Panther Party back home. Sonny grew an Afro, a haircut that was itself a political statement in its day. He wore a dashiki and a black tam, with a braid of woven bootlaces knotted around one wrist. He carried a cane, part costume, part weapon, and applied it to the ass of any white boy who gave him offense. Once, in a black mood, he snatched a can of Coke from a white GI in a poolroom. The dude turned him in, and Sonny was confined to quarters for thirty days. "Man, if I go to jail, I'm F'ing you up," Sonny told him. The honky reported that, too; the threat was added to the bill of charges against Sonny, and the MP's dragged him off to the stockade in Mannheim for three months' hard time.

It was jail, but Sonny felt at home there, surrounded by dudes as black and as angry as he was. He was tossed in the hole one day, and the first face he saw there belonged to a dude he knew from the 'hood, a guy named Michael out of Stateway Gardens. On Thirty-ninth Street he had been an enemy, a Blackstone Ranger, but the common condition of soldiering in the white man's army had bound them together in their blackness.

"Mike!" Sonny whooped, as if they were brothers parted since birth. "It's Sonny! What the F *you* doin' here?"

"Awww, you know what time it is," Mike said.

Sonny did; it was a season of black power and black pride, a time when even small acts of insubordination against the Man took on the hue of revolution, and he was whacked out on it. He was unmanageable inside the stockade and incorrigible when he came out. "I'm not doin' S," he told his sergeant. "What're you gonna do, send me to jail? I just *came* from jail."

He was restricted to an empty barracks with not much to do except read and think about blackness. In the mornings he would walk past the company formation while the sergeant was reading the orders of the day and poke his fist aloft, the black-power salute; when the sergeant looked up from his papers, every brother in the formation would have his fist up, too, and Sonny would be walking away laughing. In the evenings he would put on his tam and his braid and sit around with his partners, smoking hash and rapping about how white folks were doing them. He was, he reflected later, kind of nuts on the subject. The other guys were just there; he guessed in retrospect that they had joined in mainly to keep down the static.

He spent nearly half his tour abroad under lock and key. Doing time didn't break him. Coming home almost did. He reappeared on Thirty-ninth Street with his consciousness still wired high. He wanted everybody to be like he was, but what he found was the same S he had left behind, all these Negroes in the projects about being tough instead of smart. He ran into Mike, his stockade partner from Stateway, only Mike wasn't into the black thing anymore; he was back with the Stones gang-banging as if their bad-ass army days had never happened. He wouldn't even look Sonny in the eye when they met.

"Mike," Sonny said. "We just went through some S, man. Where's your *braid?*"

"I'm not like that no more," Mike said. "It be's that way sometime. This is a new day. *This* what I'm into now."

Sonny imagined at first that he could convert the unbelievers, given time. They haven't been where I've been, he thought; they haven't saw what I've seen. But they weren't ready to think black, as he soon discovered, and trying to persuade them was like beating his head against a wall. He was living in fantasyland, he decided finally; he had to get out of it, and the route he chose was his own private dream street, where the drugs were. The Black Panther in him died of neglect on Thirty-ninth Street. The new Sonny Spruiell was a real live-or-die nigger, a man ready for a man's pleasures and reckless of the cost. He was initiated into the brotherhood of heroin one day, in company with his man Honk, in a washroom at Trey-nine. They made Sonny's big brother show them how. "We gonna do it anyway," Honk told him. "Either we learn it the right way, or goddammit, it's gonna be your fault."

Like most of the young brothers doing drugs, Sonny figured he could handle the hard stuff, and for a time he did. He worked at intervals at the post office and enrolled in community college, the latter less for the education than for the GI benefits. A militant faction called the Mau Maus had taken de facto control of the school, and no one asked questions if you drew your government check and hung out in the lounge all day. It was a soft hustle, but there was more money in drugs than at school *or* work, and more business than he could take care of part-time.

So he dropped out of the square life for long intervals and went into partnership with Honk—Johnson & Spruiell Ltd., dealers in boss drugs, hard times, and short futures. Honk played the bad guy, the dude who could set you trembling with a look if you owed him a dollar; Sonny was the good guy, the man you settled up with when you stopped quaking. Together, they owned their corner on Thirty-ninth Street, and when the competition breathed too heavy, James Bonner was there to back them up. He disapproved of their shooting heroin; it made them slack about defending the building, and he regularly asked them, "Man, why y'all messin' with that S?" But selling it was their hustle, and so long as he was alive and they were Trey-nine brothers, they remained under his protection.

Their trouble started when they began using what they were dealing; when you did that, things fell apart fast. The partnership pulled thin and broke up. Outsiders moved onto the corner, no longer frightened of reprisal. Supplies dried up; the worst thing a hustler could have was a reputation for dipping into inventory to feed the monkey on his own back. Sonny was out there alone, broke and strung out, and it didn't matter if you kicked drugs for a few months at a time, as he did; you couldn't get back in the game. You didn't have the money or the trust. You didn't have nothing except your hunger, dragging you under again, and when you knew you had touched bottom was when you found your mama following you around the house, watching that you didn't steal nothing.

You couldn't get no further down than that, Sonny thought, but as it worked out, he was one of the lucky ones; he had someone to help pull him back up. Her name was Jean Catherine, and she had been his Trey-nine sweetheart, the girl he had nearly gone to war for back in his gang-banging days. They had married at City Hall after he came home from the army. The match was battered by his prolonged walk on the wild side and the poverty it caused them, trying to scuffle along on his unemployment and her welfare; take those two checks and put them together, he thought, and you still ain't got nothing.

He and Jean lasted four difficult years together, then split for four years more. What brought them back together was the single thing they had most in common, their daughter, Keita. They both wanted a better life for her than they had known, and they had started her in parochial school for a strict 3-R education; kids seemed to do better there, under the strict discipline of the sisters. But when Jean and Sonny split, they could no longer afford the tuition. They had to switch Keita to a ghetto public school, a baby blackboard jungle. She was being intimidated, and they could see her future dying a day at a time.

"I don't care what you and Jean have done," Effie Spruiell told Sonny one day. "Y'all work something out for the sake of Keita."

"Yeah," Sonny promised, and he and Jean came to a little understanding. There would be no more BS and no more hard hustles. They were too old and Keita was too precious for that.

He could look back on those times from a great and peaceful distance now. He hadn't forgotten how to supplement his income with a little survival money, but his basic bread came from his job at the hospital, and his home life looked less like a tale from the lower depths than like a Bill Cosby script played by a Trey-nine company. Working had restored some of his self-esteem along with his bank-roll. A nigger ain't S without a job, he mused, but with one he had a dollar in his pocket, and his family didn't have to go begging his mama if they needed something; the kids could come to him for money, and he had it to give. Keita was back in parochial school, at St. Elizabeth's. A second daughter, Nookie, had arrived, doubling the reasons for Sonny and Jean to resolve their differences. They did, and even when they fought, it was with the understanding that neither of them was going anywhere.

Sonny had settled too contentedly into his new life as father and provider. The role brought out a caring and protective side that once seemed lost under the layering of callus he had acquired in the streets. He had grown up in the ghetto, at the eye of its violence and its petty vice, and he wanted to shelter his own children from it, to make a place where they would be safe.

He came home from work one night at the usual time, 8:30, shucking his coat and popping a Colt 45 as he made for the living room. He had barely settled his weary body on the couch when Keita came at him with her seventh-grade school photos. He studied them one by one, pausing only once to interrupt Nookie in the act of filching a piece of candy. "Hey!" he exclaimed, spying her out of the corner of his eye; she was a real Spruiell, three years old and already tough to manage. She stared balefully at Sonny. He smiled and held out his hand, palm up. She slapped him five. He went back to Keita's photos, flipping through the stack and smiling his approval.

"Now let's see the group picture," he said.

"Nooo," Keita said. She was embarrassed because she was small and they always put her in the front row.

"Again?" Sonny said, but he jollied her into surrendering it and scanned the ranks of girls, cherubic in their plaid skirts and starched white blouses. "No, it's fine, baby," he told Keita, smiling a wide fatherly smile. *Life* was fine, he was thinking. He was cool. He was finally in control.

"I CHOOSE WORK"

Half Man was in control, too, when Vest Monroe found him on the South Side one day in the winter of 1986–87; if you kept your wants manageable and stayed out of trouble, it brought a kind of order to your life, a form of satisfaction. Viewed from downtown, he and

most of his old friends from Trey-nine were still stuck at the margins
of the American economic and social order, invisible men leading
expendable lives. But as Half Man called the roll in his mind, things
weren't that bad for most of them. They were getting by, and that in
itself was a victory against hard odds.

Take Pee Wee, he said; Pee Wee always had the brains and the
smarts, and now that he was finally getting his thing together, he was
working. Or Ed Hamilton—Ed might not know exactly what he wanted
to be, if anything, but he had always been a survivor, and that wasn't
too bad. Or Moose—he was a Witness now and doing great, living a
straight-up life and earning an honest dollar. Or even Honk, doing
time downstate; the man never did show no emotions, so you really
couldn't tell how he was feeling inside, but he had a nice place and
a family waiting for him, and he didn't *look* like he was hurting.

And Half Man himself—he was still scuffling, still working two
jobs so he could pay his own way through life and not depend on
strangers. You couldn't make it on welfare, he said, and he was too
proud to beg. "So I work," he told Vest. "I choose work because
I'm not lazy. That's the only way you'll get anything, man—you've
got to work."

"I've known for a long time what I wanted to do," Vest said.
"What I wanted to be. When we were kids, what did you want
to be?"

"I never thought about it," Half Man said. "I never wanted to
be a fireman, policeman, cameraman, whatever. I guess that's why I
been doing what I been doing. I never had one dream about what I
wanted to be. I just went to do the chore."

"How do you see your life five years from now? What would
you like to be doing?"

"Still working," Half Man said. "Not having *whatever* I want,
but the basic things of life. A new car, nice place to stay, and nice
clothes. Always something to eat, you know. Also, a couple of dollars in the bank. That's it. Living a middle-class life."

He guessed that was as much as most of them wanted—the ones,
anyway, who hadn't got over like Vest had. Maybe none of them had
exactly what they might have wished for, Half Man reckoned, but if
you didn't want big, you didn't hurt bad. They all had jobs, except

for Honk, who never wanted one and was now a guest of the state. No one else was in the joint, or on the street, or strung out on drugs. None of them was on welfare, either. They were doing pretty average. They were happy, Half Man guessed, all of them except himself, and he was doing what he had always done in pursuit of happiness. He was working on it.

PART V

STRIVERS

I do believe that the decks are stacked against you if you're a black man, Vest said. *If you're a black* person, *but particularly if you're a black* man. *We came through the sixties, and for whatever reason, the doors opened and a few people like myself got through. Then the doors slammed.*

And you know, there's an old saying among black people that in order to succeed, you have to be twice as good as everybody else. You have to work twice as hard. Ray Stingley has that sense, Greg Bronson has that sense, I have that sense—that you can't just be good, you have to be twice as good, and sometimes, no matter how good you are or how hard you work, it's just not going to happen.

CITIZEN BRONSON

It was the day-shift Greg Bronson, the trig black yuppie, who presented himself for a job interview at a hearing-aid company in Tampa, Florida, one day in the spring of 1986. His suit was styled by Austin-Hill, with a correct quarter inch of white peeping out from under the blue worsted sleeves; his manner was polished by Norman Vincent Peale, among other authors of the Great Books of self-improvement; his presentation was informed with numbers from *Moody's* and *Standard & Poor's;* his body was slimmed and hardened by tournament tennis. The day outside was hot and muggy, ninety-six in the shade, but no bead of sweat dampened his lean, handsome face, and no hint of a wrinkle marred the crisp line of his clothes. His résumé was attractive—he had sold copiers and cars, monitored loans in a bank, and run his own small businesses—and his bearing radiated confidence in himself.

But buttoned tight inside the worsted and the tassel loafers was a second Greg Bronson, an angry black nationalist who bore the African name Kamau Akil, and as he sat in deepening humiliation through the interview, Greg could feel his second self—his night side—struggling to get out. In the three weeks since he had moved to Tampa, he had canvassed two auto dealers, three banks, a credit union, a copier company, and a car-rental agency. He had never had trouble finding a job, *never*, but this was Florida, and he was getting a polite runaround everywhere. Nobody rejected him straight out; racism in the middle 1980's wore a smiling face, an air of pious concern for his well-being. The usual line was that they couldn't possibly pay him the kind of money he was used to making up north. That didn't matter, he told them. They would get back to him, they said. They never did.

He thought he had finally scored at the hearing-aid company, which was looking for a salesman. The white boy, the *European,* behind the desk had started out flattering him on how well turned out he looked, how prosperous, and Greg had thought, that's very positive—this is the one. And then the boom came down, hard. The prospective buyers, the man was saying, would mostly be white and elderly, people brought up in—well, the old southern ways.

So there it lay, out in the open where they both could see it. Greg believed that racism was a pandemic disease of white people; suspecting it everywhere, he saw it everywhere, a self-fulfilling prophecy. No matter how much you assimilated, no matter how well you learned to play their game, he thought, you never got there. The system *intended* that black people fail, all but a token few. The feigned concern over whether white customers would receive him or not was just one more way of showing one more black man the door.

"That wouldn't be a problem," he heard himself saying, his temper in check. He was a professional, he said; he always presented himself in a professional manner. He knew he could overcome whatever doubts or prejudices he ran into. Most of the people he had sold cars to had been white, young and old, and he had done well at it, exceptionally well. He had sold cars to 39 percent of his prospects— the national average was 22 or 23 percent—and he had been salesman of the month at his last dealership for four consecutive months.

But look at the bottom line, the man answered. "This job is based on sales commissions. You cannot make any money if they will not open the door."

The finality in his voice signaled that the interview was over. Kamau Akil, the night-shift warrior, wanted to go off on him—*grab* the man and straighten out his peckerwood mind. Greg Bronson, the day-shift striver, rose and left before he lost control.

Things had not changed for Greg since his high school tour as the one black person in the white-collar force at the steel company. He had done well in the white world, but he had never felt at ease in it,

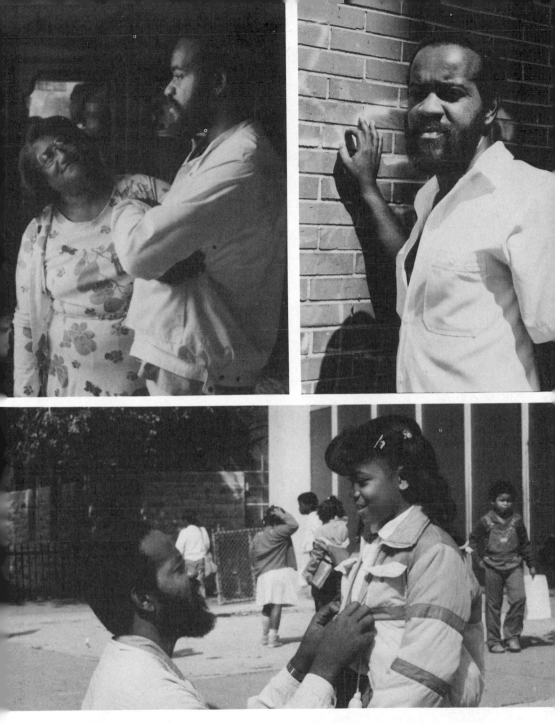

The look in Ed Hamilton's eyes, even when he was smiling, was one of deep sorrow, a look that said his very sanity had been threatened by grief. A handsome man and a good talker, Ed had begun losing the people closest to him at an early age, starting with his young brother whose death he witnessed. He withdrew to solitary safety, and protected his tough-guy image with a razor he carried in his pocket. He protected his soul with trips to museums and a favorite spot by the lake. In his loner's life, he made room for special people, his grandmother for one; and though his three children didn't live with him, he felt their presence in his basement apartment and did as much for them as his limited resources would allow (above, Ed with his daughter).

Steve Steward had determined early on who it was he wanted to be. Just himself, he'd said, that was all he could be. The only problem was that he seemed to be lacking an inner compass, and somewhere between his school years and the rest of his life he got lost. As a promising student, he'd been handed an escape route from the project called ABC. It led him to a first-rate education and a white world of prosperity he had seen only on TV. But the material comforts he found there could not compete with the more familiar comforts of home and, without conscious design, he worked his way back. Twenty years later, his material well-being rested in the reluctant hands of his girlfriend Beverly, and his spiritual well-being was nonexistent. ''I don't know what a good day is,'' he told his old friend Vest Monroe. ''I'm a failure.''

Ray Stingley's first piece of luck was that he was born without a crooked bone in his body. His second, less obvious advantage was to have been born into one of those dysfunctionally large ghetto families that in his case was headed by a hard-working father and a strong-willed mother. There was a constancy in his father's labors and his mother's rules of conduct; their lesson to their children was discipline and self-control, their message was love. When Ray was chosen at the age of fifteen to attend a military academy far from home, he was prepared. His one goal was to please his parents; they had given him what he needed to succeed, and he would never let them down.

Ray's straight-ahead vision of where he had been and where he was going was the key to his success as a father and a salesman. His inherited sense of family was strong; they would be his responsibility, not his burden, and he would see to it that their home was filled not only with material goods but with laughter as well. In his work he was a natural, well spoken and confident. He believed in making money and was aided in that by the knowledge that the medical-supply products he sold were helping people who needed help. When he was picked as the first black regional manager for ConvaTec, the lessons of leadership and comradeship from his military-school days ensured that he was a man with a future.

Half Man Carter got his name the old-fashioned way—he earned it, as he did everything else in his life. He'd had no particular dreams as a kid, which was just as well if you were a kid on Thirty-ninth Street. Instead, his ambition from boyhood on was to be a survivor, and his pint-sized frame was no disadvantage after the day he destroyed a local thug with his vicious right hand. But fighting was what he did when he had to. Work was what he did in preference to everything else; he started young, hawking papers and giving haircuts. He moved on, still in his teens, to car washes, restaurants, and factories. His progression of jobs was not aimless; they were part of Half Man's master plan for the present, which was where he lived his life. He was smart enough to get what he wanted—a nice place to live and a nice lady like Matilda to share it with. And if he didn't have anything big to brag about, he didn't have anything to be ashamed of either.

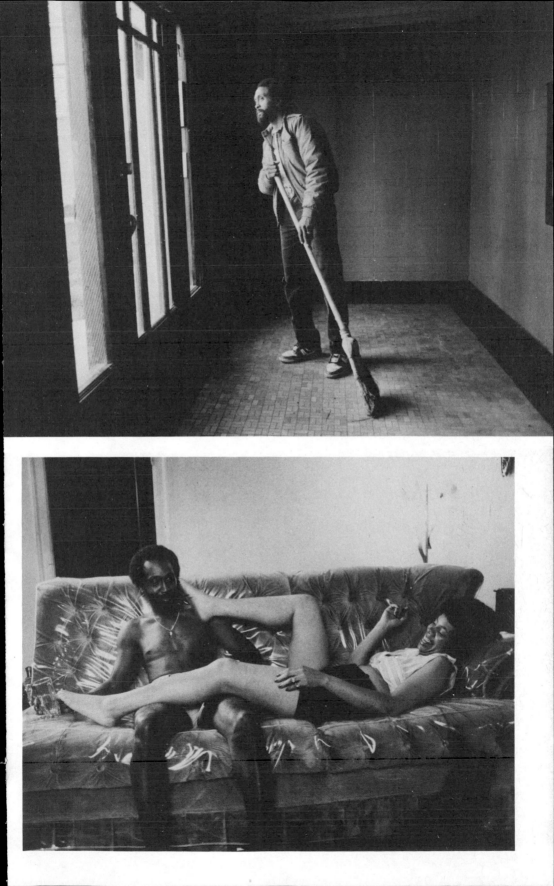

Not many boys growing up in the projects could say that their fathers had a college education. Greg Bronson was a rare exception. His father worked for an insurance company and what he brought home besides his paycheck was a humiliating view of the outside world—the white world, a place where he earned his living at the expense of his pride. Greg assumed the burden of his father's rage, and when his own life put him in contact with whites, he was armed to the teeth with hostility and distrust. But he accepted the challenge of making his way in a society he believed was bent on his destruction; indeed, he enjoyed beating them at their own game, and when he was named salesman of the month for four consecutive months at a car dealership, it was a victory not just for Greg Bronson but for his people as well.

There had been a militant passage in Greg's life, a state of mind that all but exiled him from his own country. But if his warrior's spirit was his father's legacy, so too were his middle-class aspirations. He was part of the black bourgeoisie—there was no safe refuge for Greg in the ghetto—and to live the way he wanted, it was inevitable that he would cross paths with the enemy. He had gone into their world expecting racism and, expecting it, found it. But as he got older, the anger that had given him strength began to cause him pain, and he was willing to admit that in a racist society there might be individuals who weren't. What he wanted now was peace, not war, and, wanting it, he was on the way to finding it.

Leroy Lovelace was raised in rural Alabama, where the biggest distraction may have been nothing more sinister than an afternoon of fishing, and where the greatest treat was his time spent in school. He knew from the first day that he wanted to be a teacher and, with determination and sacrifice, became one, his devotion to education complete and unshakable. But at a ghetto school in Chicago, in his very first year of teaching, he nearly lost his faith. The children who came to his classes had stronger claims on their own attention than on his: The temptations of the street and the discouragement of their circumstances were distractions beyond his control. But he believed that children were children, no matter what their address, and if he had to go to war with their environment, he would. Thirty years later, he was still fighting, but with victories like Vest Monroe, he knew he would never give up.

Before Vest Monroe started getting straight A's in school, he'd learned his lessons well at home. When he thought that half-full and half-empty were the same, his grandmother taught him the meaning of optimism, and when he wondered what he'd be when he grew up, his mother (above) assured him it could be anything he wanted. He took their faith in him and, with his own hard work, fulfilled their dreams. His debt of gratitude to them was so deep that his success seemed only partial payment. The final payment, he knew, was in the future of his children, Jason and Sherita, and so he determined to be as good a father as he possibly could. He was lucky in that task to be armed with a certain magic, a remarkable ability to be himself wherever he happened to be.

and his successes had rarely lasted very long; it was as if he wouldn't let them. His onetime lady, Sherree, who shared his life longer than any other woman and who bore his only child, came to believe in their time together that he hated white people. Greg insisted that he didn't: It was simply that he loved black people and didn't have time to go around trying to sort out good whites from bad. He was not a racist, he believed, because he had no power over other people's lives; whites did. *They* ran the system, and one of its purposes was the destruction of the blacks through second-rate schools and perishable jobs. The means might be more refined than gas chambers, but genocide, in Greg's mind, was not too strong a term for the intended result.

His rejection of white people was accordingly complete, once the workday was done. As Greg Bronson, on the day shift, he moved smoothly and confidently among them; he even found pleasure in playing their games, in the dominance he felt making a hard sale to some European who thought a black man didn't know how to count to ten. As Kamau Akil, on the night watch, he withdrew into his blackness. He refused to date white women, though there had been opportunities, or to allow a white man to cross his doorsill. He had become an expatriate of the spirit, with a new name and a new nation; it was called the Republic of New Africa, and if it existed largely in the minds of its few hundred enrolled "citizens," it was a place of peace for Greg, an armed and secure refuge from a society he could no longer abide.

His discomfort had begun almost the day he graduated from his all-black college, North Carolina A&T, to the mostly white insurance company where his father had spent most of his working life. Greg had encountered racism in its rudest surviving form in the South, at least when he left the sanctuary of the campus; in those days, the world beyond its boundaries still observed some of the tattered codes of Jim Crow. Greg encountered his first WHITE ONLY signs, long after the law and the movement were supposed to have knocked them down, and once, when he tried to buy a Coke at the bus station, a scrubwoman drove him off with a mop; he had unwittingly presented himself at the white entrance. But his time with the insurance company was his introduction to prejudice in its subtler northern guise.

Malcolm X had taught that there was no real difference between Down South and Up South, and Greg came to agree. Life and its rewards were still divided, WHITE and COLORED. Up South, they just didn't hang out the signs.

That he would begin his working life at the company was nonetheless understood in the Bronson household. The entry-level openings for blacks were a good deal better than the loading dock, where Greg's father had started, and with his rise to middle management, the way had been paved for his boys; *they* would have someone to tell them who the racists were. But Greg found the money underwhelming for a striver with a degree in business administration and a young man's ambition; it would be two years before he made as much as he had earned as a painting and janitorial-services contractor while he was still in college. He found the racial climate oppressive as well. There was, for example, the white co-worker who expressed surprise in a perfectly amicable way that there were black people like Greg. He had never met any; the only blacks he had been exposed to were caricatures like Amos 'n' Andy in a TV sitcom or criminals on the evening news.

Greg's reaction was mainly amusement, that time. But he was a child of the rebel sixties, and he did not have his father's capacity for absorbing pain in silence. He had been at the company two years when a white supervisor in his twenties fired a sixty-year-old black man for refusing to obey an order he considered wrong. It was raw, so raw that the company paid the man three years' separation pay. The settlement looked like conscience money and heightened the perception that an injustice had been done. Greg blew up. He marched on the personnel department and told them the whole place was rotten with racism. To stay would have been to acquiesce in it, and soon thereafter he quit.

His heart was in marketing anyway, and after a couple of false starts he got a job as a sales rep for Savin photocopiers in the western suburbs of Chicago. It lasted four profitable years. He liked the combat of it, the constant test of wills with white men of power. Once, he was making his pitch to a bank vice president, telling him all about the $40,000 a year he could cut from his copying bills over the long term by buying equipment from Savin instead of renting it from

Xerox. He had prepared his case well, as always, but he knew he wasn't getting through; he could see it in those blank European eyes.

"Do you have a problem with me because I'm black?" he asked abruptly.

The banker came out of his seat as if Greg had slapped him. *Bingo,* Greg was thinking, though the thrill of victory was short-lived; he could see a six-unit sale, and $3,600 in commissions, dissipate like condensation on the suddenly frosty air. Still angry, he left and, in the most businesslike tones, wrote a letter informing the president of the bank that one of his vice presidents was insufficiently concerned about saving money on copying. It worked. Within days Greg was back, repeating his spiel to the president this time, while the vice president sat by in humbled silence.

Greg's logic was relentless. The president seemed impressed. He asked the vice president why he had decided against the buy.

"I didn't think it was the prudent thing to do at the time," the vice president said.

"We'll get back to you," the president told Greg, and they did, faster than he could get back to his office. A message from the bank was waiting on his desk: He had his six-copier sale.

He was a model young businessman, a Brooks Brotherly fashion plate with *Winning Through Intimidation* on his nightstand and *The Wall Street Journal* under his arm. But his soul was restless, at work and in love, and impermanence became the habit of his life. He took a fling at the marketing business on his own and failed; he attempted marriage, to a suburban Chicago lady named Robyn, and was failing. They had settled in St. Paul in the late 1970's, and when his business went under, they found themselves working together in a bank, Greg in collections, Robyn on the teller line. Their after-hours friends, given Greg's principles, were black, and one of them was Robyn's supervisor, Sherree, a recent divorcée with a spirit as headstrong as Greg's own.

A connection formed between them, platonic at first. She found him fun to be with—unsmiling, yes, and a bit stubborn, but still bright and still fun. He found her sympathetic to the deepening stresses in his marriage, after just two years; he took to stopping by her place on the way home from work, just for someone to talk to. Sherree thought they were just friends. Robyn suspected it was more than that, and when her resentment reached the boiling point, she accused Sherree point-blank of having an affair with her husband. She was, as it turned out, technically wrong and prophetically right. Greg visited Sherree as usual that evening. She was still smarting under Robyn's attack. He was interested in her, in ways she hadn't suspected. He stayed the night, and in a matter of weeks he had moved in with his things.

He and Sherree were a strong couple, he thought, made stronger by their constant togetherness at home, at work, and—with the turn of the decade—on the radical outer edge of black politics. They had gotten swept up in a cause célèbre of the day, the arrest of a black man named Chester Sandifer for the murder of a white man named Luger during a racial confrontation on New Year's Eve 1980. There had been a rowdy party in a white saloon a half block from Sandifer's place. The police came twice, and the second time shut the bar down. The crowd emptied out into the street, looking for trouble. A pregnant black woman crossed their path, on her way to a gathering at Sandifer's house. They stopped her and beat her up. Some of Sandifer's guests heard the noise and came outside to see what was happening. A free-for-all erupted, and before it ended, Luger, a prizefighter, lay dead in the street of a gunshot wound.

Sandifer was a solid blue-collar citizen, a ten-year man at the phone company with a steady job, a stable family, and a home of his own. But his character seemed to count less than the color of his skin, and so did his apparent innocence of the charge. He was arrested, on the word of three white eyewitnesses that he had killed Lugar. The evidence suggested strongly that he could not have done it; he had in fact been dragged from his own doorstep and beaten senseless before the shooting happened, and the policemen who came to arrest him had had to carry him out of his house on a stretcher.

The case was brought to trial anyway, and a tide of anger rose in the black community, sweeping Greg and Sherree along with it. There were meetings; the two of them attended all of them. A defense fund was raised; Greg set up the bank account. When the trial got under way, black spectators packed the gallery, sitting fast through recesses so as not to lose their seats. Their silent presence was a rebuke and a warning to the prosecution; if there was to be a legal lynching, there would at least be eyewitnesses, and Greg would be one of them.

He skipped work for five days to be at the trial, to the puzzlement and finally the irritation of his supervisors. Greg was past caring what they thought. "You're not the attorney," one of them asked him. "What are you doing this for?" Greg shrugged. He was attending the trial because he was black and it was there, and when Sandifer was finally acquitted, Greg took a vicarious pleasure in his victory; it said something about what black people could do if they united around the fact of their color.

He and Sherree had found some like-minded brothers in the swirl of community meetings about the case, militant brothers with a to-gether view of the way things worked for—or rather against—black people in America. Greg sought them out and discovered that they were citizens of the RNA, the Republic of New Africa, an armed secessionist front that had been attempting since the 1960's to create an independent black state in the American South. Their numbers were small, and their territory, a decade after their founding, was not very grand: twenty acres of tax-delinquent farmland in Mississippi. Their patch of ground counted more to them, and to Greg, as a met-aphor for their hopes. It was a first symbolic step toward the birth of an African nation on American soil, and its citizens had shown them-selves willing to spill blood in its defense, enemy blood as well as their own.

Greg knew the dues he might pay for getting involved, the risks to his livelihood and perhaps his life. But he enrolled as a citizen, took an African name, and with Sherree plunged into the life of the Republic—an unending round of rallies, field exercises, and shows of uniformed force. When they ran into sales resistance to their rev-olutionary style, they organized a front with a less menacing name, Nguzo Saba, Swahili for the "seven principles" of unity and self-determination at the core of the RNA platform. Greg saw the shift as elementary marketing, something akin to a corporation changing its logo; you had to reach the people first to let them know it was nation time, and if your image scared them off, you would never get through.

The repackaging helped; the group became a respected force in the black parts of town, and Greg even got the bank to cough up

$300 for a typewriter. In fact, not much changed beyond the name. Nguzo Saba's RNA cadre led meetings and protests. They published a newsletter, Gregory Bronson, editor. They put on marches in paramilitary style, wearing uniform black and gold T-shirts and carrying big sticks—or, as they preferred to call them, batons. They organized citizens' patrols, shadowing the police in the black community with cars and cameras to watch for acts of brutality; a cop hard-timing a brother on the street would find himself playing to an audience of maybe a dozen scowling black men.

Ultimately, inevitably, they brought the fight to Greg's own bank, and when they did, his day and night personas became one. He discovered what seemed to him a plain pattern of discrimination in lending in the Summit-University section, St. Paul's main black neighborhood. There was plenty of mortgage and rehab money for white gentrifiers moving back in from the suburbs; yuppies in their Guccis and their Calvins were getting low-interest home-improvement loans meant for the working poor, while older black settlers had trouble borrowing anything at all.

Greg teased and nagged the personal bankers for a time, getting nowhere. He raised the problem at community meetings, with no strategy beyond getting people angry. Then, in the distinctly unrevolutionary pages of the *American Banker,* he stumbled on what would become his hole card: a Federal law requiring not only that banks make loans in the ghettos and barrios but that they advertise in minority papers and educate the people in the ABC's of banking and borrowing. Greg sent for a copy of the appropriate regulations and studied them down to the fine print. Then he marched on the officers of the bank, waving the regs under their noses and instructing them that they were violating the law.

His position was inarguable, grounded as it was in Federal black and white. The management began placing ads in the local black press. They posted the law in the lobby, behind a large potted plant, to be sure, but accessible to anyone with the will and the patience to find it. They agreed to put on a series of four seminars in the black quarter, a kind of elementary school in banking for people who had been shut out of anything much more exotic than passbook savings.

The seminars were Greg's idea, and he had to make a pest of

himself to get it through the bank board on the third try. His activities with Nguzo Saba outside the bank had come to the attention of the management through the daily papers, and his lobbying inside had done nothing to improve his standing; neither had his stubborn refusal to mix with his white colleagues except as business required it. In a field that favored team players, inconspicuous gray men in inconspicuous gray suits, Greg had become *controversial,* and so, by association, had Sherree.

The bank did not hide its displeasure with them. Greg missed out on a promotion he thought was his. Sherree had been promised a big raise and got a small one instead. They were victims of their own commitment and their own success at pushing through the series of seminars. By the time the third was held in the early spring of 1981, they were spectators in the crowd. They had got the intended message in their pay envelopes, and, one month apart, they had quit their jobs. The lady running the seminar didn't even give Greg credit for having thought of it; he packed a gun everywhere in those stressed-out days, and he was fighting down a sudden impulse to blow the woman away when Sherree did it for him, with words.

In retrospect, Greg felt he had been forced out of the bank. If it had been in him to conform, to play along as his father's generation had done, he could, he supposed, have achieved anything he wanted there; if he had sat on his feelings, he could have been the highest-ranking black person in the place. But he was committed, he thought, to something larger than his own success. He was black, and because he had dealt with his blackness, because he had made a bother about it, he had been punished economically as uppity black men had once been chastised with whips and ropes. He saw no choice except to leave, and if the Europeans who had run him out thought they had broken another black spirit, they were dead wrong. The fires of his animosity toward them burned brighter than ever.

They burned too brightly for Sherree. I have my principles, Greg had told her up front. They were fixed and immutable, he said. They would *never* change, he said; he was what he was. But what he saw as principle seemed to her something more like rigidity, an inability to bend on questions of color or anything else. She shared his political beliefs but not his visceral reaction to white people. She had grown up among them and had learned to coexist. Greg hadn't. He could deal with them smoothly on the job, sell them a copier or a car. Otherwise, he didn't like being around them. He and Sherree all but quit dining out at restaurants; he didn't want to be near whites in a social setting, let alone mix and mingle with them. That was one of his principles, he said, an elemental matter of self-defense. Sherree suspected otherwise; she began to wonder how comfortable he really felt inside his own skin.

Other fault lines were opening in their relationship. They were both between jobs and broke, which didn't help. Neither did Greg's wandering spirit. He took up with another woman, a lady named Carolyn he had met in the course of organizing tenants in a rundown black housing complex. He moved in with her. Sherree went home to her mother's place in the same complex. For a time, Greg commuted between the two of them. But his long liaison with Sherree was dying; she had already lost Greg when she discovered that she was carrying his child.

Their son was born in 1983, and Greg, at the high tide of his black period, named him Sundiata Malik Akil Bronson—Sundiata, "Hungering Lion," after a thirteenth-century Mali emperor; Malik, "First Born," because it was Malcom X's Muslim name; Akil, "One Who Has Wisdom," for his father. Sherree protested at first, thinking all that freight a bit heavy for a baby boy. Greg, as usual, was unyielding, and as usual, when he dug his heels in, he got his way.

What he could not have was Sherree. They made one last attempt to get their relationship back together. Greg proposed to her, begged her to marry him, but he wanted it for their son, not for them, and she told him no. She had tired of him and his principles, and was mistrustful of marrying just to be married; she believed in marrying for love. That wasn't what Greg was proposing, and she told him good-bye. She had herself grown up in a one-parent household and was undaunted by the prospect of raising a child alone. She was starting life over, she told Greg, alone with Sundiata in St. Paul.

So Greg, to his distress, became a largely absentee parent, one more father snatching visitation days with his son whenever he could and consoling himself that it was *quality* time. He took the responsibility seriously, as his own father had taught him to do. He still wished that it had worked out otherwise, that he could be with Sundiata full-time and teach him by example to be a man. But even at long distance, he had plans for his child. Sundiata would be an athlete—a pro tennis player, Greg hoped—and of course a black nationalist. He would have a sound, political Muslim education. He would be, most of all, a warrior, proud and brave, ready to go down fighting for what was his. He was not yet kindergarten age, but Greg could see that in him already.

Greg knew he would be uncomfortable at first if Sundiata one day took up the gun and joined the RNA, as he had; he vastly preferred that his son come of age in a world in which that would no longer be necessary. His own immersion in the affairs of the Republic, beginning before he left the bank and intensifying afterward, had been a harrowing time in his life, a time of paranoid dreams made real. He was on retreat with some fellow RNA citizens in the Minnesota woods when a neighbor blew out the windows with a shotgun; the gunman was found but never punished. Greg drove down to an encampment on the RNA's land in Mississippi for six weeks' military training; he was followed all the way there from Minnesota, and when he got back he felt it wise to disappear underground for a time. He went home to Chicago and was dogged across Wisconsin on the Interstate by a vanload of white boys; they didn't back off until he picked up his piece, a .38 revolver, from the seat beside him and pointed it straight at their petrified European faces.

That time was behind him now, a part of the night passage in his life. Kamau Akil survived in Greg's Manichean view of a world divided between the forces of light and of darkness. He still believed that the races were in the midst of a bloodless war in America and that to socialize with whites after the close of business was to collaborate with the enemy. He believed that geopolitics boiled down to a three-handed game of poker, the Americans and Russians colluding under the table against people of color everywhere. He believed in the example of the long-ago Guinean queen Nzingha, who stood fast against the Europeans while the rest of Africa fell; she made a boundary line around her village with their severed ears, and they left her alone.

Greg had in fact drawn just such a line in the landscape of his mind, and heaven help the Caucasian who stumbled across it; the control that got Greg through his days in the white world would come undone, and he would just go off. There was, for example, the incident at the tennis tournament in the summer of 1984, a black tournament that he and his father had helped organize in the suburbs south of Chicago. The entrants had gathered and were ready to start play when a white man walked out on the court with his woman, claiming it was their regular time. You never walk on a court when someone else was using it, Greg thought, but this man did; courts reserved in advance, signs all over announcing the tournament, people standing by waiting to start, and here he came with his arrogant white attitude as if the whole tennis club were his private property and *they* were trespassing.

Greg's father tried sweet reason, explaining patiently that a tournament was in progress and that the courts were booked. But it was plain the man was looking for a confrontation, and when he put a hand on Thomas Bronson's shoulder, grabbed him with that white paw and moved him aside, Greg exploded. He was all over the guy, so fast he knocked his own brother down getting there; the man was a head taller than Greg and maybe fifty pounds heavier, but Greg was pounding him on the back, slashing away with his Prince Pro tennis racket in a blind fury until some of the other players pulled him off.

The man called the police. The club management talked him out of pressing charges, and Greg was left alone before a higher court, his father.

"You know," the old man said sternly, "we're trying to run a tournament and we want to maintain the proper image—"

Greg was silent, marshaling his defense.

"—and you did get a little out of control—"

The judgment was in; all that remained was the sentence.

"—*but that was the right thing to do.*"

Greg smiled inwardly. Case closed.

He would never lose that warrior spirit, not while Thomas Bronson's blood ran in his veins; it was his father's legacy to him, and his to his own son. But the ardor that had brought Greg to the barricades in his RNA years had cooled a degree or two with his arrival at the threshold of middle age. Kamau Akil occupied less of his life and Gregory Bronson more.

BROTHERS

His life-style was black bourgeois, a fact he acknowledged to himself with faint embarrassment and the consoling thought that most serious revolutionaries in history had come from the middle class. He had made a great success selling cars, in St. Paul and, more recently, in Florida; his losing streak on the job market there ended abruptly when a large New York corporation hired him and put him in charge of his own used-car showroom in Orlando. His tennis game flourished in the southern sunshine—he gave it thirty or forty hours a week—and his love life finally stabilized. His latest lady was Beverly Dumas, a beauty in her middle twenties who worked for IBM in St. Paul. They had been together for two years when she got a transfer to Tampa to be nearer her parents. He had followed her to Florida for a look and had liked what he saw, well enough to stay. He and Beverly seemed to get on better living separately, but their relationship flowered, and they began talking seriously about marriage.

The duality remained in Greg's life, Bronson/Akil, the light and dark sides of his soul. He liked his job as long as it lasted, gliding through his showroom, all smiles and silken talk for his predominantly white clientele. The performance of it pleased him, the seductive small talk about golf scores and child-rearing and the bits of business wisdom cribbed from *Forbes* or *The Wall Street Journal*. So did the successive stages of play thereafter: assess the needs, address the needs, review it all, and *bang,* make the close. Greg was good at it and knew it; it brought him a mastery you were seldom privileged to feel as a black man trying to make it in white America.

But it wasn't made to last. Some of the company's promises dematerialized, pledges about money and control; he had barely got through his first summer when a new manager, a European, was brought in over his head, along with a new and less favorable schedule of commissions and bonuses. The events did nothing to quiet the voice of Kamau Akil inside him, the suspicion that corporate white America would never treat a black man fairly. He took a long retreat in the winter, driving north in Beverly's Toyota to see his parents and his son and to think things over. When he came back, he quit. The home office in New York asked him to reconsider his decision. He declined. He had thought it through and had decided to go into the construction business back in Chicago with his younger brother, Paul, as his partner.

The choice this time was more Bronson than Akil, a question of self-awareness rather than politics. Greg, in his journey north, had concluded that he simply wasn't built to work within the system. Some guys could, he thought, some *black* guys, if only they were given the chance. There was Ray Stingley, for one example, and Vest Monroe, for another; they were making it. Greg himself had been, and could still be, a first-rate salesman. But he was too stubborn, too proud, too black in spirit and soul; he took things too personally to survive comfortably in white corporate America. He had to be his own man, and the realization brought him a kind of comfort. He might always live at war with the way things are in the world, but he was finding a measure of peace with himself.

"I'M ONLY ME"

Steve Steward sat on the Chicago lakefront one day in the summer of 1986 in his old lady's Audi 5000S, gazing out over the sand and the water and seeing the waste of his own life. He had been wired on coke and PCP when he and Vest Monroe started out for the beach, and while Vest sipped a 7-Up, Steve worked on a bottle of Bartles & Jaymes wine cooler, easing himself down from his high to a soft landing. They had set out on an equal footing twenty years before, two promising black schoolboys with tickets out of the poverty of the projects. Vest had made it, to Harvard and *Newsweek*. Steve had not. He had got caught in the undertow, and all he could think of to say in his own favor at thirty-five was that he *looked* good in his designer suits, his Italian shoes, and his woman's $27,000 ride, and that he was surviving. His whole life was a front, he knew that; it brought him pleasure and pain; only now, in a car on the lakefront, it was the pain talking.

"I don't know, man," he said. "I'm a failure. I'm a failure."

What he didn't understand was why. If he could figure that one out, he might yet be *somebody,* like Jesse Jackson was always saying, instead of just another day-at-a-time brother living off his lady and waiting to hit the Lotto. "It's like you want to be more than you are," he told Vest, staring out at the water, "but why be more than you are? You know?"

A drifter wandered by the car, a tattered scarecrow with his worldly goods bundled on his back. Steve studied his passage, with something like recognition in his eyes. He knew what it was scuffling through life with your ego—your soul—on E for empty.

"Everybody has a falling point," he said, gesturing toward the derelict. "Just like this old boy right here. Look at him: cool in the game, got his backpack, movin' on out, and if he stops, he stops. F it."

Steve had stopped somewhere between his school years and the rest of his life. His father, Govenor Steward, was a janitor who burned out trying to provide for a wife and five children. He left Steve's mother alone with the kids when they were all still shorties, and Steve was raised on her welfare check and her enveloping love. Vest's mother had been a goad to his success. Steve's, with a tenth-grade education and a stalemated life, demanded nothing of him but his presence, elfin and adoring, in her train.

He became, by his own description, a mama's boy, and she in turn kept a slack rein on the mischief in him. While his pals at Prairie Courts, Greg and Vest and Ray Stingley, were hitting the books, he was strewing thumbtacks on chairs and running a penny-pool game on a desk in class. He was a bright child, a whiz at math, but his schoolwork was too easy for him, and in the peer-pressured world of boys in the ghetto, he didn't want to look like a bookworm. The worst fate in his young life was to be perceived as different, a non-member of the gang. School was something you had to do, nothing more. You didn't have to excel at it; it was best, he figured, to lay back in the pack and study just enough to get by.

It was, even then, as if he had been assembled without an inner

compass. He dawdled over filing his application for an ABC scholarship, and even when he got it, along with his ticket to Hanover
High in New Hampshire, he wasn't exactly racing for the plane. His
first concern had been that he would be leaving home; hey, the projects are where I grew up at, he thought, and the notion that it was
somehow redemptive to travel halfway across the country and live
with white folks was not wholly persuasive to him. His second reservation was his unease about being set apart from the crowd he had
grown up with. What, he wondered, was everybody else gonna think?
He was in no great hurry to find out.

As it turned out, he rather enjoyed it. His people made a great
to-do over his good fortune. His moms somehow squeezed enough
money out of her welfare check to buy him a couple of nices to wear,
a velour shirt and a pair of pants; his father showed up out of the
past with a new overcoat; his neighbors in the projects invested their
own dreams in him. "Go and show them what people from the projects are *like*," a lady at Prairie Courts had told him the day he left.
It made him feel a little important just getting on the airplane. It was
like *wow*, he remembered years later, everybody's looking at me. I'm
gonna be somebody. I'm really going to make it.

He spent his ABC years commuting between two worlds, the black
ghetto where he felt at home and the white college town where he
never quite stopped being a stranger. He had not realized how poor
the projects were until he saw how the other half lived; he bunked in
a house on the Dartmouth campus with seven other ABC students,
all children of poverty like himself, but they lived surrounded by an
affluence they had previously glimpsed only on TV. Steve went into
culture shock. He survived in part by flaunting his ghetto background, making a style of it instead of a mark of shame. He played
the tough guy, the gang-banger from Chicago with a switchblade and
a quick attitude; once he actually drew the blade on a white classmate
who made some racist remark and might have cut him if his ABC
buddies hadn't got between them. He was still more boy than man,
a gangly late adolescent, and the role wasn't really him. But it seemed
to play well with most of his schoolmates, a thousand miles from the
projects, and the ones who didn't dig it were scared to test him. Hey,
man, that dude's from *Chicago*. He'll *hurt* you.

He did well enough with his studies, and his faculty advisers urged him toward Dartmouth. He agreed to go for an interview, then dropped out of the running without even filing a formal application. It wasn't rejection that scared him but acceptance; he pictured the whole town of Hanover in an uproar because some qualified white students didn't make it while a poor black boy from Chicago did. The prospect awakened his anxieties at being set apart, at seeming different from everyone else. It was, spiritually speaking, a fear of flying, a terror of heights that would be with him all his life, and he quieted it by going to ground. He wanted a school where he could make it on his own, he told himself, and he found one in Northwestern University, a seductive fifteen-minute elevated ride from home.

Hey, I'm gonna be myself, he thought when he enrolled; his life at Hanover had been closely supervised, but he was a college man now, and he could do whatever he wanted to do. His liberation turned out to be his undoing. He lasted less than three years at Northwestern, much of the time on academic probation. His nominal major was political science. His real interest lay in street pharmacology, first doing and then dealing drugs. The taste was one he had acquired only after his supposed deliverance from the ghetto and its bad influences. He was first turned on to reefer and hash by a white schoolmate at Hanover; his off-the-books education at Northwestern, guided by a white roommate from New York, led him into stronger stuff, a witch's brew of coke, speed, acid, mescaline, and PCP.

He graduated quickly from user to trafficker and from neighborhood drugs like weed and hash to a full-service line of uppers, downers, and hallucinogens. His growing business left no room in his life for school. Not everyone was made for something, he figured, and maybe he wasn't made for college, not right then anyway. His sole surviving interests at Northwestern were the highs, the money, and the regular el trips home to the projects. He barely cared when, midway through his junior year, he was summoned before a dean with ten other failing scholarship students and expelled for nonattendance. The dean was not unsympathetic; she told him to take a year off, get himself together, and come back for a second try. He wasn't interested. Hey, he thought, drugs were cool, school wasn't—it was as simple as that.

His old partners Vest and Ray came up to help him pack and deliver him from his dorm to Prairie Courts with his things. His single worry was what his moms would say, but she as usual was forgiving. It wasn't in her to say, well, hey, I'm gonna whip your butt for getting kicked out. "Whatever you want to do, son, that's all right with me," she told him. He guessed she might be secretly happy to have him back home.

He idled for a few months, then went to work at the main post office downtown as a mail handler and later a clerk.

"Congratulations," one of his faculty sponsors wrote from Hanover, masking whatever disappointment he felt. "Make the most of it. Steve, you could be whatever you want to be." But what Steve wanted most was to be free of all that—free of choice and responsibility; free of other people's expectations of him.

His mind was still lively. He read widely and avidly, current affairs mostly, and economics; there was a time in his young adulthood when his friends rarely saw him without a book. But he had no vocation for work—nothing, that is, that the post office couldn't satisfy. The job was untaxing, the way he liked it, and the opportunities were irresistible: a steady wage, a smorgasbord of single women, and an open market for his growing trade in drugs. He was investing a whole paycheck at a time in powders and pills and turning them over as fast as he got them. The money was piling up, and he never wanted for some kind of something for himself. His favorite was mint leaf, a blend of kitchen herbs and angel dust, but he did them all. Drugs raised him to a higher level of consciousness, or so he thought; they were the source of his *outwardness,* a substitute for the glow of success to light his way through the world.

His charm when he was high was potent, even aphrodisiac, or so he imagined at the time. It was when he came down that his head got bad and his temper turned evil. No woman seemed beyond his charm when he was mellowed out; something in his eyes and his crooked smile caught them, a survival of the impishness and the vulnerability of the boy at Prairie Courts. It didn't matter what he said to them. He was sitting out on the steps at Dunbar High one day when he spied a girl in her twenties, an amber beauty named Pam, walking through the neighborhood with a friend.

"Do you smoke reefer, baby?" he sang out, skipping the verbal foreplay.

"No," she answered firmly, but the next day she was back in the neighborhood in her late-model Mustang, looking for *him*.

He was similarly direct with Beverly, lean and dark, when he met her on the night shift at the post office. They had crossed paths a number of times but had never spoken, until he finally told her it would mean something if they kept running into one another.

She smiled and said nothing, that time, but in short order they met again.

"Can I help you take your blouse off?" Steve asked.

"What are you talking about?" she demanded.

"I told you if I kept running into you, it was going to mean something," he said.

"And were you deliberately running into me?"

"No, I wasn't," he lied, and then: "Can I have your phone number?"

She gave it to him.

"I have a girlfriend, you know," he warned her.

"I'm not trying to steal you from anybody," she said.

A couple of days later, he came around to her place in a luxury high rise on the lakefront. He was stoned, but she didn't know it until he rolled a joint for her; she had never smoked reefer before and didn't know what it could do. All she saw was that Steve was dressed to kill and sweet as Prince Charming. She knew she should be on her guard; anyone that nice had to have something wrong with him, she told herself, or he'd be taken by somebody else. But Steve overwhelmed her fragile defenses. She was in love, and when Pam kicked him out a year later, Bev took him in.

Both women stayed in his power, Bev his anchor, Pam his toy. Each knew about the other, and each was aware that they were not his only ladies; it struck Bev that she had seen more of him when he was just coming around to visit than she did after he moved in. Once, in their first summer, the phone rang at her place. Bev picked it up and said hello.

"What are *you* doing there?" a woman's voice said at the other end of the line.

"I *live* here," Bev said.

She knew the caller; it was another of Steve's girlfriends from the post office. Bev was furious. She stayed home from work that day, and when Steve came in, she was waiting.

"What are you doing here?" he asked.

"I've heard that one already today," she said.

"What do you mean?"

"Your friend called," she said, "and asked me what am I doing here."

"You mean to tell me you stayed home just for that?" Steve demanded; he couldn't believe she would sacrifice a day's pay to her one-way love.

She understood that it was one-way. Once, she asked Steve how many women he had on the string at that particular moment in time, and he said, "Four," as tonelessly as if it were the time of day. He set down their names and numbers carefully in an old school notebook, a tour guide to his transient pleasures of the flesh. Bev found it once and started to cry, not out of shock—she was past surprise at his infidelities—but out of anger at being reduced to an entry in a catalog.

When Steve came home that night, he found his things in suitcases, packed and waiting at the back door.

"I'm fed up, Steven," Bev shouted through her tears. "Why don't you just get out of my life?"

"I don't need you," he shouted back. "I can go anywhere I want to go."

Her resolve was melting. "You know, Steven, you need to grow up," she said. But he couldn't, and she wasn't strong enough to do without him. He stayed.

By then he was wholly dependent on Bev, not for love but for money. She worked days as a teacher and nights at the post office. He effectively retired in 1979, awarding himself a leave of absence without bothering to notify his superiors; they responded by firing him, and he never went back to work, at the post office or anywhere else. His contribution to the economics of the household thereafter was to chauffeur Bev from job to job and draw her bath when she came home, if he chanced to be there. She bought his clothes, and furnished his ride, and advanced him money. I need $100, or $200, or $500, he would tell her, and she would hand it over. All she wanted from him was a smile, she thought, but he treated her like she was a bank; she gave everything and got nothing in return.

And yet she stayed in spite of everything—in spite of his insults and his neglect; in spite of his mint leaf and his women; in spite of a long, frightening time in which he seemed to be free-falling out of control. One day, stoned on PCP, he was arrested for bashing gays on the streets of downtown Chicago; the victims declined to prosecute, and the case was dropped. He was busted again for possession of drugs, six bags of primo Bo reefer and four tabs of preludes; this time, as a first offender, he was put in a drug-abuse program instead of jail.

But Steve was beyond rescue by a series of Saturday morning seminars. He was still doing drugs, and they brought him close to the edge of madness, so close that he was twice bundled off to a mental hospital and held down under restraint. The first time, buzzed on TAC, he whacked a drunk in a dry cleaner's, then picked a losing fight on a bus; he was kept under observation for five days. The second, flying on PCP, he got caught wandering around a shopping center wrapped in a bed sheet, with nothing on underneath. His mother brought some clothes to the hospital. He found two tabs of acid in a pocket, left over from a Funkadelic concert the week before. He took one, on top of the mint leaf he had been smoking. The next thing he knew, he was on the floor hallucinating a sniper attack, with a guard's knee planted firmly on his neck.

He spent the two ensuing weeks in slo-mo, dosed with Thorazine to keep him quiet. Till then he had rarely met a drug he didn't like, but Thorazine was zombie S, a form of walking death. On his discharge he headed straight for Pam's place, looking for his stash of mint leaf.

"Where's my S?" he asked her.

"Steve, you don't need that," Pam said.

"*Where's my S, girl?*" he repeated. Steve could be mean, even violent, when he was straight, and you didn't cross him lightly. Pam surrendered his leaf, and he smoked it for four days. He had to, he said, just to get back up to thirty-three rpm's.

To the people in his orbit, all but his adoring moms, he seemed never to make it. His life drifted in a lazy downward spiral, a commuter ride to nowhere with station stops at his mother's place, and Bev's, and Pam's, and the homes of such other women as would comfort him for a night or a week. Most of them gave him money; and the notion of work, of a career and a steady check, slid further and further beyond his powers of comprehension. A sense of failure haunted him, a pang of regret at having let down the people who, in his youth, had clothed him in their own hopes. "*Damn*, Steve, I expected to see you in a big office doing this and doing that," an old homie from the projects would tell him. He never answered; there was nothing he could say. He avoided Leroy Lovelace for years after his ABC experience came to grief. When they finally did meet, pupil and teacher, he wanted to say, "Well, Mr. Lovelace, give me another chance." The words stuck in his throat; he could not look his old mentor in the eye, for fear of the disappointment he might find there.

He did make one last pass at school, in accounting, in the fall and winter of 1985–86, putting down the last $10 in his pocket for the application fee. He could still get back in that row, he thought at the time; he could still be somebody, before he was forty.

He worked hard at it for a while, but the dream withered before he turned thirty-six, and he dropped out. His fellow ABC students were making it, Vest in journalism, Ray in medical-supply sales, and so was Greg Bronson, who had never had that helping hand. Steve encountered Greg at a dinner one night at Army & Lou's restaurant, and was impressed by his sharp clothes and his deep Florida tennis tan. "Damn, Gregory looks good," he said afterward. "If he wasn't so softhearted, he could be a pimp." The notion that a man could do so well and look so good in the straight-up life was no longer within his ken.

Beverly remained *his* meal-ticket, and his resentment toward her seemed to grow with his dependence on her two-income bank balance. He saw her as a kind of inexhaustible resource, still there even though he'd be out looking at other chicks. She wasn't one of those ifsy-ifsy women, threatening to put you out if you did this or if you didn't do that; she was more for him than for herself, and while it

caused him pangs of guilt, he came to accept her charity as his due.
I like Bev, I live with Bev, I be with Bev, he told Vest one day; I
do for her, and she does for me. But Bev was not him, he went on,
and she knew it. He had told her so. She needed a relationship, and
he gave her that. What she couldn't have was his name. He wasn't
into that. He wasn't the marrying kind.

Bev's goodwill was not in fact as limitless as he imagined. He
bruised her feelings daily with his carelessness, and she had begun
to look on him as her enemy. They were sitting in her car one day
when a black woman walked by, pretty and petite, on somebody
else's arm.

"*That's* the type of woman that I'd like to marry," Steve said,
and then: "You know, Bev, I could never love you."

Bev wanted to melt, sitting there in her anger and shame. She
was a damn fool, she thought, for putting up with him, and yet she
could not help herself. She hated Steve and loved him; she liked him
and didn't like him. Sometimes she thought she should see a psychi-
atrist, except that she *knew* what she was doing. It was just that she
could not stop.

Neither, it appeared, could Steve. His real home, to the extent he
had one, was his mother's flat in Prairie Courts, back where he began. Vest and his *Newsweek* colleague Vern Smith visited him there
one day in the spring of 1986, rapping repeatedly at the broken screen
door before Steve finally appeared.

"Hey, Monroe," Steve said, as casually as if the distance that
had opened between them could be measured in minutes instead of
light-years. "What's poppin' with you?"

"Nothin' much, bro," Vest answered. "Just looking for you."

They had interrupted Steve cleaning up after his kid sister Leslie's
four little boys—"trying," he said half apologetically, "to help my
moms get these little shorties squared away." Leslie was in the joint,
doing time for petty larceny; she had been in and out since 1981, and
Mrs. Steward had crowded her sons into her Spartan three-bedroom
apartment. She had just fed them a lunch of red beans and rice, and
Steve was mopping up the mess they had left on the dinette table.
The boys scattered to the living room, bare except for two worn and
soiled sofas. Two of them, Lance and Phelano, had had meningitis

of the brain. Lance, the older, stared out a window. Phelano sat on one of the sofas. Neither spoke. A third brother, Antonio, a toddler, leapt into Vest's arms, hugging him tight around the neck. Vest hugged back and tried to set him down. Antonio wouldn't let go.

Steve's mother appeared from a back bedroom, a short, plump woman in her fifties with a look of permanent weariness in her smile and her eyes. She greeted Vest, her manner friendly and wary all at once. Vest talked about the story he was working on. He would need to speak with her, he said; he wanted her perspective on how Steve had turned out.

"My son turned out just *fine,*" she said. She smiled broadly, but there was an edge of accusation in her tone. "You got something up your sleeve, Sylvester?"

Vest said no.

"Steve's the only one of my children that hasn't left me," she said. "He's never going to leave me. Are you, baby?"

Steve busied himself wiping the last crumbs of rice from the dinette table.

"Steve's *never* going to get married," Mrs. Steward said, " 'cause I don't want him to get married."

She was still smiling, making a joke of it. Steve swabbed the table, saying nothing.

Alma Steward was in fact central to his life, the only woman he knew, he liked to say, who could get his money without asking for it. He had been born sickly, like too many children in the ghetto, and she had cosseted him back to health; he had always been her favorite, and if he felt rooted anywhere, it was in her sheltering presence.

Otherwise, there was an insubstantiality to his life behind the front of prosperity he had so carefully built, or, rather, borrowed from the women who looked after him. He was, he thought, totally non-existent so far as the workaday world was concerned; it was as if he cast no shadow. All he had to show for his trackless passage was his person and his depleted inner resources. All I am, he thought, is *me.*

"I wasn't a venturer," he told Vest, sitting out on the lakefront in Bev's Audi. "I didn't have an ego. So without an ego, you can't go nowhere. I guess that was my downfall. I didn't think of myself as being no more than just me. So when you're just for yourself, satisfied with what is, you say, well, hey—it's cool. Maybe I could have had it, but then I didn't, so why cry about it?"

Steve nursed the last of his Bartles & Jaymes. Vest said something about ego being the fuel for a man's ambition.

"Right, right, right," Steve said, "but who supplies the fuel?" No one had for him, not his moms or his teachers or his peers, and he had come to that falling point like the bum on the beach; he didn't give a F anymore, and he had quit. "It's like being on a basketball team," he said, "and a MF says to you, 'Hey, man, you gonna play today?' 'Naw, man, I'm not gonna play today. F it.' " So things had got F'd up, and he was a failure.

"At what?" Vest asked.

At life, Steve was saying; it had all been easy-grab, easy-give, and he had nothing to show for it. "I mean, I'm *surviving*," he said. "I'm at that level where a MF will say, 'Well, he might not have any money, but he *looks* OK.' But if you ain't got no money, you can't go nowhere. If you don't have any skills, you can't go anywhere. I got lost in the shuffle. I got lost in the shuffle because I didn't want to shuffle along. I didn't give a F. I didn't care. It didn't matter."

"I wouldn't call you a failure," Vest said. The gloom in the car was getting heavy.

"Well, you know, a failure in the respect that . . ." Steve paused. "I would love to say that this is my car. But it's not. I have to manage the situation to have it be considered my car. I only equip myself for what I want. You know, when you don't have to do nothing for anybody but yourself, why do anything for anyone? You know? I'm only me. Laissez-faire. That's the approach that I took, man, and it's F'd up, but it's cool with me."

"Are you happy, man?" Vest asked.

"Happy? What is happy?"

"You say it could be better, but it could be worse."

"Yeah, it could be worse," Steve said.

"But are you satisfied? Are you *content?*"

"Content? Naw. I would like to springboard into something. But what? That's the challenge. It's like *damn*—can I still bounce back? Make a supermiraculous move?"

"What's a good day for you?" Vest asked.

"A good day?" Silence filled the car while he thought about it. "Damn, I don't know," he said at length. "Maybe I never had a good day. I don't know what a good day is."

They talked for a while more, two old friends from the projects musing on life and love, drugs and money, success and failure. It was all a playground, Steve said, and he was playing it for what it was. "If you want to get big," he said, "you have to get bigger. If you don't want to get big, that's cool; life is just life. Prosperity doesn't fall for everybody, man. Everybody can't get the bright lights. Really, man, I don't have it, but I'm cool. Situations pursue me to the point where I say, 'Well, hey, Steve, you made it through another day.' "

The Bartles & Jaymes was gone, and so was the last of his high. He turned the ignition key in his lady's Audi and put the radio up high, a blast of synthesized soul. "You wanna go by and see Pam?" he asked. "I'm wondering what's up with this chick." In the worst of times, he thought, you could have the best of times. F it, he thought. I just want to be me.

THE ORGANIZATION MAN

Ray Stingley had never wanted to walk through life with just RAY STINGLEY on his business card. He wanted a title, something to hand that sucker on the other side of the desk authenticating who he was and how far he had come from the projects. When he was asked during a job evaluation where he wanted to go next in The Company, he was not bashful about his ambition. Regional manager, he said. Period. He made himself not think about it thereafter, knowing it would get in the way of his work if he sweated it too much; instead, he did what he had always done, which was take care of today's business today and worry about tomorrow tomorrow. But when the call came from the home office in New Jersey in May 1986, advising him that there was an opening for manager of the Gulf states region, Ray had his answer rehearsed and ready. "I would like to have that job," he said. "What do I have to do to get it?"

What he had to do, besides clearing it with his wife, was to be himself—the quintessential Organization Man, restyled in black and updated for the eighties, climbing up the corporate ladder toward that state of well-being called success. He had not precisely been born in rags and had not yet attained riches, but his life was nonetheless a page out of the Horatio Alger canon: the kid from the ghetto with empty pockets and dim eyes getting over in a world once as distant and mysterious to him as China. He had been helped at critical points by the vogue for affirmative action of the 1960's and 1970's, when the situation of the black poor weighed more heavily on our national conscience than it would in a less generous present. What made those measures work for him was that he was himself an affirmative actor, a bright, tough, competitive man with a straight-ahead sense of where he had been and where he wanted to go.

He sometimes wondered if his success might have come earlier and more easily if he had been born white. He supposed that it would have. Face it, he thought, white folks run this thing; there was no getting around it, it was the way things were. He reckoned further that there was no point dwelling on it. Coming up poor in the projects taught you not to cry about what you didn't have or couldn't change; you just did the best you could with what you had and trusted God to do the rest. Ray's blackness was a fact of life he couldn't alter even if he had wanted to, which he didn't. He was living with it, comfortably, thank you; he was going to do all right.

He had, he thought in retrospect, been one of the lucky ones. The doors enclosing black people in the ghetto had opened a crack and he had squeezed through, into a life he hadn't even known *existed* until he got there. He had grown up in the projects thinking that that life was off limits for black men—that you had to be a ball player to make it up and out—and his years in white schools had not greatly lifted his sights. He was working in a cable factory in St. Louis, his B.A. and his teaching certificate gathering dust in some drawer somewhere, when he heard a radio ad for blacks interested in careers in sales. What the hell I got to lose, he thought, and with no more hope than that, he applied.

He had already begun a family, little more than halfway through Albion College. He and Aline Thomas, then a freshman from St. Louis, had met across the steam tables at the college cafeteria one evening in the fall of his sophomore year; she was serving, and as he paused on the line with his tray, they exchanged a flirtatious few words. Their eyes met, hers warm and smiling, his large and innocent behind his thick glasses. It was, they realized afterward, love at first sight.

Ray had been a skylarky student till that moment, about work and women. He had coasted along enjoying his independence of his parents and his deliverance from the all-male, no-nonsense life he had led at military school; his mornings no longer began in the half light with some little plebe sounding reveille and singing out the uniform of the day, and his nights no longer ended with his folks fussing over what time he got to bed. At college he was free for the first time. There were black students at Albion, some of them girls, and Ray had spent most of his first two years chasing them; he was like a kid in a candy factory, partying nonstop.

But as his romance with Aline ripened, his intentions turned urgent. He had found the woman he could take seriously enough to love; she looked pretty, spoke the truth, and had good sense, and she loved him the way he loved her. They could, he supposed, have moved in together like a lot of people their age were doing. Ray wasn't made that way. He was responsible—his parents had taught him that—and he was possessive; if you're going to be my woman, he thought, then come be my woman for *real*.

They were sitting in her dorm room one Saturday evening when, almost casually, he broached the subject to her. That was Ray: Jump right in with both feet and see what happens.

"Hey," he said, "why don't you call your mama and tell her we're going to get married?"

"OK," she answered, just as casually, and she did.

When Ray told his parents, they were distressed, not by his choice but by his timing. His father, who rarely called him at school, was on the phone that night.

"Hey, man, whyn't you wait and get out and have some *fun* first?" he asked.

Ray wasn't budging, and his father didn't argue the matter further; he had raised his son in his own resolute image, and he could tell from the tone of Ray's voice on the phone that his mind was made up.

His mother was more persistent. She wrote him, begging him to reconsider. She was afraid that he would leave school if he married so young, and that his prospects for a better life would be gone.

"Mama, I promise you I'm going to finish," he told her. "I'm not going to let you down."

He didn't, though his new responsibilities made a herculean labor of it. He and Aline were married on New Year's Day 1972, in St. Louis, with Ray's old friend Vest Monroe as best man. A baby girl, Dione, was born a year later; two boys, Corey and James, would follow. Ray suddenly found himself a family man, studying days, working nights in a foundry and napping when he could. Not surprisingly, his grades dropped to bare survival level; one more year, he guessed afterward, and he might not have made it through at all. In his last semester, he was student-teaching besides, working toward that certificate as a kind of doomsday insurance on the future. Growing up in the ghetto left you with a contingent sense of life; he had no intention of teaching *no* damn body, he thought, but he wanted the credential in case he had to.

He never used it; he graduated instead from Albion to the cable factory at twice what he would have made as a teacher and stayed until that radio commercial piqued his interest in sales. Corporations were actively shopping for black faces then, trying to improve their equal-opportunity numbers, and one of the food industry giants took Ray on as a beginning salesman back home in Chicago. Affirmative action had got his foot in the door; the rest, he figured, was up to him.

The on-the-job training was excellent, much of it supervised by his district manager, Rich Green, himself a black man of hard-sell

technique and ferocious temper. Green yelled and threatened and bul-
lied like a drill instructor in boot camp, and his people quaked at his
approach, the blacks no less than the whites. He was if anything
harder on the brothers under his sway than on anyone else, on the
theory that you didn't help anyone with preferential treatment.

But Ray learned a lot from him, about ingratiating manners and
unobtrusive dress, about hitting the street early and hard and staying
there, knowing that the answer was going to be no more often than
yes; about doing your homework the night before a call and selling
with facts and figures instead of that Willy Loman shine on your
shoes. Green's most valuable lesson of all was that a black man *could*
aspire to management and didn't have to be Superman to get there.
Hey, S, Ray thought, sizing up Green like a rookie shortstop measuring the incumbent, if you can be the boss, I can be the boss, too,
somewhere—only, he promised himself, I'll try not to yell so much.

His path there was long and his résumé checkered. His gyroscope
never faltered, although, for a passage early in his career, it looked
as if it might. His two-year apprenticeship in Chicago was a costly
one. The pay was low, $12,000 a year, less than he had made in the
cable factory, and the city was expensive. The bills for his young
household were piling up faster than he could pay them.

He was used to coming home nights to a house filled with laughter, but the burden of debt was straining his marriage, and he realized
one day that the laughter had stopped. This isn't *us,* he thought. The
sense of family he had inherited from his parents was strong, almost
in his genes; his wife and children were his responsibility, and he
could not bear the possibility of losing all they had struggled so hard
to build. He did what he had to to save the situation. He quit the
food company and moved back to St. Louis, where the living was
cheaper. Then he went into bankruptcy to get the posse of creditors
off his heels.

The armistice got him on his feet again, and the same agency that
had placed him with the food company put him in a new and more
rewarding line, health-care products, first pharmaceuticals, then medical supplies. He found a professional home as well, after several
bounces, with a new home-health outfit called ConvaTec, a division
of the Squibb Corporation with a specialty in paraphernalia for osto-

mates—people who had had surgery for cancer and other disorders of the intestines and the urinary tract.

Ray was a natural salesman, well spoken and confident, good at selling himself as a prelude to selling a product. He had the additional gift of being an intensely competitive man, as sore a loser in business, he reckoned, as Vince Lombardi had been in football. But his new line made life easier for him. He loved his wares and his work with an ardor far beyond the store-bought loyalty of the company man. He really *believed* that the items in the sample case he lugged around his six-state territory were the best on the market, and because he believed in them, he sold them better. His way was further eased by the fact that he was dealing with professionals who understood his products and with patients who needed them to survive. There was no BS about the color of his skin, no room for that S whatever. People had to look past him at his product. All they judged you on was whether what you were selling could help someone in trouble. Petty prejudices melted; no one cared what color you were when your business was adding years to people's lives.

His fortunes took off with ConvaTec's. Its sales force quintupled in five years, and Ray himself was doing more business in less territory; he was working the St. Louis area and its surrounding counties in eastern Missouri and southern Illinois instead of his old six-state sprawl. He was prospering nicely when the call he had been waiting for came in the spring of 1986, offering him the Gulf states territory. He would be the second youngest regional manager in the company, and the first black man ever to rise so high in sales.

The corner of America they awarded him was, on its face, a mixed blessing, the weakest in sales among ConvaTec's seven districts. The eleven reps working the territory regarded his arrival, moreover, with wary eyes, not so much because he was black as because he was an outsider. Yes, his numbers were good, but two of the salesmen who would be working for him had wanted the job themselves and thought they should have got it.

But his manner was winning and his competitive spirit contagious. His first campaign promise to his people was that they weren't going to stay seventh in the standings; just because you start last doesn't mean you have to finish last, he said. He did a reinforcing swing around the circuit, making calls with his reps and putting them at ease with him. He had a temper but had mastered it over the years, with great effort. It was a matter of pride with him that he no longer yelled at anyone except his dog.

He meant to keep it that way. He didn't want his reps to dread his arrival, as he had once lived in terror of Rich Green. He was an informal man, underneath the Kuppenheimer pinstripes, the starchy white shirts, and the generous applications of cologne. He liked a Marlboro Light and a beer or a brandy, and the comradeship of the road; the life ought to be about having fun, because if you were having fun, he believed, you were going to do a better job.

He wanted to work with his reps as his peers, not his employees, a point he made in small symbolic ways on his first tour of the territory. He carried his own bags and opened his own car doors; the message was that he thought of the field force as his equals, not his servants, and that he hoped in time to make them his friends. He didn't want them losing sleep about seeing him, thinking, Oh, S, here comes that son of a bitch. He wanted them to be *glad* to have him in town and to bring him their problems, not hide them from him. He wanted relationships with them. He wanted them to see their stake in his success, as he saw his own stake in theirs.

His formula appeared to be working in his first months on the job; his team climbed from seventh to sixth on the sales charts by summer, and he meant to keep them moving on up. He could remember a time in his childhood when he had no idea that there *were* jobs like this, let alone that he might hold one. All he had known then was what he wanted. He promised himself, when he was a very young man, that he would have a house of his own by the time he was thirty-five. He didn't have a master plan for getting there; he had no idea what he would be doing for a living. He knew only that he wanted that house. If he achieved that measure of size and place in the world, he figured, everything else would take care of itself.

He turned thirty-five in the fall of 1986, and the house he occupied, in Atlanta, was his third. He was not the sort to brood about whether, except for the accident of his birth and his boyhood poverty, he might have gotten there sooner. His career curve was upward-bound, his family was whole and healthy, and his life, so far as he could see into the future, looked groovy. He wouldn't trade places with anyone. The kid from the projects in Chicago was alive and well, and living the American Dream.

A PAUSE IN A JOURNEY

In the winter of 1986–87, twenty years after they had first left the projects for the larger and scarier world outside, Ray and Vest sat down to talk about what they had made of their lives. It had been a long and difficult journey, one they could not even have imagined when they were boys coming of age in the ghetto, and not everyone who began it with them had got over. There was Steve, for one example, all the way back at the starting line, living on borrowed love and money. There was Greg, for another, his promise still rich in his middle thirties and yet never quite fully realized. Ray had had dinner with him one night on a business trip to Florida, at a point when Greg was still job-hunting and feeling discouraged. He was as bright and talented as ever, but he was still hovering at the edge of success like a kid peering in a toy-store window; something in his genetic code, some strain of stubbornness or pride, seemed to keep him from going inside.

And there were the others, the men whose dreams had died in childhood or perhaps at birth. The ghetto is a place of stunted hopes and blighted aspirations, a city of limits in which the reach of realistic ambition is to survive. Ray and Vest had escaped. They had been both gifted and lucky. They had been nurtured by teachers and helped along at critical moments by affirmative action, but their success had begun at home, they agreed, with families who would not let their dreams die.

"A lot of my motivation came from that," Vest said. "From not wanting to disappoint people that I loved."

Ray agreed. "If I had a dime for every time I'd said, 'If it weren't for my mother,' I'd be rich right now. I could not have taken the looks of disapproval if I had given up."

So they had kept going, the two of them, and when they met again twenty years on, each had achieved a measure of success in the American mainstream; they were middle-class men with homes, kids, possessions, debts, and well-launched careers. It seemed like ages ago, Vest said, when they were boys sitting out on a snowbank in the ghetto, drinking rum and promising one another that they were going to make it.

"We've come a long way," he said.

"I agree," Ray said. "Got a long way to go."

"True," Vest said, but the promise in the snow still stood between them, no longer needing to be spoken. They would keep on keeping on.

PART VI

REFLECTIONS

It was homecoming time at Trey-nine, a Labor Day barbecue for some of the brothers who had come of age in the projects of Chicago twenty years before, and Half Man Carter, not wanting to miss anything, showed up early with his lady, Matilda, and an-

other couple. His friend's wife
announced that she wasn't getting
out of the car; she had grown up
in the Taylors, she said, and she
was scared she might catch some-
thing. But Matilda made straight
for the beer cooler—"I can hang
anywhere," she said—and Half
Man moved bandy-legged into the
crowd, sharp in red pants, a
white silk shirt, and a pair of Air
Jordans he was breaking in for
his son.

Old homies greeted him like
lost family, and Half Man an-
swered in kind, clasping their out-
stretched hands in both of his.
His eyes were bright, and a little
smile played at the corners of his

mouth. *He felt like a celebrity, a* rock *star or something, coming home to the old building, which was one reason he didn't visit that often. You come down here every day, he told himself, and people think you regular. Like* them.

Half Man wasn't like them, not those, anyway, who had got mired in the poverty of the projects. He had made a life's work of the difference. He wasn't no millionaire or nothing; the paint plant was on a seasonal shutdown, so one of his two paychecks had stopped, and his creditors were gaining on him. But he had lifted himself out of

the ghetto, paid *his way out with
his own hard, constant, and often
menial labor. He had a little
money in his pockets, and, just as
important to him, he had respect.
He could feel it in the way people
welcomed him back to Thirty-
ninth Street, treating him* special,
*he thought, 'cause he had moved
out to somewhere nicer and never
slipped back. They think I made
it, he guessed. Way they see it,
I'm doin' cool. Got a car, got a
roof over my head, got a nice-
lookin' woman, and they think
I'm high society. I might not have
much, he thought, but that's
more'n most of 'em got.*

Half Man Carter was born to what we have lately taken to calling the black underclass: a caste of men, women, and children tenanted largely in the private slums and public housing of our aging inner cities. Viewed from one angle, he does bear some of what are thought to be the identifying marks and scars of his beginnings near the low end of our social order. He grew up poor in tenements and projects, enclosed in the want of the ghetto; his only window on the larger world outside was television. He chanced to have been raised by two parents, but a majority of his friends were not, and his own mother and father were too careworn just getting by to provide him with much more than food and clothing. He quit school young. He got involved in drinking, gambling, and gang wars. He became a husband, a father, and a divorcé before he had reached manhood. His marriages and liaisons since have been numerous and short-lived. He has fathered three children, two of them out of wedlock and none living under his roof or his care. His jobs have typically been low-paid and impermanent; there have been so many that he cannot easily remember them all.

His life, in all these respects, could be said to be the fulfillment of statistical prophecy. The data weigh like a judgment on men born in the black core of our cities. They tell us that half to two thirds of the boys in the poorer ghetto districts will drop out of school; that one in six will have been arrested before he turns twenty; that black men are twice as likely as whites to be unemployed at any given moment; that they are far more often stuck for life in what Half Man calls ass-and-elbow labor, when they can find work at all; that a majority of their own children will be conceived out of wedlock and raised at least part of the time by single women on welfare; that they are disproportionately prey to all the sicknesses of our culture, from crime to drug abuse, and to all the ills of the flesh from cradle to early grave.

The statistics are daunting, to the people they portray and to the larger society. In our discouragement, we have all but given up trying to reverse them as an objective of public policy. The war on poverty is over—poverty won—and affirmative action is under siege everywhere. It has become our tendency, even our fashion, to see the underclass as permanent, its material and spiritual depression self-sustaining and beyond cure. It is said that the ghetto is in some ironic degree the victim of black success—that the flight of the best and brightest from the tenements and projects to better neighborhoods has drained the inner city of middle-class leadership and middle-class values. It is said that only the poor are left, and that they are caught in a pathological culture of poverty; their world is, the numerologists tell us, another country, a flip-side America where babies are made for bounty, work is a sometime thing, crime and welfare are the twin staffs of life, and law and order are impediments to the business and the pleasures of the street.

Yet charts and graphs can be another form of invisibility for black men, a handicap as well as an aid to understanding. To view the life of Half Man Carter as sociology is to see it in two dimensions: a life begun in poverty, stunted in adolescence, marked in adulthood by erratic patterns of work and marriage, lived without hope, plan, or regard for the future. There are no surprises in it for students of urban demography, except perhaps for his physical escape from the ghetto. The rest can be found in the *Statistical Abstract,* among others of the prophetic works of social science. Half Man was sentenced at birth to life on a treadmill; the numbers told us so.

The complications lie in that third dimension called the human soul. To meet Half Man unencumbered by numbers and theories is to discover a bright, competent, and likable man who *believes* in the bedrock values of American society and has tried all his life to live by them. He is the work ethic made flesh, a believer in paying his own way; he would take any job, however menial, at any wage,

however small, in preference to begging, borrowing, stealing, or subsisting on the dole. He has never asked much in return, only enough
to provide for himself and his family and to indulge a few modest
creature comforts on the side. But he has never quite achieved even
that for any sustained period of time. He has always worked, and has
seldom been much better off than working poor.

What was missing in his life was not the will but the way. There
was a certain shrewdness in his eyes, a street wisdom that had been
there when he was still only half a man growing up at Trey-nine. He
had looked into the future, contrary to the common judgment of social science on men like him, and concluded early on that there was
nothing in it for him—nothing, in any case, worth waiting or planning for. There were not many success stories in the projects, not
many middle-class men leading middle-class lives. People were there
because they were poor, and if their luck turned, they got out.

Yet working-class values somehow survived, stubborn and hardy,
in men like Pete Carter and his son Edward, known as Half Man.
Like most of his friends, Half Man wanted to work, and own a home,
and provide for a family, all classic elements of the American Dream.
But life in the projects gave them little ground for hope that they
could make it. Half Man and his friends grew up surrounded by unhappy endings, by men who were barely afloat and men who were
drowning. It was easy for a boy coming up in the projects to see
wasted lives as a judgment on black people, and unless you were Dr.
J or Marvin Gaye, with a talent tradable on the white entertainment
market, it was easier still to accept it as inevitable. Half Man read,
or sensed, the actuarial arithmetic and did not challenge it. Instead,
he dropped out of school and retired behind the boundaries around
his dreams.

His victory was that in the city of destruction, he never surrendered. Instead, through fat times and lean, Half Man kept on scuffling. That state of material grace we call success was beyond his
reach; he had not prepared himself to chase it, and white Americans
had never shared it freely with blacks, particularly the sons and
daughters of the black poor. So he settled early for what he could
get, which was the *appearance* of success. He liked having good
clothes, and a clean ride, and some paper in his pocket to buy his

friends a beer instead of having to beg one for himself. He liked having a nice lady on his arm, too, and the newer they were, the nicer they tended to be. It was when relationships got old that they tended to get stressed by questions of money, constancy, and child-rearing, *family* questions that mainly made you uncomfortable when you worked for a not-quite-living wage. A new lady didn't look too hard behind the surface of your prosperity and didn't nag you to do more; so long as the honeymoon lasted, you could keep her happy just sharing what little you had with her.

Men didn't ask questions of one another. They knew the game and played by common rules, each accepting the others at face value; if you didn't challenge somebody's earning power—which in America meant his manhood—he wouldn't challenge yours. In truth, except for Vest, the Trey-nine brothers were mostly just scraping along, working perishable jobs for nondescript money. But Half Man could come home for a cookout at the project that Labor Day and be received as if he were high society, not just a dude filling cans at a paint plant for his bread and doubling as a janitor in the predawn hours to keep a roof over his head. By unwritten law, nobody looked at your bank balance or your credit rating. They took you on your own terms.

Half Man, by those standards, was a success merely for having escaped the projects; he was the prodigal son come home. He mixed and mingled with the old crowd for a while, then drifted over to the basketball court and got into a game, Half Man and Honk against the world. His game was a little rusty, but when a rebound squirted out of the pack under the basket, Half Man scooped it up, dribbled clear of traffic, pulled up for a little jumper, and—*yes!*—knocked it down.

Off to the side, Sonny Spruiell and Ed Hamilton watched with appraising eyes.

"Ain't that Edward Carter over there?" Sonny asked.

"Yeah," Ed said.

"Good," Sonny said. "He owes me five dollars."

There were no illusions in the projects, either. A five was still money among the brothers, worth remembering and even carrying a grievance about. But Half Man, caught up in the game, didn't hear; he was enjoying the rediscovery of his jump shot and the glow of somebodyness he felt back at Trey-nine. He wasn't measured by the white man's standards there. He didn't have to be a doctor or a lawyer to be counted a success, or have a million dollars in the bank. Back home, among the brothers he had grown up with, he *counted*. He had a job, and a woman, and some walking-around money in his pocket. He was making it. He was a man.

Honk Johnson had come around fashionably late in the morning, walking his slo-mo walk, scanning the set with his face blank and his eyelids lowered to half-mast. His hair still flowed long then—his former friend Marvin had created the style for him—and the billed Big Apple cap riding the waves was made to match his beige linen leisure suit. More than any of the others, except maybe Pee Wee, he belonged at Trey-nine. Most of them had left, but not Honk, not really. Trey-nine was still his home, or anyway his family's, and his business territory as well.

The other guys had mostly scattered, moving up and out, the way the social engineers who built the projects meant for them to do. It was Honk who had stayed behind, the player clinging to the game like a great athlete hanging on past his time. The others had all changed. They had had their little walks on the wild side, a lot of them, their dalliances with gangs, hustles, and drugs, and some of them were still doing a little business on the side to stay above the poverty line. But they had started drifting away early, going into jobs and marriages and S, some while they were still in their teens. Half Man Carter, for instance; in the old days, Honk thought, Half Man was about the baddest little MF you wanted to see. And Sonny Spruiell; Sonny was kind of rough himself back then, a tough enough nigger to be Honk's partner on the corner for a while. But Half Man got married, and then Sonny, and after a while none of the old brothers were left on Thirty-ninth Street. They were mostly about working, and you hardly saw them around the 'hood anymore.

So Honk had had to look elsewhere, recruiting his mob. There were always plenty of willing bodies around the projects; these young niggers be tough, Honk thought, and in the good days he had been a kind of role model for them, his style and flash an advertisement for what money could buy. Guys wanted to run with him and did, studs with names like Chicken and Ca Ca and Midnight and Shotgun Al and Big Ed, or, as they sometimes called him, Dum-Dum, for the wide gaps in his jailhouse education. They were bad dudes, all of them, only they *began disappearing, too. Big Ed got iced in that dope-house robbery, his blood puddling on the pool table downstairs. Ca Ca was in jail, caught dirty sticking up a store; he was looking at forty-fifty years for armed robbery. Midnight went to the joint, too, a winehead and a dopehead when he checked in, an ordained minister when he came out. A reverend and all that S, Honk thought wonderingly, out here on Forty-seventh Street with his pamphlets and books and stuff; he was the only dude Honk ever knew to go to the penitentiary and come out clean.*

They kept vanishing, one by one, their hard lives and bad endings becoming the stuff of legend. Most of the niggers I come up with, Honk was thinking—the big majority of 'em dead or in jail. And now Honk himself, the prince of players, was penitentiary-bound; just when his boyhood friends from Trey-nine were getting their lives together, his was falling apart. He wondered what his legend would be, and how long it would last; how long before some young dude who had never liked him anyway said, "F it," and all the other players quit talking about what a hell of a nigger ol' Honk used to be.

Even at the low ebb of his life, one more soul on ice in the Shawnee slammer, Honk Johnson wasn't the kind to blame his environment for the way his biography had come out. His view of the world he grew up in, and the power arrangements that govern it, was deeply cynical. He accepted the dogma of an older generation of

Black Muslims that white folks were the devil, really believed it on the evidence of the ruin all around him on Thirty-ninth Street—them girls starving up in the projects with they babies; them studs drinking wine out on the block with nowhere to go beyond the bottom of that next bottle of Rose. The honkies put roofs over they heads for $80 or $90 a month, and gave them just enough welfare checks and food stamps to keep them fed, but all that benevolence was meant to keep them in the projects. You can't move out the MF. White folks don't want you out, and it's *they* world, he thought; *they* the ones made all this S.

Still, Honk did not favor a world view that portrayed him as victim, of economics, sociology, or anything except bad luck and a poor choice of companions on his last job. He was a believer in free will; he had sorted his options early in life and had made his choice—sure money now rather than smaller and less certain rewards later on. In this, he shared some of the spirit of his generation of Americans with certain younger traders on Wall Street and preachers on television, among other subscribers to the get-it-now ethic. The difference lay in the scale of their appetites and the means to their fulfillment; the ends of rich and instant gratification were approximately the same.

Honk had never seen any other kind of gratification worth pursuing. The most striking single fact about the world he grew up in, after its poverty, was its encapsulation—its remove from the world of possibilities open to whites and, lately, the black middle class. His analogy of Trey-nine to a prison was inexact, though only slightly; in spiritual fact, it more nearly resembled a concentration camp, where the larger society housed a population it feared, despised, and wanted out of sight. A boy stepping out his front door in the morning saw downtown Chicago, with its options and opportunities, through the barrier of penitentiary-grade steel mesh enclosing the project galleries. It was not a view that encouraged dreaming. That ambition survived at all owed to the stubborn refusal of a parent here or a teacher there to surrender their children to the odds. They urged, against the weight of the available evidence, that there *were* possibilities for a poor black child. They taught further that to seize them you had to be twice as good and work twice as hard as anyone else, and in this the visible record seemed to support them.

Honk couldn't wait that long. He was a believer in probabilities, not possibilities, and nothing around him suggested that he could satisfy his hunger by what society considered legitimate means. He saw in earliest boyhood that his teenage heroes were making better money in The Life than his daddy was earning straight up. In adolescence, he watched his walking buddies leave the corner for the world of work and come back holding chump change for frying burgers on a grill at Sally's or humping cartons on a loading dock at Precision Valve. There was school, of course, but you had to be a bad MF just to *get* there past the niggers waiting to beat your brains out going and coming, and there didn't seem to be anything waiting at the other end—nothing, that is, worth studying *for*.

School was for a dude like Vest, old Brainiac, a guy with brains and plans and a gift ticket out of the projects. Like most of the brothers at Trey-nine, Honk respected Vest and took a certain vicarious pride in his achievements; a lot of them thought it was college he was going off to at fourteen, not prep school, and they puffed up a little at how smart he was and how well he was doing. *Lots* of genius-ass niggers in these schools, Honk thought, but you got to be *strong* as well as smart to do what Vest did, to stay with it and then go out and get over in the other world. It was a lot of studs wouldn't want to be into that, wouldn't even want to *try* it. The fact that Vest had made it didn't mean that everyone could. His Trey-nine friends were bright youngsters for the most part, but there had been no one at home or school to flog them on and no faraway white benefactor with alphabet-soup initials to pluck them out of the projects. Most gave up too soon, before they had finished high school; higher education, for those few who did stick with it, usually meant a two-year community college across town. The brothers regarded Vest and his success as wonders of nature rather than as examples they could follow. He had always been the neighborhood prodigy, and their affection for him coexisted with the sense that he was different, that his way out had never been available to them.

Honk, like most of the others, found it easier to stay inside the perimeter of their world. To venture outside was to risk one's manhood—to work the meanest jobs in the American economic order, existing only at the sufferance of the Man, and still not bring home enough to live on. Some of the brothers accepted that risk. Honk would not. *He* had brains, too, and hopes; he hungered for money, not just as a medium of exchange but as a measure of size. His theater of operations had its own dangers: A single misstep could cost you your freedom, your sanity, or even your life. But it operated by its own outlaw code, a body of rules that were fixed and knowable, as against the encrypted language and laws of the white world outside. Honk saw early that white people were not greatly troubled by what black people did, up to and including murder, so long as they did it to one another. The lesson was confirmed by his own experience, so he put his entrepreneurial gifts to work where he was: on a street corner in the ghetto on the South Side of Chicago.

He did achieve size there, the kind of rogue honor extended by the brothers on the corner to anyone who beat the odds by any means necessary. Vest Monroe was a man of respect in his way at Thirty-ninth and Federal, and so was Honk, in his. It was possible, even logical, for them to become brothers-in-law; they had taken radically different paths in the world, one making it as a downtown journalist, the other as a side-street hustler, but they had their success in common, and their standing among the brothers they had left behind.

It was only with encroaching middle age and the prospect that he would enter it in prison that Honk began to understand how small a stage he had played on, and how fleeting were its rewards. White people had long since deserted Thirty-ninth Street, and after them the black middle class; they had left behind a mined-out colony, and the men who rose to primacy over what was left, men like Honk, had few remaining resources to exploit except one another. To become chief of this and that on Honk's corner, and to defend one's position against rival outlaws, was a dangerous game. It was, on the other hand, the only game in town, at least so far as Honk could see.

He was impatient for wealth and prestige, a character trait much admired in finance, say, or politics. His misfortune was to have been born on the underside of the American Dream, the dark side, where the avenues of advancement were fewer and narrower. The doors open to half-schooled black men like himself led most often to subsistence jobs or to dependency on welfare or women, and Honk found all three alternatives degrading—*trifling S*, he thought, that did not satisfy his need for cash or, more important, for self-esteem. His calling was banditry. He had a vocation for it, and he saw no other course, no way for a black man from the projects to achieve his ends both quickly and honestly. To be patient required a belief that there was a future worth waiting for, and Honk was never sure. It was not clear from his vantage point that there would *be* a future—not for him anyway.

So Honk became a player, a man of moments, living in the sweet now instead of the uncertain by-and-by. He shuddered a little thinking about the times he had taken that ultimate risk, throwing his life at a dream that wouldn't even last into the next day. Lay down and it'd be right there in your face, he thought, but you better enjoy it while it's there, 'cause a dream wasn't nothing but an overnight thing; wake up next morning with your head all bad and ain't nothing there, nothing worth having staked your life on. There was only that next dollar to be hustled, and Honk, in his middle thirties, was tired of all that S. When you get my age, he thought, you really done got *old* out there. I ain't got no business even being *around* that S anymore, he thought. It was time to let it go.

He didn't regret his past or its pleasures, except maybe the drugs and the paper he had spent buying them; he was always better at making money than keeping it, and when he needed some, bad, his fortune had vanished with his luck. Good-bye to a boss dude: Old Honk was history, bighouse bound, and all the studs he had left behind on his way to the top were surviving. Maybe they weren't rich; maybe surviving was all they were doing. But that put them ahead of him in the game. The day was gone when he could sit back with his big hat broke down mean and tell them idly, "My man—see? Didn't I tell you this was better?" It was twenty years later, and this stud with the job been steady getting raises while Honk was steady getting busted. I've lost all the way, he thought, seeing the brothers again at the barbecue. He had the feeling that he was passing them again, this time on the way down.

His gaze swept the gathering, lighting on familiar faces. Half Man over there, looking sharp; you hardly ever saw him around Thirty-ninth Street anymore. And Pee Wee, alternately sipping a Colt 45 and turning half chickens on a big tub barbecue like a contented suburban buppie; he had had his problems, his personal post-Vietnam syndrome, but he was trying to get it together now with a job and a steady lady. And Sonny Spruiell, boogying with Jean on the sidewalk to the music blasting from a parked van; Sonny had come to play, but he was dressed for work, in his green orderly's shirt from Lakeside Hospital. And Moose Harper, looking out of place and sad behind that fixed Kingdom smile; the project till then had been a place he pointed out to his wife and son from the Dan Ryan Expressway, a bad patch in the landscape of his past, and when they found themselves actually there, they wouldn't even get out the car.

Some of the other brothers were trying to put Moose at ease. Ed Hamilton came diddybopping around with a stogie and a smile; he had a job now, nothing but a funky little old job, he was telling everyone with a stylish wave of his cigar, but at least it was something, and this time he meant to keep it.

"I don't have to be to work until four P.M. tomorrow," he told Moose, making conversation. "I work the four to twelve shift. You work days?"

"I work nights," Moose said. "The midnight shift." His days belonged to Jehovah.

"Moose was always a good boy," Half Man said, mostly for Moose's wife's benefit. She was sitting with Armond in the car, a blue Chevy Citation, looking uncomfortable.

"You remember the time we were up in the hallway smoking Lipton tea?" Ed said.

If he did recall it, Moose wasn't saying so.

"Aww, we never did anything *real* bad," Half Man said. "You know, just drinking wine and stealing stuff out the Del Farm"—the grocery store over in the shopping center.

Moose looked like he wished he were somewhere else.

Ed said something about what a good time he was having.

Moose smiled and said he was, too. He wasn't. I used to *love* down here, he was thinking, but no more; all the old relationships had died the day he became a Witness. His past had died. He was a new man. With God's great help, he had picked himself up off the street and re-created himself—had become a husband, a father, a provider, and a bearer of the Word. There's nothing here, he thought, surveying the country of his childhood. He mainly felt depressed.

He wasn't alone. Honk felt another sort of melancholy, sipping wine and surveying all their faces across the distance that had opened between his life and theirs. Seeing them was like being at a picture gallery, looking at a retrospective of his own past, except that only he was what he had been back in their days together. He had laughed at them once for buying all that okey-doke about the work ethic; they could slave all their lives filling paint cans or pushing food carts, and unless they hit the Lotto, they wouldn't make as much as he had already spent by age thirty-five.

But they were all successes in their way, victors by the mere fact of being alive with some change in their pockets and a smile for a new day. Honk was the one tapped out now, his bankroll gone and his freedom going. You can't be hustling and ain't got no money, he mused; it was enough to make him think he might have came out better with a job, 'cause, he thought, a working man puts in his eight hours and *know* what he's going to make. A hustler never did. A hustler worked harder than a businessman for his success, on call twenty-four hours every day, and still might not have a dime in his pants. He could be in jail or an early grave.

Honk had spent his life dodging bullets, but he was fresh out of everything now except bad luck and hard times; society, fearing him, was about to put him out of sight, under lock and key, about as far from Chicago as you could go and still be in the state of Illinois. There would be more like him, more young men who hungered, as he had, for wealth and reputation on the same small patch of concrete he had ruled. The ghetto kept producing them, out of its poverty and demoralization, and a new generation of them was ready to claim its inheritance.

The younger studs on the block had come up, mostly, as children reared by children, untamed and lawless to a point that frightened even Honk; they would be, if anything, less fastidious about what they did and more dangerous doing it than he had been. Thirty-ninth and Federal was *their* corner now, or shortly would be. The prince of the ghetto had finally been devoured by it, as all his friends in The Life had been; they had disappeared, one by one, till only he was left on the street, and now his number had come up, as he had known it had to. Honk's figurehood as a hustler had proved as perishable as Billy Harris's celebrity as a ball player, and he didn't even have a scrapbook to show for it. It had all been illusion. I ain't *nobody*, Honk thought morosely, casting an eye over his lost estate. I don't care who run nothing. I'm through with the world.

R*ay Stingley, corporate middle manager, was flying in for the barbecue, an interplanetary traveler descending from a distant world, and his old homies from Prairie Courts formed a welcoming committee to meet his plane. Greg Bronson was up from Tampa, taking a weekend away from his auto show-room; Vest Monroe, Big-Time Vest, had come from Washing-ton between political assignments for* Newsweek; *and Steve Steward—well, Steve had all the* trappings *of success if you didn't know they were borrowed. They were waiting at the gate at Midway Airport when Ray deplaned, his thickset body briefly filling the exit door. He was dressed for the cookout in shorts and a striped polo shirt, but he was carrying a leather portfolio full of ConvaTec business, and he had another plane to catch in a few hours for a meeting on the Coast.*

The rendezvous at Midway was a reunion within a reunion, the first time the four of them had been together since their freshman year at Phillips High, and they greeted one another warmly. They were the ones who got out while there was still time, the achievers who had left the projects and set out in pursuit of the dream twenty years before. All except Steve had achieved a piece of it; they had started out as boys racing one another hungrily through the success stories in their grade school library, and three of them had gone off and written their own—stories of hard work and solid achievement in the American mainstream. Only Steve had stayed behind, home in the projects, where he knew his way around.

"You're looking good," Ray told him, watching him nose Bev's Audi out of the parking lot and start south for Trey-nine.

"That's 'cause my woman takes good care of me," Steve said. "Even though I don't take such good care of her."

Only Vest among the four of them was really at home at Trey-nine, having grown up there. Some of the Thirty-ninth Street brothers were fleetingly irritated with him for having brought the Prairie Courts bunch; the projects had always been suspicious of strangers. "Hey, Vest," one of the picnickers said peevishly, sizing up Greg's careful grooming and his tan baggies, "I thought this was a Trey-nine thing. Who're these outside MF's?" Vest smiled and said they were OK, and the issue was settled; his word was good enough.

Still, there were curious stares, and the visitors moved with the awkward step of tourists in somebody else's country. Ray moved through the crowd, meeting the people, but he was constantly stealing glances at his watch, worrying about his plane and his meeting. Greg stood apart, sipping a beer, a soft-spoken man with a bemused smile and an oddly formal bearing. He was Kamau Akil, citizen of the Republic of New Africa, a warrior in the defense of black people; he could quote Malcolm X and take down an AR-15 rifle, but he lived his daily life in a different world, light-years away from his childhood in the projects. He had just come off the tennis courts, where he had split a match with his father, one set apiece. He had expatriated to another country, far from home.

It was Steve who belonged, though he had never lived in the Taylor Homes. He came from the projects, and while he had been handed a passport out, he had not made it; he had got a few steps across the frontier, but the terrain on the other side had frightened him, and he had retreated to safe ground. He was at ease anywhere there, with his gregarious nature— his outwardness—*and his disarming smile. He had pulled up at Trey-nine early in that gunmetal blue Audi, music up and sunroof back, profiling as if the ride belonged to him, not his woman. Heads turned as he parked and stepped out. Showtime.*

His eyes found Honk in the crowd. They came from differ-ent 'hoods, but they had some tastes in common, and their circles intersected.

"Hey, Roy," Steve said, "what's up with you?"

"Hey, brother," Honk said. "You got it."

"I hope these gangsters down here don't F with my ride,"
Steve said, glancing back at the Audi.

Honk grinned. "We already moved on them MF's," he said. "They know better than to bring that BS around here today."

Steve grinned back, that little I'm-cool smile. He felt as easy at Trey-nine as if he had lived there all his life. He knew where he was.

It was easiest never to leave home. Ghettos were created to hold their inhabitants inside, but their boundaries were a defense perimeter as well, a secured border within which people felt as if they *belonged*. The world beyond that line was terra incognita. The white people who owned and occupied it seemed afraid of young black men and, being afraid, made them feel unwelcome or worse. To walk into a store or hail a cab in the street was to risk humiliation; to apply for a job or a promotion was to invite rejection and never know why; to mingle with whites was to enter a country where a smile could be an open invitation or a coded warning. The projects and the streets could be places of great physical danger, but their perils were mostly known and predictable and were subject in some measure to commonly understood rules. There were, for example, places and situations one avoided and hours of night at which one preferred to be indoors among friends.

The white world downtown didn't operate that way. It had rules, to be sure, but they were like the bylaws of a restricted club: You had to become a member to know them, and you had to know them to become a member. Violating them could, in extreme circumstances, be a corporal or even a capital offense. In the winter of 1986–87, three black men were assaulted by whites for the crime of having stopped for a pizza in a white enclave called Howard Beach in the out-boroughs of New York City; one, fleeing the attack, ran into the path of a car and was killed. The vastly more common danger for a young black man was to be judged, silently, by his color and to be prisoner to certain widely held assumptions about it—that he was probably less capable than whites and quite possibly armed and dangerous. The fact that not all white people shared those prejudices was small comfort as against the great number who did—most of them, if one believed one's elders, with their tales of life in the Jim Crow South and in Miss Anne's kitchen. Sorting good whites from bad could be an intractable puzzle, a Rubik's cube rigged against solution. The easiest thing was to give up, put it down, and walk away home.

Most of the Trey-nine brothers had done precisely that; they had surrendered halfway through high school and had led lives outside the frontiers of the white world, with its standards of judgment, risk, and reward. Some had shown promise in school, up to a point. Sonny was quick at his lessons; Honk's drawings hung in the principal's office; Moose had a writer's imagination, in search of words to give it expression. But it took more than intelligence to break out of the cycle of despair. It required the belief that it was *possible* to break out when the stale smell of defeat in the air you breathed told you daily that you could not.

To sustain that belief would have demanded stronger support systems than many of them had, at home, at school, and in the community. Their parents—mothers alone, as often as not—struggled valiantly to feed and clothe them and raise them right. But the fight exhausted whatever small resources of money and hope were available to most ghetto families. It took a particularly stubborn soul to imagine, under the circumstances, that life could or would be much better for one's children. The schools, for the most part, had already surrendered. The peer pressure against learning was furious, and the argument for it—that it would lead somewhere—bumped against the pervasive expectation that it would not. Boys growing up in the ghetto were made aware daily of how little value the larger society placed on the lives and, in a postindustrial age, the labor of poor black men. Their own fathers, too often, were casualties, those who stayed home and those who disappeared. The defeat of one generation begat defeatism in the next.

For most of the Trey-nine brothers, the odds favoring real success in the outside world seemed about the same as the possibility of hitting the Lotto, and the risks were a good deal higher than the price of a dollar ticket. Most preferred the game of chance, even knowing it was mathematically stacked against them; in the other, larger competition, the Man controlled the cards and the rules, and it was accepted as a given in the ghetto that he would never willingly deal black folks into the action—certainly not *poor* black folks.

Accordingly, most chose not to play. It was easier to stay behind and scuffle; in a world conditioned to defeat, merely to survive was a triumph of sorts, and if the payoff was small—service jobs, mostly, for subsistence money—so were the risks of being judged a failure. In the white world, you were made to feel marginal, one in a caste of men consigned by their color to work and to housing that no one else wanted. Among your own, nobody except maybe your woman held you to blame for what kind of job you had or how little you made doing it. You didn't have to be a banker or a brain surgeon. Merely getting by was enough; doing it with a touch of style was, in the eyes of the bloods on Thirty-ninth Street, a triumph.

That any escaped was remarkable. Steve Steward had been handed the keys, thanks to the ABC program, and still hadn't made it. He had walked out into the larger America beyond the ghetto, looked around for a while, and then fled home. He persuaded himself over the ensuing years that there was nothing much out there he wanted anyway. In fact, the world had frightened him. He was fifteen years old when he first glimpsed it at Hanover High; he had wondered all through his boyhood in the ghetto whether white people really existed and then was made suddenly and forcefully aware that *hey!*—they're *predominant.*

He got through his three years among them playing the role he knew by birthright, the tough kid from the projects, an image gentled by his wit and charm; the motto next to his picture in the school yearbook was "Black Power," but the descriptives were "easygoing" and "talkative." The entry further noted that he "likes Chicago," and once he got back there, he stayed, where he grew up at, he liked to say; where he could feel safe. He had never wanted to be more than what he was, and no one in his world demanded it of him, not his doting mother, or his absentee father, or his lovesick women, or his partners in the street. White people and white standards became unreal again. He had traded the danger he felt among them for the security of the reservation, and if he was still role-playing—if his prosperity was borrowed from his ladies and his self-esteem was mortgaged to his drugs—it didn't matter to anyone except himself.

Greg Bronson had ventured even farther from home and had found that he could manage nicely, at least in that daylight world where the deals are done. He took an athlete's pleasure in the game, in closing a hard sale and, in the process, confounding all the white man's European notions of what black men could and could not do. He did not otherwise like being around white people, not unless he was in competition with them; he never lost the sense that every day he spent among them was a day behind enemy lines. The only way he could manage it, psychically, was to armor himself against them and at intervals to secede from their company entirely.

It caused him pain to be thought a racist in reverse. He sometimes wished he could be more flexible on the subject; he even conceded the possibility, out of his own experience, that at least some *few* white people were honest and sincere enough to deal with a black man on terms of mutual respect. The problem, in Greg's suspicious eyes, was that so many could not. In his middle thirties he was still the lonely black teenager in the steel-company office, seeing hostility in the white faces all around him and burning with anger and shame under their gaze. His defense mechanism, then and now, was to act on the working hypothesis that *all* of them were his enemies. It simplified his relationships with them, sparing him the difficult exercise of sorting out which few meant him well. If you shut them all out, none of them could harm you.

His world view was, of course, disabling to his progress and his prospects in corporate America; he could handle any job he was given, but he could not easily work for white people, presuming as he did that they were dedicated to his failure and perhaps his destruction. Not many boys coming of age in the ghetto were immune to doubts about the intentions of the Man; they had the word of their parents and grandparents on it, and the impressions of their own daily lives. Most internalized these feelings and reached a kind of inner accommodation with them, sometimes at great cost. They submitted to the limits on their hopes and possibilities as if they were ordained and maybe even just, the judgment of nature or God.

Greg strained against them. His habit of mind was not surrender but war, and so he entered upon his double life, his three-button daytime persona serving as camouflage for the soldier he became after dark. As Greg Bronson, he was one solitary man, alone and vulnerable. As Kamau Akil, armed, disciplined, and dangerous, he was one with the nonwhite majority on earth. His anger and his ambitions made a bad match, and there was a price for his militancy, in his life, his career, and his inner peace. Still, he preferred living inside his vision, as a citizen of New Africa; it seemed to him preferable to submission to the ways of a world ordered on the white man's terms. When he and his brother opened Gilead-Angelo Construction, Inc., in the Chicago suburbs in the spring of 1987, it was at once an act of entrepreneurship and a declaration of independence.

He was one of a dozen black teenagers who had set out from the projects of South Side Chicago twenty years before, each in quest of his particular version of the grail. Their hopes had not been very different from those of boys on the far side of the ghetto walls; they aspired to jobs, homes, families, cars, and a little in the bank for a rainy day. But practically all the circumstances of their lives conspired against them, starting with the color of their skin and the poverty of their beginnings. If success means material well-being, a full share in the affluent society, only two or three among them could be said to have achieved it. One had died in a fight, a casualty of the meaningless violence of the ghetto. One was in prison. One was a burned-out basketball player with only his scrapbooks to show for his glory days. One was an underground man, a dropout dependent on drugs and women. One was living in the psychic no-man's-land between his middle-class life-style and his revolutionary black rage. Most were marking time at the margins of the American economy, working-class men in a contracting job market.

And yet there was a measure of victory in most of their lives, not least the fact that they were alive at all; sudden death is a commonplace among young men in the ghetto, and violence is its leading cause. Some had been hustlers and outlaws and had gone straight. Some had been addicted to drugs and had got clean. Practically all were working most of the time. None was on unemployment or the dole. Most had children, and some were trying hard to be fathers to them. The others fit the statistical profile of family life in the ghetto, with its rising numbers of births out of wedlock and families headed by women on welfare. But they did not neatly fit the stereotypes of black men as irresponsible babymakers, uncaring about the love children they had left behind. Those who had failed at fatherhood were only too painfully aware of their failure. They had had neither the money nor the skills to succeed at it, and when they walked away from their women and children, they were not denying their responsibility; they were, rather, conceding defeat.

That some succeeded at life was more extraordinary, given the obstacles in their way. Their stories were the stuff of American myth, the immigrant experience reproduced in the projects of the South Side; they had found hidden springs of strength in the ghetto and in themselves and had made it out into a wider world. Ray was starting up the corporate ladder in marketing; Vest was reporting politics and public affairs out of Washington; Greg was bringing his construction business to a promising launch. Their workaday lives differed in detail, not in kind, from the lives of young, upwardly mobile white men of their generation. They had, of course, to consider the fact of their blackness in moving through the day and make the appropriate course corrections if they were to prosper or even survive. The burden of having to do so was more than Greg, for one, could tolerate, and he seceded from America into his black republic of the mind. Otherwise, the strivers bore a strong family resemblance to the whites they encountered daily in the workplace. Their cares ran to such matters as debt, divorce, child-rearing, and work anxieties, the standard stresses of life in the middle class.

It was not difficult to isolate the advantages they had had, beyond the mysteries of genetics. Each began life with strong, demanding parents, whether a mother alone, as in Vest's case for much of his boyhood, or a married couple, as in Greg's and Ray's. Hope had a high mortality rate in ghetto families, the casualty of poverty and resignation to the way things were. Not many parents protested when their sons slacked off in their studies and finally dropped out of school; the common assumption was that a boy born black in the projects faced a life sentence at hard labor whether he did his lessons or not. The Stingleys, the Bronsons, and Mrs. Monroe were quite aware of what their sons would be up against; they lived in the projects and were not blind. But they had aspirations for something better for their sons than they themselves had known, and they did not merely expect an extra measure of effort—they *required* it. So did a precious few teachers like Leroy Lovelace, gallant men and women whose classrooms were little redoubts of learning in schools where teaching more often resembled a pacification program.

Still, parents and teachers were too often overmatched against the city of destruction; just as Lovelace himself had imagined, the decisive turn for the boys who made it was getting out of the ghetto. Greg's family moved out to the suburbs. Ray's and Vest's could not afford to; their letters of transit were their ABC scholarships to faraway prep schools and then to quality colleges.

The journey was a painful one, since it meant leaving home, and not a little frightening, since it placed them among white people for the first time in their young lives. It was not in fact the company of whites that was redemptive so much as the quality of education and the wide range of options available to them. The doors open to them had largely been closed to the children of the inner city until the black revolt of the early sixties forced them ajar. The youngsters who slipped through might shrink from whites as a class, as Greg did, or move among them easily, as Ray soon discovered he could. In either case, it was important to know them and their folkways—they were, after all, the majority—and it did not hurt to be standing on the same platform when the train to tomorrow pulled in to board passengers.

The ABC boys were the children of the first generation of affirmative action, when the conscience of the nation was still smarting at the situation of the blacks a century after Emancipation. That impulse has cooled since the 1960's, under challenge in the courts and in the journals of modern political and social thought. The fashion twenty years later was to talk more about its failures, like Steve, than about its successes, like Ray and Vest. Success, of course, had never been guaranteed. Programs like ABC promised only the right to play, not to win; the outcome depended on the wit and sinew of the individual player. Ray and Vest had it. Steve did not; the leap from one high school in the ghetto to another in an Ivy college town was measurable, psychically, in light-years and was too long for him. He fell back. The others made it, and so did the great majority of ABC youngsters from the ghettos, the barrios, the reservations, and the white backwaters of poverty in America. Their experience argued for better chances for more people, not fewer; the issue was not whether some might sink but whether any might be helped to survive.

The times no longer favor generosity. We have grown accustomed to, and even comfortable, thinking of the last decades of the twentieth century as an age of limits, on both the resources and the imagination we apply to the ills of our society. We still tend to talk and think, politically, in the vocabulary of the Kennedy era; we tell ourselves that a country capable of putting men on the moon in a decade should be able to buy a solution to this terrestrial problem or that, and when quick results elude us, we give up. The signal of our surrender came when politicians and social scientists began speaking of a "permanent" black underclass. The problems of the inner-city poor may or may not be remediable, but to call them permanent is to surrender without a fight.

We live now in the America that a presidential commission once warned us against: two Americas, really, one black and one white, separate and unequal. The boundary between them is not absolute. We have not entirely abandoned the ghetto and its children to failure as a self-fulfilling prophecy; we have in fact admitted some few achievers to the social and economic midstream of our society. But the gates have never opened wide for the majority of young people growing up poor in our urban black quarters, the Sonny Spruiells and the Pee Wee Fishers and Half Man Carters. They, too, had had promise once, but opportunities were scarce, and they had not prepared themselves to seize what chances *were* beginning to materialize. They grew up in isolation from middle-class America, cut off from its choices, its affluence, and even its understanding. All they had in common with whites and well-to-do blacks was their dreams.

Their lives are formed now, as they approach middle age. They existed in their own age of limits, and except for Honk in his prison cell and James Bonner in his unmarked grave, most were doing well—as well, anyway, as their circumstances allow and as well as they are likely to do. Their hope for something more rested with *their* children, little ones coming up, mostly, as their fathers had in the waste and want of the inner city. Their inheritance was not, on its face, a hopeful one, but their challenge to the larger society was plain. It is in the generation of the children that the ideals of America will be tested. It is in their lives that the dreams of the brothers will or will not come true.

Vest Monroe moved busily among his old crowd at the barbe-cue, part co-host seeing that the party was going well, part reporter checking out the happenings. His success showed in his bearing and his sporty clothes, the glasses that turned dark as if by alchemy in the sunlight and the sharp gray jacket with the sleeves pushed up his forearms in the mod style. He had journeyed farther from Trey-nine than any of the others.

He had covered Jesse Jackson's first campaign, among other major stories, and was preparing for his second; his work had taken him to the far corners of the world.

But the old two-way connection remained strong between him and the project. Standing there on the grounds, within sight of his old back bedroom window in apartment 1201, he was still a homeboy. For his old crowd, his prosperity was proof of the talent in the building, undiscovered, maybe, but still there. His success was the confirmation of their own worth, and they liked the fact that he had come back to share it with them. The spotlight on him had always been big enough for them, too, even when they were little ones and he was the brain in the house.

"Ves' used to always hang out and try to be with us," a brother remembered. Vest had it but didn't flaunt it; he had always been one of the guys.

"That's who I should've married," a long-ago sweetheart whispered to a friend. She nodded toward Vest. "Him, right there."

Vest drifted past them, borne along on the tide of his memories, as he was every time he came home. He thought about the boy he had been and about all the people who had helped him get over. He thought about his mother, flogging him to school with patches on his sweatshirts and jeans, telling him against the secret doubt in her own heart that he could be whatever he wanted to be. He thought about his absentee father—Vest was twenty-eight when they met—and about the uncles who had stood in as the men in his life. He thought about the brothers, the schoolboys who had been his partners in learning at Prairie Courts and the gang-bangers who had been his protectors and friends at Trey-nine. He thought about Mr. Lovelace, sending him off alone and scared into the world, and about his first days at St. George's, Hattie Monroe's homesick boy, sure he was dying of a malady called nostalgia.

He thought less about his disadvantages in life than his good fortune. He had been born in a world where every day was dangerous, every step a venture into a free-fire zone, and yet he had never been alone; he had found resources where modern sociology proposed that none existed. His grandmother, for one; she was an unlettered woman, unable to read her own name, but she had shared her strength with him, and her cast-iron resolve. If she caught him pouting about being poor, she would run some tap water into a glass and ask him if it were half full or half empty. It's the same thing, he would answer, and she would tell him no, it wasn't—the glass was half full. So, boy, she would say, what you moping for? You got a roof over your head, something to eat, and a family here that loves you. You got nothing to be sticking your mouth out about.

*The worm of doubt had never stopped gnawing at his in-
nards. Like any child of the ghetto, he had been born with a
contingent sense of life; he still dreamed that all he had
worked for could disappear at the whim of white strangers.
He knew guys who had tried the same leap he had and hadn't
made it, guys driven to drink, drugs, and even suicide. He
knew guys who had never left Thirty-ninth Street at all. He
had been luckier. He had the answer to the riddle of the glass
now: It had been half full and, as things turned out, maybe
just a little bit more. He felt at home back at Trey-nine, surrounded by old faces and old friendships. But he lived in a
larger world. Trey-nine was not so much where he belonged
as where he was from.*